How to Write

EDITED BY PHILIP OLTERMANN

Published by Guardian Books 2009

2 4 6 8 10 9 7 5 3 1

First published in Great Britain in 2009 by
Guardian Books,
Kings Place, 90 York Way,
London N1 9GU

www.guardianbooks.co.uk

A CIP record for this book is available from the British Library.

ISBN 978-0-85265-138-4

Text design: www.carrstudio.co.uk
Printed and bound in Great Britain by CPI Bookmarque, Croydon,
Surrey CR0 4TD

Disclaimer
We have taken all steps possible to ensure the accuracy of the data
in the Writers' directory.

Contents

Introduction

I t wasn't a great omen. About two days after I had been asked to edit the Guardian's series on writing last May, the paper printed a short news item with the headline "Creative writing courses: the new mental hospitals". The novelist and scriptwriter Hanif Kureishi had given an interview in which it had seemed to him that whenever there was another instance of a young person going on a gun rampage, "it's always a writing student."

It was hyperbolic stuff, for sure, but between the lines lay a feeling that many might secretly share – including me. Wasn't there something sinister about creative writing courses? About those ever popular 'How-to-write-a-novel-in-three-weeks' manuals hogging the shelves at the bookshops? About that happy-clappy line they peddled, that "everyone has a novel inside them"? (It must be quite a downer when you've paid a fortune on a creative writing course only to realise that yes, you did have a novel inside you, but no, it wasn't a very good one. No wonder some lose the plot after having polished their plot to perfection.)

Another thing that made creative writing manuals suspicious to me was that none of them seemed honest enough to break the bad news about their line of work: writing doesn't pay the bills. I know some writers; a select few of them make a living from words, most of them have to do something else to support themselves. That vital sideline tends to be teaching creative writing.

Slightly perturbed by this riddle, I called one of these friends for a chat and some advice. Shortly before I rang off, I apologised to him. It must be terribly dull for him to talk about teaching – we would definitely chat about his new novel next time.

There was a disbelieving silence, and then a chuckle. I had got it all wrong: as turns out, most writers absolutely love teaching creative writing – a discovery confirmed as I approached several well-known novelists, poets, playwrights and comedians to contribute to this book. In fact, some of them enjoyed teaching more than actually writing novels. Teaching fiction to them was the creative process without all the smoke and mirrors of the publishing process. It was about the pure adrenaline of making a plot resolve, a paragraph work, a character whole, a line sing, without the talk about marketing strategies and target readers, without the fear of a reviewer tearing your work apart in the nationals. There's a New Yorker cartoon of an in-store book signing, in which a woman walks up to the author and says: "I really, really enjoyed your hype". Teaching creative writing is the antithesis of that.

The other thing I discovered about creative writing courses is that they can actually work. There is a line of thinking which says that good writing cannot be taught. Writing a novel, or a poem, or a play isn't like building a table: it requires great talent, a stroke of genius, a flash of inspiration. Writing is a mystical process, more akin to alchemy than carpentry.

Granted, there's magic to writing. But then there is also magic to building a really good table, or making pastry. Of course no manual – this included – will ever be able to write your screenplay, memoir or children's book for you. It's never going to be a case of plot + character – boring descriptive bits = page turner. Even once you have closely read all the advice presented in this booklet, taken on board all the lessons and completed all the exercises, you will still need to find that elusive extra something which will make the equation resolve.

But writing also has tricks which can be learned just like those of any other trade. The aim of the tutorials and exercises in this book is to show you some of the mechanics of writing and break down a overwhelmingly complex process into manageable chunks that you can get your head around. I have found the advice of our tutors and special experts enlightening and inspiring. I hope you do too.

Philip Oltermann, May 2009

Fiction

What's the story?

Producing a novel should be fun even though it's difficult, says writer Robert Harris. And while there are guides to help you along the way, fundamentally it's all down to you

Writing a novel – unlike operating a piece of heavy machinery, say, or cooking a chicken – is not a skill that can be taught. There is no standard way of doing it, just as there is no means of telling, while you're doing it, whether you're doing it well or badly. And merely because you've done it well once doesn't mean you can do it well again. The whole process is a mystery, devoid of rules or fairness.

That doesn't mean that guides like this are without value. On the contrary. Having the urge to write a novel, especially if you've yet to be published, is like having a medical condition impossible to mention in polite company – it's a relief simply to know there are fellow-sufferers out there.

In the 20 years that I've been writing fiction, three pieces of published wisdom, each offered by an eminent American novelist, have helped me along. The first was from John Irving, who maintains that any writer who embarks on a novel without knowing how it is going to end is a fool and a knave. A novel, he argues, recounts something that has already happened; therefore you cannot just make it up as you go along. This practical approach had a profound effect on me: indeed, it enabled me to complete my first novel, Fatherland which, in classic rookie fashion, had trailed to a baffled halt somewhere around page 50.

The second was from a 1995 interview with EL Doctorow: "You have to find the voice that allows you to write what you want to write ... It's a writer's dirty little secret that language precedes the intentions." On the face of it, this contradicts Irving ("I don't begin with a plan," insists Doctorow), but actually they are both saying the same thing, which is that the shape and style of a novel is determined by the thought you give it beforehand: that the way you approach your material is at least as important, maybe more important, than the material itself. This process of settling on an angle of attack may take months, even years of frustration and false starts, during which many writers – and certainly most writers' families and friends – believe the author may be going slightly mad.

> "This process of settling on an angle of attack may take months or even years"

Have courage, and remember the words of my third authority, Philip Roth, in 2003. "Over the years," he observed, looking back on his career on his 70th birthday, "what you develop is a tolerance for your own crudeness. And patience with your own crap, really. Belief in your crap, which is just 'stay with your crap and it will get better, and come back every day and keep going'."

To these three dictums, Polonius-like, I can add a few more. Don't try to write too much in a single session. One thousand words a day is quite enough. Stop after about four or five hours. Remember that most writing is done in the subconscious ("the boys in the basement," as Stephen King calls his unseen helpers) and that inspiration is only a posh word for ideas. Pace yourself, get some recreation, avoid tiring yourself out. Cut your manuscript ruthlessly but never throw anything away: it's amazing how often a discarded scene or description, which wouldn't fit in one place, will work perfectly later. Resist the temptation to show off your research (one of Tom Stoppard's maxims is, Just because it's true doesn't mean it's interesting). Be economical: Noel Coward's definition of good writing was the art of conveying something in as few words as possible .

Finally: enjoy yourself. "A writer who hates the actual writing,' Raymond Chandler once observed, "who gets no joy out of the creation of magic by words, to me is simply not a writer at all." That's the essence of being a novelist, and if you don't feel a surge of recognition on reading those words, it might be advisable to do something else.

Robert Harris is the author of several bestselling historical novels, including Fatherland, Archangel and Pompeii. His most recent book is the political thriller The Ghost (Arrow Books).

Where do ideas come from?

How do writers know what to write about? Your tutor Kate Pullinger says the best way to learn about writing is to do it

Writers are often asked the question, "Where do you get your ideas from?" as though there is a special place where you can buy them: Asda for chick-lit, perhaps, Waitrose for literary fiction. But, even though this question gets asked a lot, most writers find it difficult to supply a decent answer. The truth is that ideas are all around us, in the people you meet, in the things you read and see and hear and experience, in your own childhood and family, in the wilder reaches of your imagination.

But a good idea isn't the be-all-and-end-all. As anyone who writes will tell you, writing is primarily about graft. It's about a willingness to put in the hours it takes to make your story work. Some writers write very quickly while others labour over projects for years, but neither would deny that writing requires dedication, and that the difference between someone who dreams of being a writer, and someone who gets on with the absorbing and frustrating process of getting the words down, is vast. "Being a writer" is itself a weird idea, really, as though there exists a permanent state of glorious writerliness,

About your tutor

Kate Pullinger's books include The Mistress of Nothing, A Little Stranger and Weird Sister. Her digital works include the award-winning multimedia fiction Inanimate Alice. She teaches creative writing and new media at De Montfort University.

when in fact writing is not a state of being, but an art, a craft, a set of technical skills.

Many writers write because they feel compelled to do so; because if they don't, they aren't happy. In some ways, this is the best place to start: have a good idea and then feel guilty every day you waste not working on it.

All serious writers are also serious readers. Writers read for a huge variety of reasons; for research, of course, and for pleasure, but also to learn from writers we admire. While creative writing degrees have helped a lot to professionalise the way we learn to write, there's still much to be said for the auto-didactic approach of intensive, prolonged reading across genre, across period, and across the market as well. It's important to develop your reading skills – when you read something you like, spend some time figuring out why you like it, what the writer is doing to produce this effect. Conversely, when you read something you don't like, think about what it is that displeases you as a reader.

> "A good idea isn't the be-all and end-all. Writing is primarily about graft"

But really, the best way to start writing is to start writing. Get the words down onto the page. For many writers the most productive technique is to push on, regardless of what crap they are spewing. Bad writing can be improved upon, can be polished and cut and shaped and revised. A blank page is just that, and the only thing it is good for is driving you crazy. Whereas a page of writing, well, then you've got something to work with, something that, hopefully, will lead to better things.

Before you get started

● Turn off your word count. So what if you wrote 500 words today? When tomorrow arrives, you'll probably have to cut 450 of them. Only count words when you are in need of reassurance; only count words on those desperate days when knowing you've written a bunch of words will make you feel like you've achieved something, regardless of the quality.

● Find a simple but compelling way to describe to people what you are writing. When you tell people you are writing a novel they will, inevitably, ask "What's it about?" If you reply, "Well, I'm not really sure, it's kind of about a guy who isn't all that happy and is thinking about maybe moving someplace else, but can't make up his mind," you'll panic as their eyes glaze over and their smile slowly fades, and you'll end up thinking, "God that sounds awful, why am I even bothering to write this thing?" about your own novel, which is never a good thing. Instead, have a good line, something like, "It's about a woman who establishes an independent republic inside one of the pods on the London Eye," to which people will reply, "What happens to her?" and you'll have your first potential sale. It doesn't matter that much if you are, in fact, writing a novel about a guy who isn't all that happy and is thinking about maybe moving somewhere else, as you'll have spared yourself one of life's tiny humiliations. Writing is a kind of confidence trick – you have to con yourself into thinking you can do it, into thinking that what you are writing is the Real McCoy. Finding a way to describe what you are doing and protecting your own fragile ego isn't such a bad idea. Write your one-liner on a piece of card and stick it up where you can see it while you work; when the going gets tough and you are trapped in the extended labyrinth of words that all novels comprise, you'll be able to look at it and remind yourself of the simple brilliance of your story.

● Try not to worry too much about your desk or your window or your computer or your pen or whether or not you have any of these things. The thing about writing is that it is easier not to do than it is to do, and there are an infinite number of ways to prevent yourself from doing it. Obsessing about chairs and notebooks and whether or not it is such a good idea to always write in bed is counter-productive. The trick with writing is to do it. Shut yourself up and get on with it.

Genre and market

I n the world of publishing, works of fiction are marketed according to genre. Broadly speaking, they include historical, romantic, science fiction and fantasy, horror, crime, and the genre-with-no-name, otherwise known as literary fiction or contemporary fiction (writing for children will be covered elsewhere).

Most of the big prizes are for literary fiction; even so, the literary has taken a battering in recent times as the exquisitely-written-but-no-story slim volume has given way to the Richard-and-Judy inspired preference for big books with big stories. Unless you are aiming for the most formulaic of reads, it's impossible to second guess the market and predict what will sell, so you are better off pursuing whatever genre speaks to you as a reader.

Each genre has its own set of conventions that are there to be both obeyed and ignored. With crime, plot, character and action are key; with science fiction the imagined world and its landscape are primary; historical fiction almost always takes on historical fact and places its fiction in the cracks and gaps of historical knowledge; romantic fiction is in league with its enormous child chick-lit, which takes a world of archetypes and uses these to dramatise the contradictions and problems of women's lives; Horror is the genre that barely dents the consciousness of the mainstream reading world, except when written by Stephen King. Out of all of these, crime is the genre that is most respectable, with its

Dames Rendell and James, and its epic occupation of our television screens. The techniques and tricks described in this pamphlet can be used across all these forms of writing; at the end of the day a good story is just that, a good story, no matter the setting.

The market for all fiction is under increasing pressure as publishing becomes ever more corporate and the range of titles that sell the required amount becomes ever more narrow. In today's highly competitive market it is important that novels contain strong narratives that are compelling to readers. In an article written for the Summer 2008 edition of The Author, the in-house magazine for the Society of Authors, Serpent's Tail publisher Peter Ayrton wrote, "...a beginning novelist can make a good start by making sure they write a book with a strong narrative, with subjects for readers' groups to get their teeth into." He added, "...today's fiction writer is going to need very steady nerves and plenty of luck," when it comes to navigating the route to publication.

> "A good read has convincing characters, strong stories, fluid and original prose"

There are many elements that contribute to writing a book that qualifies as a good read. Convincing characters; strong stories; fluid and original prose; writing that conjures vivid mental pictures for the reader; writing that evokes all our senses – touch, taste, smell, hearing, seeing; writing that packs an emotional punch. As Elmore Leonard wrote in his manifesto, "Writing: The 10 Deadly Sins", "Try to leave out the part that readers tend to skip." This is important: if you are bored by your story, what hope is there for your reader?

Research

A good idea will often require additional knowledge that you don't possess and you'll discover you need to do some research in order to make your story convincing. Research comes in many shapes and sizes, from seeking out a forensic pathologist and requesting an interview so you can pin down that serial killer, to spending hours searching through history books, contemporaneous accounts and academic articles over the internet and in the library. Writers of fiction usually aren't academics and so often have a magpie approach to research, going for the shiny bits, easily distracted, forever poking at one idea with their mucky beaks before dropping it and moving on to the next glittering thing. Other writers take it upon themselves to become experts in their chosen subject. But whichever your favoured approach, the most important thing is to pursue your interests. If you think something is absolutely fascinating, it's likely that passion will come through onto the page.

Sometimes the most difficult thing about research is knowing when to stop, when to let it go so that you can concentrate on your story. We've all had the experience of reading a novel where the research is too evident on the pages, where the writer feels compelled to jam in every last detail about what kind of buttons that regiment wore on their jackets and where, in fact, those buttons were made, and what, exactly, was the correct way to polish them. It's as though the writer is thinking, I took 10 years to learn all this stuff, so I'm going to damn well share it with you.

There's a particular type of very important research that writers often find necessary but don't like to talk about too

Philippa Gregory on how to research a historical novel

The first rule I apply when writing a historical novel is that it has to work as a novel, as well as be absolutely based on the history. The broad narrative of the history imposes the story of the novel, all I can choose is when to start and stop. The only time I invent an occasion in the life of an historical character is when we simply don't know what they were doing – and then I choose the most likely explanation.

But the details of research I only use in service to the story-telling. Thus if a conversation occurs at dinner and we know what is said, that conversation goes into my novel and if we have the exact words so much the better. But the detail of the table setting, the food, and the entertainment only come into the description if it really helps to set the scene, give the atmosphere, animate and illustrate the scene. This means I don't use strange words or technical terms without explanation, and actually, I only use them at all if they help the scene to work as well as a scene in any sort of fiction. However pleased I am to have learned something arcane, it only ever goes into the novel if it adds to the understanding and enjoyment of the reader.

Ideally, I should know more as an historian than I tell as a novelist. I should see the scene, and the background to the scene, I should know the means of transport waiting outside the window, and whether the window is glazed. The reader only knows to see the scene, everything else should only help them to see it vividly and to understand its importance. It is called historical fiction and I believe it has to be both: well researched history and well written fiction.

Philippa Gregory's novel, about Mary Queen of Scots, is The Other Queen (HarperCollins)

openly. It's called lying on the sofa, or staring blankly out of the window for ages. This type of research is as important as the time spent observing schizophrenics at the secure unit or hard at it on Wikipedia. Like everyone else, writers need time to dream, and this dream-time can be highly productive and useful. In an interview about how she writes Val McDermid explained how the unconscious plays "a huge role" in her work; "This is the only job (apart from being a sleep-research guinea pig) in which you can work while you're asleep". If you don't spend time lying on the sofa immersed in the world you are imagining, why would any reader want to lie there as well?

Character and style

Strong, well-rounded characters who spring from the page fully formed are the most valuable currency for every writer, from Nobel prize winner Elfride Jelinek's masochistic piano teacher to John Grisham and his lawyers. Without good characters, a story will not be memorable. Writing good characters depends on creating people who are both real and interesting to the reader.

However, the way that writers we admire do this varies hugely and is often a matter of style. In his masterpiece of a short story, Hills Like White Elephants, Ernest Hemingway never describes what his characters look like beyond referring to them as the American and the girl with him. Nothing is spelt out and everything is suggested. In less than five pages we are given their story and, despite the lack of description, we can see them both with perfect clarity.

It is important to know as much about each character as possible, no matter how minor that character might be to the overall story. The reason we see Hemingway's couple so clearly is because he had them firmly fixed in his mind's eye.

The way you go about creating convincing characters is very personal – many writers create characters by finding out about them as they go along, while others cut out pictures from magazines and make lists of what their characters like for breakfast. Many writers create characters by coopting details from people they see around them; some characters emerge fully formed from the unconscious – the idea for

"Writing good characters depends on creating people who are both real and interesting"

Dracula came to Bram Stoker in a nightmare. Regardless of your method, the way to make characters believable is for you, as a writer, to inhabit their skin – imagine what it is like to be that person, no matter how unlikeable, corrupt, or

Freya North on romantic fiction

In reality, falling in love or in lust is not in the least bit magical, it's purely chemical – merely the presence of phenylethylamine in the brain. In fiction, the reader doesn't want to know that. The reader will be gladly conned into trusting that the magic of attraction between two people exists and can happen to them too.

It is safer and more usual for us to fall for people with whom we have things in common. In fiction, however, we are perfectly happy to believe in Jane Eyre and Mr Rochester. Between the sheets of a novel, opposites attract the reader as much as they do each one another.

Good dialogue is crucial: don't just describe characters smouldering at each other, let the reader eavesdrop on what they say. The dynamic of the characters' relationship can be bound up with how they communicate. Devastating arguments that would have a real couple storm off in a huff can have the reader stay put for pages. Give the characters those declarations of love we've always fluffed, or filthy talk we're too shy to try.

For author and reader alike, characters in a novel should do all the things they'd never dare do, make the mistakes they hope they never would – but also experience the apotheoses of love and lust to a degree we possibly never will. To this end, the main asset for any characters is for their author to be a hopeless romantic and an inveterate daydreamer.

Freya North's Pillow Talk won the Romantic Novel of the Year award 2008. Her new novel, Secrets, is out now.

from the front line

creepy. Detail is important here: the telling detail can give us as much if not more than any amount of description. Examples include Hannibal Lector and that bottle of Chianti, Proust's narrator and those madeleines, Miss Havisham and her wedding dress.

Hemingway is a master of concision; however, on a sliding scale of prose style with the economical Hemingway at one end, writers like JK Rowling and Arundhati Roy reside at the opposite end, with heavily descriptive prose. Rowling's books are successful because of, not in spite of, this style; legions of readers love her characters. As readers we don't have to choose between Hemingway and Rowling, but as writers we do need to think about what we want to achieve – studied elegance or a breathless ability to make the reader turn the page. The very clever writer combines both these things, their style adding to the pleasures of a rattling good story, like Philip Roth and the novels he has written over the past decade.

For many writers, style is innate; they write the way they do because they write the way they do. Here the boundary blurs between "style" and "voice". With some writers that voice is hugely distinctive – Cormac McCarthy and Flannery O'Connor and James Kelman come to mind. Finding your voice is an important part of learning to write but, as with so many writing skills, this is most often something that emerges gradually, with practise, as you gain confidence, as you discover the stories that you most want to tell.

"The way you go about creating convincing characters is very personal"

George Saunders on the art of keeping it short

When I was a kid, writers and writing gave me the creeps. In our English book, which had one of those 1970s titles that connoted nothing (Issues and Perspectives, maybe, or Amalgam 109), the sentences repulsed me the way a certain kind of moccasin-style house slipper then in vogue repulsed me. The sentences in Amalgam 109 or Polyglot Viewpoints seemed to have given up life, or to never have taken life sufficiently personally. They weren't lies, but they weren't true either.

And then a nun gave me a book called Johnny Tremaine, by Esther Forbes. Forbes suggested that the sentence was where the battle was fought. With enough attention, a sentence could peel away from its fellows and be, not only from you, but you.

A person can write: "There were, out in the bay, a number of rocks, islands of a sort, and upon these miniature islands, there resided a number of gulls, which, as the sun began to rise, gradually came to life, ready to begin another day of searching for food."

Or she can write, as Forbes had: "On rocky islands gulls woke." The first sentence is perfectly correct but is the increased information justified by the greater number of words? The second sentence credits our intelligence. Where else would the islands be, but in a bay?

The second sentence has been loved by its creator. She has given it her full attention. That missing comma? She meant it.

George Saunders' short stories have appeared in The New Yorker, McSweeney's and the Guardian's Weekend Magazine

from the front line

Developing character

1. Think of a character, a character with whom you have little in common: if you are a man, choose a woman; if you are very young, choose someone middle-aged, etc. Establish the basics: name, age, nationality, appearance. Next, start to think about who this person really is and make notes:

　a) What does he/she like to eat?

　b) What is her/his favourite item of clothing?

　c) What does he/she smell like?

2. After establishing these facts about your character, go on to ask three more questions, making more notes:

　a) What is his or her greatest fear?

　b) What is the first thing everyone notices when this person walks into a room?

　c) What is his or her relationship with his parents?

3. Now that you have him or her clear in your mind's eye, write a scene with this character in it. Keep it simple; write about an ordinary activity, for example, washing the dishes, walking to work, getting ready for bed, talking to someone. Don't tell us what kind of person this is, show us through their actions – body language, tone of voice, the telling detail.

Exercise

Place and atmosphere

I n fiction, place does not simply mean location, it means landscape, history, and community as well. Many of the most admired writers produce work that is firmly tied to place. North American writers excel at this: for instance, Alice Munro in rural Ontario, Philip Roth in New Jersey and Willa Cather on the central plains. Naguib Mahfouz and Ahdaf Soueif bring Cairo to us, while Orham Pamuk gives us Turkey. In the UK, London is recreated over and over again in fiction, while over the past 20 years Scottish writers like Denise Mina and Alasdair Gray have revivified the literary landscape through their use of both dialect and place.

In the novel evocation of place is wholly tied up with the creation of atmosphere; it's almost impossible to deal with these elements separately. Place can help determine atmosphere; where else could Stephen King's The Shining be set apart from an isolated snow-bound mountain hotel? A wonderful example of a description of place that uses the tricks from the following exercise while giving the reader a vast amount of information about the characters as well as a strong sense of atmosphere comes early on in F Scott Fitzgerald's east coast novel, The Great Gatsby.

"...The windows were ajar and gleaming white against the fresh grass outside that seemed to grow a little way into the house. A breeze blew through the room, blew curtains in at one end and out the other like pale flags, twisting them up toward the frosted wedding-cake of the ceiling, and then

"In the novel, evocation of place is wholly tied up with the creation of atmosphere"

rippled over the wine-coloured rug, making a shadow on it as wind does on the sea ... The only completely stationary object in the room was an enormous couch on which two young women were buoyed up as though upon an anchored balloon. They were both in white, and their dresses were rippling and fluttering as if they had just been blown back in after a short flight around the house."

In this example the "enormous couch" contrasts brilliantly with the blades of grass, while the young women back from their "short flight around the house" provide a strong sense of the uncanny, laden with foreboding.

It picks up on a number of themes that run throughout the novel, including whiteness, Daisy Buchanan's otherness, both in terms of her wealth and her femininity, and the transience of the world these people inhabit. The writing in The Great Gatsby is rich with metaphor and imagery while remaining highly economical; like all the best books it rewards repeated reading.

Writing about location

From your story (use either a work in progress or something entirely new) choose a geographical location that is integral to the book.

Be precise: choose not the entire house, but a specific room. Then write a description of this place that uses the following elements:

1. include something huge in the picture – if you are outdoors, the sky, or a mountain; if you are indoors, the largest thing within that room.
2. include something tiny or minute
3. include something odd or uncanny or strange

Exercise

Point of view

Point of view is one of the most important basics for any piece of fiction; not having a firm hold on point of view can cause no end of problems. There are two types of point of view that tend to dominate most current writing: first person, or stories that are narrated by the "I", like Lionel Shriver's narrator in We Need To Talk About Kevin, and third person, where the point of view, using "he" or "she", is limited to one or more characters, a technique used, for example, by Jonathan Frantzen in The Corrections. Less common are the second person, or "you" and "we" – used to good effect in Joshua Ferris's recent first novel, Then We Came to the End – and the third person omniscient, where the writing moves in and out of various character's points of view fluidly, of which Virginia Woolf's Mrs Dalloway is a tour de force. Many novels use multiple points of view, for example, alternating between first and third.

A useful exercise is to look at a selection of your favourite novels and see what point of view the writer has used. First person can lend a story intimacy; when combined with the present tense this can contribute hugely to narrative pace, while multiple third person can give a story a rich, polyphonic density. When you begin to write a piece of fiction, choose which point of view, or points of view, you are going to use, and then stick to it. It's important that you control point of view; don't let it control you.

"When you begin to write choose which point of view, or points of view, you are going to use and stick to it"

Five provocations

Creative writing students often hope that there's secret truth about how to write that will be revealed once they start their course, and that published writers possess the keys to the kingdom. But the sorry truth is that there is no secret, there is no magic formula, there is no mysterious How To Write Fiction book that will suddenly make it easy (apart from this one, of course!).

The fact is, there are no rules for good writing. Matters of taste and fashion apart, good writing these days can be as structurally conventional and yet deeply satisfying as Colm Tóibín's rewarding look at Henry James in The Master or as original and ground-breaking as Ali Smith's anti-novel Hotel World. So, in the absence of a secret formula, here are five rules to provoke you into thinking again about what and how you are writing.

1 Try to avoid using adjectives and adverbs. Adjectives and adverbs are for lazy writers. (A quick reminder here: adjectives are descriptive words attached to nouns, like "lovely nouns" or "gorgeous nouns", and adverbs are attached to verbs.)

Well, adjectives might be necessary from time to time, but adverbs are definitely to be used as sparingly as harissa paste, she said brightly. She gazed longingly at his adverb-free piece of writing.

2 Avoid exposition. Don't explain things to us; we readers don't like to have things explained to us. We like to see things, we like to imagine things, we like to draw our own conclusions, we like to be illuminated, we like enigma and mystery. We don't like to be told what to think.

3 Use the words "seem" (and its evil cousins seemed and seems) and "just" carefully. Beginner writers just always seem to rely very heavily on these two words. Just is like a verbal tic, I think; we hear it in our heads, so we put it on the page. Just stop. Seemed, well, either something is like something else, or it isn't. Be definite. Be specific. Vagueness is your enemy (NB: Vagueness is not the same thing as enigma and mystery).

"Try not to ignore that little voice in your head that says 'oh, that doesn't quite work'"

4 Don't repeat words ... unless you are going for a specific, repetitive style or voice, like Thomas Bernhard in his novel The Loser where we hear about Glenn Gould's genius, and the narrator's corresponding lack of genius, over and over again. Some writers appear to believe that because novels have lots of words in them, they can be lazy about word choices, patterns, and rhythms. Every word counts in a novel, as it does in a short story, as it does in a poem.

5 Try not to ignore the little voice in your head that says, "Oh, that doesn't quite work." A big part of learning to write (and this is an ongoing process) is figuring out the difference between the loud internal voice that says "THIS IS ALL RUBBISH AND YOU SHOULD NEVER WRITE ANOTHER WORD EVER AGAIN" and that somewhat quieter internal voice that says, "Hmm, that's not quite right, but let's pretend we didn't notice." Learn to trust your gut instinct – listen to that little voice, while ignoring the big pushy one.

The trick with writing well is to convince yourself you can do it, while at the same time telling yourself you can do it better. But you can do it better, and when you do it well, there is nothing more exciting.

Checklist

■ **Is the beginning too slow?**

The first few pages of any novel are crucial to its success. A brilliant opening line like 'Last night I dreamt I went to Manderley again' can hook your reader and draw them directly into your story. Too much scene setting can bog things down when most readers like to get straight to the heart of the story. But while you are getting a book started you will likely find that you return to the opening pages over and over again, polishing them so hard and bright that they end up rather inert and lifeless. A good tactic is to forget about the beginning until you get to the end; many writers find that they have to get to the end of a book before they can write the beginning.

■ **Have I "killed my darlings"?**

"Killing your darlings" refers to knowing how and when to make serious cuts and alterations in your story. When you have laboured long and hard over a passage of writing, it can be heart-breaking to realise that it doesn't work within the context of your book. One of most useful attributes for any writer is ruthlessness, the ability to write and then cut, write and then cut, and then cut again. Some writers write with an ideal reader in mind; others write for themselves alone. It doesn't really matter either way, provided you stay true to what you are trying to do. Take a step back, draw a deep breath, and sharpen that knife. This is what editing and rewriting and polishing are all about.

■ **Have I checked my grammar and punctuation?**

When your work is being read by people in the publishing industry, they will use every excuse possible to discard your manuscript and move on to the next one. Do not underestimate the weight of unpublished manuscripts that bear down on agents and publishers. Writing that isn't up to scratch on this basic but crucial level will find its way to the dustbin faster than you can say "But I spent five years writing that thing and it's a work of genius!" Good writing is clean writing.

■ **Have I laid out my dialogue properly?**

There are many ways to indicate dialogue, from the standard new-paragraph-new-speaker with double speechmarks common to many novels to the more radical approach of, for example, Jose Saramago in his novel Blindness where the dialogue is not separated in any way from the rest of the prose (in fact, this gripping novel pulls off a stylistic double whammy: the characters do not have names). The basic rule is this: it doesn't matter how you place dialogue on the page as long as it is clear to the reader who is saying what when. And the key to getting this right is consistency.

■ **After my compelling beginning, am I keeping my reader interested?**

There are many tactics for keeping your reader keen, not the least of which is having a strong narrative drive peopled with great characters. One useful trick is to think in scenes, utilising what we have learned from the cinematic jump-cut; move from one scene to another without worrying too much about how your character actually gets there, without getting bogged down in setting things up. Your reader will make the connections without you having to labour the point.

■ Is it finished?

Most writers write many many drafts of their fiction. In general it seems to be a mark of the less serious in this world who baldly state, "It came out perfect. If I touch it, I'll ruin it." A redraft can be as simple as a run through the entire manuscript to tighten it up or as complex as an entire restructuring of the narrative flow while changing all the third person passages into the first person. Maintaining objectivity on one's own work is extremely difficult and most published writers rely on a first reader of some description – a writer friend, an agent or editor, a mentor or tutor – to help them figure out when a book is actually finished (as opposed to when you wish it would stop). The writer who can do this all on their own is a rare beast.

What next?

Your novel is finished, so should you send it to an agent or straight to a publisher? Editor Vanessa Neuling says getting the right agent could be key

F rom completing your manuscript to glimpsing your novel on the shelves of Waterstone's can feel like an impossible leap. So, what's the best way towards it for you and your book? In the competitive world of fiction publishing it's almost always finding a good literary agent.

Having the right person on your side can prove indispensable as you navigate your way through the publishing process. While you may feel more than capable of approaching publishers directly it's increasingly rare to meet with success this way, and strong representation will ensure that your project is read by the most relevant and talented editors in the industry. Not only will a skilled agent have a thorough understanding of the market and how to pitch your book most successfully, they will have dedicated time to building relationships and getting to know editors' individual tastes and the strengths of different publishing lists. They may well work with you to shape your book before submitting it and they should also be keeping your future career very much in mind.

In the happy event that you receive an offer, or more than one, for your work, your agent will negotiate the best possible deal and will then finalise the contractual details, a crucial stage where a little industry knowledge, experience and negotiating power can go a very long way. Details such as high-discount clauses or ebook royalties are a world away from the creative process of writing but they have the potential to make an enormous difference to your income, and unagented authors can find themselves in a much weaker position here. During and beyond your first deal the agency will assist you in managing the business side of your affairs, and will often be well set up to sell foreign rights and other subrights. As you build a new relationship with your editor, a match that any conscientious agent will have considered carefully, your agent will continue to support you as and when needed.

Approaching literary agents can be daunting at first – while there are plenty of them out there, not all are actively seeking new clients, and for those that are you will almost certainly find yourself competing with other aspiring writers. So it's essential that you are professional and focused in your search, researching agencies as fully as possible and making considered approaches to individual agents. Take the time at this early stage to look at client lists and see who authors writing in a similar area to you have paired up with. Might your novel appeal to those agents too? Keep an eye on the trade press, and look beyond the high-profile names striking significant deals – it might well be a more junior agent with a passion for literary or crime fiction who is best placed to dedicate time to working with you. When you do send in work present it clearly; most agents are kept very busy with their existing clients and are much more likely to be won over by a well-written, concise letter and biography than a quirky one.

The agent who shares your vision and is passionate about your writing is the one most likely to lead you in a direction that's right for you, and to remain dedicated to helping you build a successful and rewarding career. So, tempting as it may be, try not to settle for the first person who shows an interest in your work. You'll need to find someone you trust and can communicate openly with, so seek a face-to-face meeting if you can – and choose a companion you'll enjoy going on this journey with.

Vanessa Neuling has worked at Virago and most recently as a commissioning editor at Random House

Books for children

Child's play

Writing for children means thinking about your own past, while staying in touch with young people now, says Michael Rosen

We've all been children, we all know a parent or parent-figure. This makes us all potential writers of children's books. I think of children's books as not so much for children, but as the filling that goes between the child world and the adult world. One way or another, all children's books have to negotiate that space, whether it's thinking about how the text of a picture book will sound when read aloud, or how the child views him or herself in a world run by adults. And before it reaches the hand, eye or ear of a child there are many adults to deal with: editors, illustrators, publicists, marketing people, the buying adults. And of course, more than likely, you're an adult reading this, so the moment you think about writing something for children, you'll be handling something or other from your own childhood. This may be something you read, experiences of being read to, pleasurable or painful experiences from when you were young.

There is also an interesting line between the child you once were and the children you know now. If you want to write a book for children, you will find yourself travelling to and fro along this line, wondering one moment about what kind of child you were, why you had those particular tastes and interests, what depressed or excited you, what you were afraid of, what you yearned for; the next, looking, listening and thinking about the children you know or meet. Are there big differences, or is there some core child-ness that is unchanged?

"You need to get that child who is now the age of your target audience into your head"

Is the culture and background you came from, similar or different to the kinds of children you know and meet now? If so, how does your writing reach them?

So you know you want to write something. As you'll read in the rest of this section, children's literature has very specific forms or genres. It may sometimes seem to you that editors can only think inside specific boxes, whereas a book you liked, The Little Prince, say, defied such boxes. So you'll hear from editors, comments like: "There's no point in writing a picture book text that's longer than a couple of hundred words", "That story is too 'old' for a picture book audience", "Your story is too short" and so on. Bafflingly, if you go to the library and pick up a pile of books, you may well find some that seem to defy such boundaries. Nearly always, that's because it's a famous author who's been granted leeway to write what they want – Roald Dahl's The Minpins is an example of that. Or you've got in your hand a book produced by an independent company, a firm like Tamarind, Frances Lincoln or Barefoot Books.

What this means is that any of us who write for children have to do homework. We have to be very aware of both what is being published and how people are telling stories these days. The writer Morris Gleitzman told me that he sets himself one golden rule when he writes for children: "Start any scene as 'late' into the action or dialogue as you can." In other words, don't hang about. That's his perception of today's audience.

If you're serious about writing, you'll need some kind of axiom (or several) like that so that you put yourself in control of what you're putting down on the page.

We also have to spend time in bookshops, libraries, nurseries, schools and with reading children, seeing how the books work with the audiences. You are of course the first audience for what you write, but you want to make yourself the kind of reader who can pretend to be the reading child. You've got to build in a sense of your audience as part of the way in which you're tough with yourself about what you're writing. Part of that reading child will inevitably be the reading child you once were. That's no bad thing, but quite often, I would suggest, this is not sufficient. You also need to get that child who is now the age of your target audience into your head too.

The world of children's books is a very friendly, decent place to be. It's full of people who are desperate to enlighten, interest and excite children in ideas, imaginary worlds and contemporary issues. Everywhere you look in this world, you'll find very committed, low-paid people, who will go the extra mile if it means reaching a child who might not otherwise come across a book. There are a whole host of organisations trying to foster a love of reading and the moment you've got something written and published, no matter how modest, there are all sorts of places that will be interested in inviting you to share your book with some children. A very important part of writing for children is appearing at book festivals, and in libraries and schools. An important part of becoming a writer for children is seeing what published writers do and say when they appear. Writing children's books may be as lonely as any other kind of writing, but there is a big social element in how the books are taken to the readers. There are thousands of people out there doing this – parents, librarians and teachers mostly – so part of being a writer for children is being among these people at the events they organise. If you get the balance right, this will be part of what motivates you to go back into the cell and write some more!

Michael Rosen is the Children's Laureate (2007–2009). He has written 140 books of poetry and fiction for children

Why write at all?

Writing for children is not an easy route to becoming published; your tutor Linda Newbery explains why

About your tutor

Linda Newbery's publications range from Posy, a picture-book illustrated by Catherine Rayner, to novels. Set in Stone was Costa Children's Book of 2006; Sisterland and The Shell House were Carnegie-shortlisted. Recent publications include The Sandfather and Flightsend, and a novel for younger children, Lob, will be published by David Fickling Books in 2010. Linda has tutored for the Arvon Foundation.

Books can change lives – we know that. And if you're lucky enough to write and publish books for children, there's the potential of changing young lives in various ways. Yours might be the book that turns a child on to reading; maybe it's a favourite bedtime story, or the first book a child reads alone. It might give a child an absorbing new interest, or bring insight, reassurance, or the determination to confront a doubt or a fear. Yours might be the book that's loved literally to pieces, the story that's read and reread and almost known by heart. Your book, once published, will reach farther than you'll ever know.

These are powerful reasons for wanting to write for children, but let's get rid of some that aren't likely to get you far.

It can't be difficult – anyone can do it. No: anyone can't. This misconception hasn't been helped by the current crop of celebrities publishing children's stories. A household name certainly helps with the marketing, but most of us don't have that flying start. Shelves and tables in editors' and agents' offices sag under the weight of unpublishable stories sent in the belief that anyone can write for children.

I'm writing the next Harry Potter. You may think so; so do countless others. As Philip Pullman has put it, no one was looking for the first Harry Potter (nor for His Dark Materials).

The best books often come as if from nowhere, not from an examination of market requirements. Publishers' lists reach at least two years into the future, and what you see as a hot trend may be nearing the end of its run.

I've written this short story and my friends say I should get it published. But why? You may be able to cook a reasonable pasta dish, but you don't therefore see yourself as rival to Gordon Ramsay or Nigella Lawson. Yet, for some reason, it's a common belief that any coherent piece of writing deserves publication. Publishing isn't a reward for effort; it's a business.

It must be an easy way to make money. It isn't. A recent survey by Mary Hoffman for the Society of Authors revealed that most children's writers earn less than the minimum wage. An exceptional few sell books by the million; most of those who make their living by writing have worked hard at it for years.

So why write for children?
- Because you have the germ of an idea that might make a story, and you can't wait to explore it
- Because you've had such pleasure from living in other people's stories
- Because you love playing with words and ideas
- Because you can live inside the head of a child or teenager and be fascinated by what happens there
- Because inside your adult self there's a child's playfulness and sense of wonder
- Because you know that children's reading is so important that only the best you can offer is good enough.

> "You have the germ of an idea that might make a story and you can't wait to explore it"

Genre in children's writing

C hildren's books cover a huge range, from books for babies up to young adult fiction. You can easily get a sense of the various ranges by looking at publisher websites or catalogues, and by looking at stock in libraries and bookshops. Specialist review magazines such as Books for Keeps and Carousel will introduce you to the best current books and authors, as well as making these age distinctions clear.

Many would-be children's authors start off with little or no knowledge of the current market – maybe with a nostalgic memory of their own childhood favourites. The results are sometimes completely impractical: a 60,000-word novel for five-year-olds, say, or a story about talking tractors which requires the reading ability of the average 12-year-old. Some familiarity with the different areas of publishing will help you to avoid this kind of mismatch between story and assumed reader.

Picture Books
These are not to be confused with illustrated chapter stories. Picture books usually contain minimal text and are illustrated in full colour, most often in large 32-page format. Some artists write their own texts, for instance Shirley Hughes, Emily Gravett and Lauren Child, but if not it's the editor who

matches author with illustrator. If you've written a picture-book text, don't think you have to find an artistic friend before you can submit it – your words will stand more chance of catching an editor's attention on their own. Editors often have illustrators they want to use, and are looking out for good stories for them. And, as specialists, they'll have their own ideas about design.

A common mistake with would-be picture-book authors is to use too many words. There's no need to describe things that can be shown in the illustrations – for instance, it's redundant to say that someone is shocked, when the picture can dramatise their expression. On the other hand, Rosie's Walk by Pat Hutchins works brilliantly by setting uneventful text (and very few words) against dramatic images; the reader sees all the dangers to which Rosie the hen is oblivious.

Don't be misled into thinking that picture books must be easy to write because there are so few words. It's a very specialised area, and because full-colour books are expensive to produce, publishers need to sell foreign rights to justify the costs. Rhyming texts may be difficult to translate, so publishers often turn them down for this reason. However, there are many successful exceptions, including Julia Donaldson's The Gruffalo.

"Don't be misled into thinking that picture books are easy to write "

If you intend to write picture-book texts, it's worth installing yourself in a good library or bookshop where you can spend a couple of hours browsing. Look at layout and design and the flow of text across pages, to see how picture books work. Especially, notice how the turning of a page is used to create drama or build a surprise.

First Readers/Chapter Stories

Many of the larger publishers have a series of short illustrated books for children aged from around four to seven – for example, the Banana books published by Egmont, or Young Corgi and Corgi Pups at Random House. These are usually paperbacks, with colour illustrations on every page; often an author will base a series on one human or animal character. Most are humorous, pacy stories written in short chapters. Some publishers issue guidelines as to word length (usually between 2,000 and 5,000 words) and other requirements. Again, these should be written with illustration in mind.

The advantage of writing this kind of fiction is that as a new author you'll instantly become part of a known brand, as these series always have a distinctive look. Your book is likely to appear in the catalogue alongside work from established, big-name authors, many of whom produce work for these series.

"Too much market awareness can take your attention away from the real business of writing"

Junior fiction

Here we have novels for children aged from seven to 12, and there are two sections here: the seven to nine books, and the nine to 12 category, which is a core area of children's publishing. Obviously books at the younger end tend to be shorter: 15,000–20,000 words, say (though there aren't any rules). For nine to 12s, you have enormous freedom with regard to length, subject and style. There are plenty of trilogies and series published for this age group, but editors will also be looking for really good standalone novels.

Teenage/Young Adult fiction

In bookshops and libraries, what's known as teenage fiction includes books aimed at readers of 10 or 11. This younger end is known to publishers as aspirational fiction – ie it appeals to children who aren't teenagers yet, but want to engage with characters older than themselves in easy, accessible stories. Also on these shelves you'll find the more sophisticated novels of adolescence with appeal to adults as well as teenagers: for instance Tamar by Mal Peet, Postcards from No Man's Land by Aidan Chambers, or A Gathering Light by Jennifer Donnelly. If you doubt that the best writing for young readers can stand up against the best fiction for adults, take a look at these excellent novels.

Crossover fiction has become increasingly prominent in recent years, with novels such as Before I Die by Jenny Downham, Across the Nightingale Floor by Lian Hearn and The Curious Incident of the Dog in the Night-Time by Mark Haddon achieving high sales in adult editions as well as winning major children's book prizes.

In adult fiction, most fantasy is firmly directed to a separate shelf in bookshops, whereas various genres mix happily in the children's and teenage sections.

So, where to start? You may have an idea that already suggests characters of a particular age. Use your own childhood and teenage years. Which point in childhood can you remember most vividly? You might have clear memories from when you were 15, or 12, or eight. If you can recall the doubts and anxieties and excitements of being 10, maybe this is where you should place yourself fictionally. When asked by an interviewer how he managed to convey an eight-year-old's world so convincingly, Roald Dahl famously said: "I am eight years old."

Most authors have been asked who they write for; some say that they write for an imagined reader of a particular age, while others write for their own children. Many say that they write for themselves.

It's not fair

All children have a highly developed sense of injustice. Thinking back to your childhood, and whatever age you arrive at, write a short first-person account of an experience that struck you as unfair. Try to recapture the feelings that gripped you at that time – whether you were the victim of the injustice, or an observer.

exercise

from the front line

Meg Rosoff on how to write crossover fiction

Crossover fiction is a slippery category, neither fish nor fowl, sometimes published for adults but read by teens (The Life of Pi), other times published for teens but read by adults (His Dark Materials). It's a category that didn't exist when Edith Wharton published The Age of Innocence or Jane Austen wrote about Elizabeth Bennet. I had no idea I was destined to write crossover novels, but an obsession of 35 years' duration with coming-of-age stories might have provided a hint.

As for advice on how to do it? A bit like the priesthood, it may be more a calling than a choice. It helps to be in touch with your inner adolescent, though I've found my inner mid-life crisis helpful as well. Think of books like Marjane Satrapi's Persepolis and Cormac McCarthy's All the Pretty Horses if you aspire to brilliant modern versions of the form, though the oldies – To Kill a Mockingbird and Lord of the Flies – work just as well. Don't worry about pleasing your audience, don't dumb down, don't pull your punches, and don't try to think like a teenager or you'll end up moody, angry, and confused.

If you can remember what life was like when the world seemed to be perpetually out of focus, when the sort of issues that interested you were existentialism, sensation, falling in love, and the shape of the universe, you're probably part-way there. An adolescent protagonist is not actually required by the form, though most crossover books seem to have one. Pages and pages of description may be deemed boring, but Yann Martel got away with it in spades. When in doubt, ditch what everyone else says and make up your own rules.

My best advice is to write fiercely. Your audience craves intensity, passion, catharsis, sex, extreme experience, philosophy, relationships, hallucinatory revelations. And that goes for the teens as well as the adults.

Meg Rosoff's How I Live Now won the Guardian's Children's Fiction Prize in 2004

Whatever your approach, it's essential that you find pleasure and satisfaction in the writing, and feel challenged by it; otherwise you'll be writing down to your readers, which is patronising, and will detract from the immediacy of your story.

It's as well to have an idea which section of the market you're aiming for – but, once you're under way, too much market awareness can distract you from the real business of writing. The late Jan Mark, twice winner of the Carnegie Medal, tutored a number of courses for adults, and once remarked of her students: "You get the ones who want to be published, and the ones who want to write." Undoubtedly, it was the latter group she was interested in. While working on a book, don't be sidetracked into thinking about marketing campaigns or your Carnegie acceptance speech; your attention must be focused on telling the story as well as you possibly can.

So – if you're serious, think of yourself as a writer first, a writer for children (or teenagers) second.

From idea to story

"**W**here do you get your ideas from?" Every author who gives talks to children or adults has been asked this question hundreds of times, and of course there's no simple answer. Ideas are everywhere – the trick is to recognise a promising one when you get it, and not let go. Your starting point may be something that's happened to you, or to someone you know; a news item; a fear, or a dream; something from the past; a fascinating character; a painting or poem; and of course our heads are crammed full of ideas and images from books we've read, stories we've heard and films we've seen. Several of my own books have begun with a particular place or atmosphere: an intriguing old house (Nevermore), a wartime airfield (Flightsend), an out-of-season seaside resort (The Sandfather).

When a promising idea grabs hold of you, hang on to it and see if you can turn it into a story, or at least the beginning of a story. You can build on it by asking yourself questions and thinking of the answers. Who? When? Why? will get you started; then more and more questions will follow: But why doesn't he tell anyone? Who could possibly help her? Where have his parents gone? What's he hiding from? At this stage, it's a game: you haven't committed yourself to anything, and can enjoy playing around with ideas and possibilities. When you're ready, you can start making notes on the characters and their situations.

Every story, whatever the genre, must involve conflict, and it's useful (though not necessarily at this early stage) to be able to convey the essence of your story in a single phrase. As the agent Carole Blake, author of From Pitch to Publication, puts it, any story can be boiled down to: What does the main character want, and what's stopping them from getting it? If there's no conflict, there's no story.

• Macbeth: What does Macbeth want? To be King of Scotland. What's stopping him? There's already a king, with two sons as his heirs.

• Far From the Madding Crowd by Thomas Hardy: What does Gabriel Oak want? To marry Bathsheba Everdene. What's stopping him? She becomes a woman of property, and falls in love with the wrong man.

• Tom's Midnight Garden by Philippa Pearce: What does Tom want? To explore outside, instead of spending the summer holidays cooped up in his aunt and uncle's flat. What's stopping him? He's in quarantine for measles, and expected to stay indoors.

A story is driven by the facing and resolution of the central conflict. Too early a resolution means that all tension is lost. Too easy or convenient a solution means that the story won't convince. Let's look in detail at a 32-page picture book, Dogger by Shirley Hughes. What does Dave want? To be reunited with his favourite toy, Dogger. What's stopping him? ...

In the opening pages, we're shown how important the toy dog is to Dave. His sister Bella sleeps with several bears tucked up next to her; Dave has Dogger with him in bed. No other toy will do. The first crisis comes when Dogger is dropped in the street while Mum and the children buy and eat ice-cream cornets. At bedtime, when Dave can't find Dogger, the whole family is involved in searching; but the toy can't be found.

Next day, at the school fete, Dave is unhappy, missing Dogger. Meanwhile, Bella's enjoying herself, coming first in a

> "What does the main character want, and what's stopping them from getting it?"

Stepping stones

Using numbered points, make a simple outline of a story you know well – Cinderella, for example – showing the main plot events.

Now do the same for a story or your own, using stepping stones to show the unfolding of conflict and how it will be resolved.

race, winning a raffle prize. Dave is jealous, because his sister's having such a good day while he's miserable. Then he sees Dogger, sitting on the back of the toy stall, with a price-tag. Dave hasn't got enough money, so he runs to find Bella. Now the second crisis: as they hurry back to the stall, a little girl has bought Dogger and is walking away with him.

The resolution doesn't come immediately; we have to see the possibility of Dave being parted with his toy forever. Bella offers to buy Dogger back, but the girl refuses – she's paid, and now he's hers. Dave is distraught, crying as the girl marches off with Dogger. The answer doesn't arrive out of the blue, either – it's already been built into the story and is there in the pictures. Bella is clutching a big teddy-bear, her raffle prize. Although we know that Bella likes bears, she offers to swap the teddy for her brother's toy; the girl agrees, preferring the brand-new bear to battered old Dogger, and everyone's happy. The final picture shows Bella in bed with her row of bears, and Dave tucked up with Dogger. The story is expertly paced and dramatised, and we've seen the swings of resentment and affection between brother and sister. Needless to say, Shirley Hughes' illustrations give character, warmth and charm to a story crafted from the stuff of ordinary family life.

Try applying this simple what does he/she want formula to novels you've read recently, or to films, and then to the story you're thinking of writing. The dilemma set up, and its resolution, give you the main thrust of the story. In a picture book like Dogger, one plot strand is enough; in a novel for juniors or older, more will be going on. If, for example, your central character is a keen footballer desperate to be picked for the local team, there can be scenes at home and at school, perhaps involving a division of loyalty or clash of responsibility, so that the football detail isn't overwhelming.

Sometimes writers, especially inexperienced ones, come to a halt simply because they've lost sight of where the story is going. Authors vary tremendously in the amount of planning they do – some like to know exactly how the story will unfold, and have a chapter-by-chapter plan; others prefer to gather their ingredients, then let the story develop, leaving room for surprises. There's no right or wrong way, of course, but when you embark on a story for the first time you're more likely to feel confident if you can always see where to go next. This route can be plotted via stepping stones (see panel above) – you don't need to plan every detail, but at least you know what the next major episode will be.

> "Sometimes writers come to a halt because they've lost sight of where they're going"

Julia Jarman, author of Hangman and Peace Weavers, says that writing a novel is like making a film, "but you're taking charge of every aspect of it. The casting, costumes, locations, dialogue, special effects, pacing – everything, and you do it all with words." If you think of your unfolding novel as a film being privately screened inside your head, it will help you to establish the setting with enough but not too much description, like the mise-en-scène of film, and to vary the pace of the narrative. For instance, a scene that consists mainly of people talking can be followed by one that develops the plot through action or a shift in location, or moves more quickly through time. Some writers plan through storyboards, another way of thinking in filmic or dramatic terms.

Nicola Davies on how to write non-fiction for children

Writing non-fiction won't get you onto any literary high tables, but it is still a noble calling: your words could instill lifelong curiosity in your readers. Start with thorough research; don't skimp because it's "only for kids" – it'll make your writing superficial.

Once you have assembled everything, be prepared to cut. Don't worry that you aren't telling your readers everything.

It's better to tell them one thing they'll remember than ten things they'll forget. The most basic information can be interesting for young children; how a foot makes a print in sand is more exciting to a two year old than the geology of the beach. And don't be scared to say what is not known – it's important that children see knowledge as an ongoing project that they could contribute to.

Lists don't make readable books, so find a narrative thread to string your information on. One way to do this is to describe what your book is about in one word. I found my book about blue whales was about "bigness", but my turtle one was actually about "memory".

Make sure you use the right language for your audience. Translating complex information into words that children can understand takes time and lots of thinking. Use examples from the child's world to help. Always remember that the only way writing non-fiction differs from fiction is that you don't have to make up anything up. Keep your writing rich and interesting.

Nicola Davies' latest non-fiction book is Just the Right Size (Walker Books)

from the front line

Characters and viewpoint

The main characters in fiction for children and teenagers tend, not surprisingly, to be children and teenagers, though it's not hard to find exceptions, such as Philip Pullman's Once Upon a Time in the North. To write convincingly, whether in first- or third-person, you need to position yourself inside the head of one or more characters. In Tom's Midnight Garden, we share Tom's thoughts all the way: his frustration at being cooped up, his interest in the old grandfather clock, his surprise at finding that the midnight garden is different from the daytime one.

One way of getting a sense of your characters as rounded human beings, rather than as cardboard cut-outs, is to build them through questions and answers. For example: What's in her pocket? Who does she dislike, and why? What's her best subject at school? Who would she most like to get a text message from? What's she most anxious about? and so on. And it's important to hear your character speaking, and to see his or her body language.

Adults will almost inevitably appear, but children's writers are adept at getting rid of them, or at least keeping them on the sidelines, so that the children have to confront their own difficulties. Health and safety consciousness can curtail the activities of children in present-day stories of the real world,

"What's crucial is that the child characters are central to the action"

from the front line

Michael Lawrence on what makes kids laugh

Adults who haven't read any of my books about Jiggy McCue and his pals might imagine that they are relentlessly rude crowd-pleasers. With titles like The Killer Underpants, The Toilet of Doom and Nudie Dudie I can hardly blame them, but in fact I avoid extreme vulgarity, and scatological humour in particular. Kids love a little gentle rudeness, though, and this I do supply, because it appeals to me too. A good example is 'The Fellowship of Ancient Rights for Trees' in The Snottle. Jiggy refers to the organisation's members as 'FARTers', always emphasising the first syllable to irritate his mother. Well, isn't that what you would have done when you were 11 or 12?

I don't go out of my way to keep up with the times in these stories. Mobile phones, DVDs, famous film stars and so on are mentioned, but Jiggy's school experiences are essentially my own from over half a century ago. I base his lessons on the lessons that I remember so well. (Some of his teachers were my actual teachers – and yes, I use their real names). You might think that this would date the books, but children can't have changed much, as they write to me in droves to say how much like Jiggy's world theirs is. I find that rather pleasing.

Michael Lawrence's latest book is Jiggy McCue: One for All and All for Lunch! (Orchard)

which may account for the huge amount of fantasy published in recent years; in imaginary settings, child characters can be magicians, warriors, seers, time-travellers, or whatever the author wants them to be. Similarly, children in historical fiction can plausibly face huge responsibilities and go on dangerous journeys with only their own resources to depend on.

What's crucial is that the child characters are central to the action, and play a decisive part – they can't just have things happen to them. In Dogger, it's the children who sort out the problem – the outcome would be less satisfying if Dave's parents had swooped in to take charge.

In some settings, children – and adults – seem powerless. Continuing the tradition of stories about children caught up in war, oppression and persecution, the author Elizabeth Laird has written, with great success, novels featuring street children in Addis Ababa (The Garbage King), a Kurdish refugee (Red Sky in the Morning) and a Palestinian boy living in the Occupied Territories (A Little Patch of Ground). Importantly, Laird makes her child characters more than passive victims of persecution. Karim and his friends convert a patch of wasteland into a football pitch, defiantly raising a Palestinian flag; their game of football is unlikely to challenge Israeli dominance, yet the novel humanises the situation and engages the reader by showing us one boy's very ordinary aspiration.

"There aren't any rules, but you should know what rules you've made for yourself"

Most important of all is that your readers must care about your character. Endow your hero or heroine with skill, beauty and undentable self-confidence and you risk alienating the reader. Flaws, self-doubts and weaknesses – in even the most spirited of characters, like Philip Pullman's Lyra – engage reader sympathy. Winnie-the-Pooh is endearing because he's well-meaning, but easily confused; Jane Eyre because she considers herself to be plain and unremarkable. Christopher in The Curious Incident... is aware that his Asperger's syndrome marks him out as different, but makes us see people and events with his own logic and dogged determination.

A problem frequently seen in students' writing is viewpoint-hopping. Without realising, they've changed the point of view from paragraph to paragraph, or even from sentence to sentence, so reading the story feels like jumping in and out of

Lauren Child on how to illustrate a story

There are millions of talented illustrators out there who would love to illustrate books for children. They are creative, they are original, they are skilful. And yet they have to suffer one rejection after the other.

I know, because for the first five years of my career, I was one of them. It was only when I realised that I could write my own books that I got my first manuscript accepted.

Normally, as an illustrator, you are taught to treat text with a lot of respect, reverence even. The books that you illustrate tend to arrive paginated, with the text already fine-tuned. But in a good picture-book, the pictures should be as important – if not more important – than the text. I never finish the text before I am done with the illustrations.

When you illustrate a story, don't try to show what the words are already telling you. You have to add something new. I try to do this by changing perspective, or by engaging with my characters' imagination. In one of my books, Charlie tells Lola that she has to go to bed "because all the birds have gone to bed". To which Lola replies: "But I'm not a bird". Rather than showing Lola in the kitchen, where the conversation is taking place, I showed Lola sitting in a bird's nest.

The simplest drawings of characters are the often the most successful: think of Miffy or Peanuts. But even the simplest human face has to show more than one expression over the course of your book. If you want your character to be liked, you have to give them an emotional inner life.

I always know when I see a good illustration: I get jealous. The tricky thing is that you have to actively resist the temptation to imitate the illustrators you like. Many publishers will pretend that they want your book to look "more like Quentin Blake" or "a bit like Shirley Hughes". But deep down they want to see something new.

Lauren Child's collected Clarice Bean stories are published by Orchard

from the front line

various characters' heads. This is unsettling for the reader, and rarely works.

Of course you can use more than one viewpoint: children's fiction, like any other fiction, can have omniscient narrators, multiple narrators, unreliable narrators. There aren't any rules, but you should know what rules you've made for yourself, know when you're breaking them, and do so for good reason.

Openings

Opening pages are so important. You can capture a reader's interest, or immediately lose it. (And before you have any chance of reaching readers, your work must catch an editor's interest.) Where does your story begin? Why there? Is there a decisive moment – a phone call, a meeting, a discovery – that sparks off the whole thing?

It is advisable to get into the story quickly, rather than loading your opening pages with explanations and information. The unpacking of relevant background can be done bit by bit as the story moves on; and you may not need as much of this as you think.

Let's look at some openings to novels for children and teenagers. See if you agree with me that these first paragraphs are written with a confidence and authority that make you want more:

"Her delicate skeleton was lifted from the stand on which it had hung for longer than anyone could remember. The leg and arm bones made hollow, musical sounds as they knocked against each other gently. Like bamboo wind chimes in a breeze. For a moment she seemed to be dancing. Her legs moving, her arms lifting and her body swaying to some strange music only she could hear.
She was dancing again after being still for so long.
At least, that's how I imagined it had happened, even though the photograph showed nothing of this."
Fish Notes and Star Songs, by Dianne Hofmeyr

"I have been in love with Titus Oates for quite a while now – which is ridiculous, since he's been dead for ninety years. But look at it this way.

In ninety years I'll be dead, too, and then the age difference won't matter.
Besides, he isn't dead inside my head. We talk about all kinds of things."
The White Darkness by Geraldine McCaughrean

"When the Dead Man got Rachel I was sitting in the back of a
wrecked Mercedes wondering if the rain was going to stop. I didn't
want it to stop. I was just wondering.
It was late, almost midnight."
The Road of the Dead by Kevin Brooks

"Remember? I can still smell it. I met her in the Aldwych Underground
Station, at half past six in the morning, when people were still busily
rolling up their bedding, and climbing out to see how much of the
street was left standing. There were no lavatories down there, and with
houses going down like ninepins every night there was a shortage of
baths in London just then, and the stench of the Underground was
appalling. I noticed, as I lurked around, trying to keep inconspicuous,
that there was someone else doing the same. I was lurking because I
wanted to stay in the warm for as long as possible, without being one
of the very last out, in case any busybody asked me tricky questions.
And there was this girl, as clearly as anything, lurking too."
Fireweed by Jill Paton Walsh

What marks out good writing is hard to define. To me, it says:
"I know what I'm doing. Come with me. I won't let you down."
It's not trying to show off, but it has an energy that is
unmistakable, and a sense of living in the moment.

First page

Pick some books at random from the children's or teenagers'
shelves in the library. Read just the first page of each. Which
ones catch your attention and make you want more? How?
Which ones don't work so well, and why?
Now look at your own first page in the same way.

Exercise

Checklist

Revising your work is an essential part of writing, and should be enjoyable. You'll only improve your writing if you're self-critical; if you develop a sense of the best writing, and tune your ear. This is the time to make significant changes to your work. You're not facing the pressure of reaching the end of the story; it's all there, and everything you do now will be an improvement.

■ **Is the story as good as it can be?**
Don't be in too much hurry to send your work to a publisher or agent. The euphoria of reaching the end can be misleading; you're too close to the work to judge its quality. Leave it for a while – a week, a month, longer if possible. Then read it, trying to forget that you're the author. This will help you to notice problems of pacing, scene-setting, etc and also you'll appreciate which parts of the story work well.

■ **Are my opening pages engaging?**
Are you expecting your reader to plod through stodgy explanations before the story really begins? If your opening pages are cluttered with information, consider ditching that chapter altogether. Bits of background can be dropped in later.

■ **Would the writing be stronger with fewer words?**
Cutting is an important part of revising. Don't patronise your reader by spelling everything out. Use adverbs sparingly; they're often not needed, particularly when applied to speech.

■ Read your work aloud.

And don't rush it – spread the reading over several days, if necessary. This way, you'll notice clumsy repetitions, nonsensical sentences, accidental rhyming or a phrase that's difficult to get your tongue round, and you'll get a sense of whether or not your dialogue sounds convincing. It helps develop your ear for rhythm, too because rhythm is just as important in prose as it is in poetry.

■ Do key events carry enough weight?

Inexperienced writers sometimes rush through the most dramatic events, which has the effect of making them seem ordinary. Allow for pauses in conversations and, in action sequences, the moments when time seems to go into slow-motion.

■ Is the tension sustained?

There will be rises and dips, but don't let the tension fall away altogether, or there's no reason for the reader to continue. Plotting this as a graph, chapter by chapter, will show you the shape of your story.

■ I'd like an opinion of my work. Who shall I give it to?

It can be tempting to show your work to your friends, or to various members of your family, but don't try to please everyone. If you have a trusted friend whose opinion you value, it's more productive than getting vague or half-hearted responses from people who don't know what to say.

"Don't patronise your readers by spelling everything out"

■ Make it happen

Finally: many people have a dream of writing a novel. It's not going to write itself; you'll have to make it happen.

What makes good writing stand out?

- "The kind of writing that catches my attention is clear, uncluttered prose, with pace and momentum." Jon Appleton, editoral director, Orion Children's Books
- "A young, contemporary outlook. Even historical novels need to feel as though they're of now in the way they're written – the old reporting/telling styles of the past can feel so dull." Anne Finnis, editor, Usborne
- "I'm impressed by the ability to convey a lot concisely and to move the story along, an intelligent sense of humour, and an understanding that what makes human beings tick is just as magical as anything in or out of this world." Catherine Clarke, literary agent

What next?

Don't want to end up on publishers' slush piles?
Read out loud before you get read, advises editor
David Fickling

Not everyone can sing. Not everyone can write. Even fewer people can sing professionally. Even fewer can write professionally. Do not be like those poor deluded souls who audition for the X Factor and clearly can't sing for toffee. There are far too many hopelessly written typescripts sloshing about on publishers' slush piles. They clog up the system and are a waste of everybody's time, particularly if you are a good writer yourself. There is a mistaken view that writing for children is easy. It isn't. There is another view that children's books today are of generally poor quality. They aren't. On the contrary, the rest of the world is queuing up to buy children's books published in the UK. If you do not yourself know in your innermost soul that children will enjoy your story then please I beg you do not send it (or even show it) to anyone. Before you send it, it is an excellent idea to read stories aloud to children. But, for an honest opinion, not your own children. They are biased. You don't need to like children yourself, but they need to like your work. No, strike that, they need to LOVE your work. Getting published is a paradoxical business. To get published your work needs to be recognised by someone else. Your champion! You are in the peculiar position of an egg looking for a particular sperm among thousands. Apologies if that is a ghastly thought, but it shows you how the odds are stacked against you. Every publishing success story has a different route. Nowadays, professionally speaking, your

> "The rest of the world is queueing up to buy children's books published in the UK"

champion will in all likelihood be either a commissioning editor in a largish publishing house, or a literary agent.

Getting your typescript to either and having them actually read it are necessarily tortuous and difficult. Personally speaking I wouldn't waste a second worrying about it all. Your job is to make your story irresistible. Concentrate on that. It is surprising how many really brilliant things are never lost.

As an editor at Oxford University Press, Transworld and Scholastic, David Fickling worked with writers including Philip Pullman and Jacqueline Wilson. He founded David Fickling books in 1999, which is now an imprint of Random House.

Memoir and biography

Step back in time

There's nothing like immersing yourself in a bygone era and bringing it to life, says historical biographer Antonia Fraser

Gibbon was inspired to write The Decline and Fall of the Roman Empire sitting on the steps of the Capitol at Rome one evening, listening to the sound of monks chanting vespers. My own inspiration to become a historical biographer came in rather less elevated circumstances, as a teenager one rainy Oxford afternoon: I began to read Lytton Strachey's Eminent Victorians, and as a recent convert, was in particular fascinated by his essay on the worldly Cardinal Manning. This was going to be the life for me! Once back at school I plunged into further research in the convent library. A very different picture emerged. Gradually as I pursued the topic, I became aware of Strachey's daring sallies into artistic truth (as opposed to historical truth). Nevertheless I never forgot my original sense of being transported into a world more vivid than my own.

An ability to convey this sensation is, I believe, at the heart of the matter. If you, the biographer, don't thrill to your subject, you can hardly in all fairness expect the reader to do so. In a sense (not of course the commercial sense) the choice of subject is irrelevant so long as it meets that requirement. You could say that I was extremely lucky to choose Mary Queen of Scots for my first foray since there proved to be a worldwide public for the troubles of the ill-fated Queen. But you could argue equally that I made my own luck, since I had been obsessed by Mary's story from childhood. Nor was success foreordained. It was, after all, the leading publisher Mark Bonham-Carter of (then) Collins who said to me when I confessed my project: "They say that all books on Mary Queen of Scots sell and no books on South America do", before adding with a laugh, "Perhaps yours will be the exception."

Nevertheless I did have luck. In the 60s, so-called narrative biography was said to be out of fashion. Mary Queen of Scots was an early beneficiary from the fact that the public continued to have an appetite for it, so long as the research was felt to be solid.

The actual research for a biography – now that's a whole other matter. The paramount need for it – historical truth not Stracheyesque truth must be established – means that biographers discover for themselves the reality of Dr Johnson's wise dictum about the greatest part of a writer's time being spent in reading in order to write: "A man will turn over half a library to make a book." And what about those fabled things boasted of on blurbs: hitherto unpublished documents? Obviously it is every researcher's dream to discover such papers, and their discovery once again may make a project commercial which would not otherwise be so.

There is also no excitement like that of viewing the piece of paper on which the subject actually wrote. The delicate white gloves now demanded by conservation made it particularly exciting when I inspected the single surviving Wardrobe Book of Marie Antoinette in the archives nationales in Paris – to say nothing of the presence of armed gendarmes behind me, quite ready to defend this treasure of France to the death (mine).

At the same time I would issue a caveat about hitherto unpublished documents (HUDs). HUDs are not in themselves more valuable than the printed sources – it's a historical coincidence that one set has become known early on, the other not. One needs to evaluate them even more closely. Here I speak

> "According to Dr Johnson, a man will turn over half a library to make a book"

from personal experience. A series of chances led me to discovering some hitherto unpublished letters of Oliver Cromwell just as I was finishing my manuscript. I blazoned my finds across the text: only to realise at the proof stage, that they might be unpublished but they were not very important in the grand scheme of things … an expensive mistake.

Where the perils and pleasures of writing historical biography are concerned, there are two perils which seem to me to raise points of principle. The first is the peril of anachronistic judgements. For example, in the 16th century more or less everybody took astrology seriously, and more or less everybody enjoyed a jolly afternoon out to see the bears baited. It's no good dismissing the former as meaningless and cringing from the latter as disgusting. In the same way, political correctness is dangerous. The importance of James I of England's allegedly homosexual tastes is their political consequences if any, not an opportunity for a 21st-century historian to display liberal values (let alone the reverse).

I would further cite the peril of hindsight. We may know that Henry VIII will marry six times, but he didn't, and he would have been amazed if it had been predicted at the time of his first marriage to Catherine of Aragon.

And the pleasures? Manifold! Principal among them, however, is the opportunity to lead a life less ordinary. As a biographer, I can rule over kingdoms, lead the cavalry into battle, patronise the great artists of the past and all without leaving my chair.

Antonia Fraser has written more than a dozen award-winning biographies including Mary Queen of Scots and The Six Wives of Henry VIII. Her latest book is Love and Louis XIV: The Women in the Life of the Sun King (Weidenfeld & Nicolson).

Where do I start?

Ever had a yen to write about someone real? Your tutor Midge Gillies explains how to pin down your subject matter

About your tutor

Midge Gillies's books include biographies of pilot Amy Johnson and music hall star Marie Lloyd. Writing Lives: Literary Biography and her book about prisoners of war in World War II will be published in 2010. She teaches at Cambridge University's Institute of Continuing Education and Anglia Ruskin University.

According to the main character in Stephen Poliakoff's Perfect Strangers, a TV drama about a family reunion and the secrets that it unearths, every family has at least three great stories waiting to be told. If you want to write a memoir or family history you only need one to get you started.

Perhaps you've stumbled upon a marriage certificate that shows your mother was a GI bride before she married your father, or maybe a birth certificate reveals that your grandfather – who was something big in the City – was Jewish but changed his surname in order to fit in.

The motivation to write a family memoir often starts with a desire to understand. Does your mother's carefulness with money relate to something that happened to her mother (you've heard whispers of a financial scandal) or maybe the fact that your father came to Britain as a refugee in the 1930s explains why he's a workaholic?

Writing a biography is even simpler: all you need is someone you're passionately interested in. (If you want the biography to be published you will need to convince an editor that other people will find him or her just as enthralling.) You'll be spending the next few years living with your subject, so it's vital that you begin the relationship under their spell.

Memoir, autobiography and biography

"Memoir" is often used interchangeably with "autobiography". The blurb on the back of cookery writer Nigel Slater's account of his childhood, Toast, describes the book as a "memoir" and yet it won the British Book Awards Biography of the Year. Memoirs rely more on memory than fact and often concentrate on one period in a life. Toast's subtitle is "The Story of a Boy's Hunger" and the book focuses on Slater's childhood and his relationship with his parents.

Autobiography usually covers more of the author's life and follows a logical chronology. Within autobiography and memoir there is a huge range of approaches and styles from Laurie Lee's description of his Cotswolds' childhood in Cider with Rosie to Vera Brittain's poignant account of the way the first world war wrecked so many lives in Testament of Youth.

A biography tells the story of a life other than the author's. Traditionally, this has taken the form of a straight narrative arc from birth to death. Recently biography has started to take on more exciting and imaginative forms than this traditional, "cradle to grave" approach.

"When writing a biography all you need is someone you're interested in"

Choosing your subject

You can't choose your relatives but you can choose which ones you write about. Deciding on whose lives you will research – whether as part of a family history or as a single biography – will depend on several factors. Ideally, your interests and skills should match theirs. If you want to write about a Nobel Prize winning economist but you failed maths GCSE you may struggle to appreciate their work. On the other hand, ignorance can be the ideal starting point from which to demystify a complicated subject.

Weigh up the type and availability of sources before choosing your subject. There should be enough material to allow you to get to know the person you're researching, but not so much that it would take you your lifetime to read it. When Michael Holroyd was researching the life of George Bernard Shaw he began to think that Shaw, who wrote 10 letters every day of his adult life and had the benefit of shorthand and secretaries, could write more in a day than Holroyd could read. By contrast, if you're interested in an early professional footballer you may discover that he didn't write a single letter and you will have to find other ways of giving him a voice – perhaps by quoting from newspaper interviews or speaking to someone who knew him.

Much research can be carried out on the internet but you will still have to interview people, consult collections and probably make at least one trip to somewhere such as the National Archives in Kew or the Imperial War Museum in south London. How far you live from your main sources will affect the time and expense involved. If they are abroad both will rise and you may also face language difficulties.

Copyright

If you intend to quote extensively from a particular source don't wait until the last minute to see whether you will be granted permission. You may be refused or the price might be prohibitively high – in which case you will have to rewrite the book. The use of song lyrics, even if you want to use just one line, can be particularly expensive.

You can't quote a "substantial" part of a copyright work without permission, but what constitutes "substantial" is open to debate. Four lines from a short poem might be "substantial", whereas several sentences from a novel would not be.

Letters belong to the recipient but the writer holds the copyright which is passed to their estate after their death. When travel writer Paul Theroux wrote a memoir about his one time friend, Nobel Laureate VS Naipaul, he was only allowed to quote tiny amounts from Naipaul's letters to him and was not allowed to see his replies. He was, in effect, denied access to his own letters.

Whether a work is still in copyright depends on factors such as when the author died and their nationality. Most archives should be able to advise you on how to ask for permission to use material they hold or you can contact the publisher of a writer you want to quote. The Society of Authors publishes two useful guides: Copyright and Moral Rights, and Permissions.

What's out there already?

• Consult the British Library catalogue (http://catalogue. bl.uk/F/?func=file&file_name=login-bl-list) to see if any books have already been written about the person or topic you're interested in; check when they were written and who published them. If they appeared a long time ago or were published by a specialist press you have a greater chance of interesting a publisher in a new account.

• Do an online search for your subject and make a note of sources to follow up, for example, archives, academic publications or appreciation societies.

• Check an online bookseller, such as Amazon.com, to see if any books about your subject are scheduled to be published.

• If you want reassurance that no one else is working on the same subject contact the main sources or experts – for example, family members, copyright holders of material such as letters or diaries, or archivists – who may know. However, this is not foolproof and carries the risk of alerting a biographer in search of a subject.

Is my idea commercial?

If you want to get published, consider how commercial your idea is before you devote the next few years of your life to it. Your grandchildren will probably enjoy reading your account of how their great-aunts and uncles survived in the poverty of 1930s Ireland because of their personal connection to the people you're describing. But the book

exercise

Blurb

The blurb is the writing on the back of a book which tells the potential reader what the book is about and encourages them to buy it. Write a blurb about the book you intend to write. This exercise will help you to spot the highlights of your story and any themes that you might want to explore.

is likely to be too similar to Frank McCourt's Pulitzer Prize-winning Angela's Ashes to interest a publisher.

Likewise, finding a publisher for a biography of a well-known person is very difficult unless you have something new to say. Most publishers would be reluctant to commission a new biography of someone like Winston Churchill. However, if your father was Churchill's driver and kept a diary of his working life they might be interested in an account told from the chauffeur's perspective. Alison Light took a startlingly fresh approach to the Bloomsbury Set – a group which had been written about exhaustively and exhaustingly – in her book, Mrs Woolf & the Servants: The Hidden Heart of Domestic Service.

Conversely, sales and marketing departments (both have a huge say in whether a publisher commissions a book) are likely to be wary of a subject that no one has ever heard of. However, there are plenty of examples of individuals dragged out of obscurity to delight modern readers. Kate Summerscale became fascinated by Joe Carstairs when she wrote her obituary for the Daily Telegraph. When she started work on her biography very few people had heard of Carstairs, an oil heiress who dressed like a man, held records for speedboat racing in the 1920s, owned her own island and poured her affection into a rag doll. But Summerscale told her story in such a compelling way that The Queen of Whale Cay became a bestseller.

Sometimes the quality of the writing is enough to secure publication. On paper Bad Blood by Lorna Sage, a memoir written by an academic about growing up in the 1940s in a bleak vicarage on the English/Welsh borders, may not sound compelling but it won the Whitbread Biography of the Year in 2001 and was praised for its lyrical writing and dark humour.

"There are plenty of examples of individuals dragged out of obscurity to delight modern readers"

Research

Getting started

- The basics. Gather together as many official documents as you can. These might include death, marriage and birth certificates; census returns; wills; divorce records and details of service in the armed forces. The Family Records Centre in London, the Church of Jesus Christ of Latter-day Saints' family history centres and many county record offices and larger public libraries (which often have family or local history specialists) are all good places from which to start your search. Although official documents aren't infallible they will provide you with key dates on which to build.

- Draw up a family tree. Include as much basic information as you can: first names, dates of births, deaths and marriages, professions and causes of death. Pin it up where you can study it and add question marks if you're unsure of information. As your knowledge grows so will the family tree and you will have a clearer idea of the point at which to begin your biography or family history. Trends and questions will also emerge. If you're writing a biography of a music hall star and several of her relatives married jockeys perhaps you need to explore the connections between the two ways of earning a living? Or maybe several members of your family died from a similar disease – was this hereditary or caused by a life working down the mines?

- Start a timeline. Include dates from the family tree and expand it so that it covers the period you will be writing about. Compile it on a computer so you can easily add new events as your research progresses; include both minor dates such as when they started university or school as well as bigger events – for example, when they were arrested for chaining themselves to the railings in support of votes for women. If you're researching a particularly dramatic moment – perhaps when the Titanic sank with your grandfather on board – you may want to add hour-by-hour details.

- Know your competition. Read similar books so that you can tell a publisher why your biography will be different. Pay particular attention to the footnotes and notes on sources. Photocopy the bibliography and work your way through it.

- Contact family members. If your subject has any surviving family members you are going to have to be very, very nice to them. They may be able to provide valuable information and you will probably need their approval to quote from letters or diaries or to reproduce photos. They, however, may be suspicious of someone nosing around their family. Write them a reassuring letter and ask if you can visit them. Timing is crucial: you should have learnt enough about the subject to make the meeting worthwhile, but don't leave it too long to interview someone in their 90s.

- Befriend an expert. No matter what your subject, the chances are someone will already have studied it – perhaps for years. This needn't be bad news. Many archivists and local or specialist historians are keen to share their enthusiasm and will provide valuable leads – who to interview and which archives to use. Special interest groups such as Researching Far East Prisoners of War (researchingfepowhistory.org.uk) can also put you in touch with useful contacts.

- Start your own journal. Research is as much – if not more – fun than writing a biography or family history, and you may decide to weave a sense of this drama into your book.

"Start a timeline. Include dates from the family tree and expand it"

How did it feel to lay a wreath on your grandfather's grave at Passchendaele or to meet the last descendant of the famous woman whose life you want to write? You can also use the journal to speculate, or to remind yourself to follow up leads: "Was Maud having an affair with Thomas?"; "Why did Gosia leave Poland?"; "Visit the Jewish Museum".

At the coalface

Despite the importance of the internet, there is still nothing quite like the thrill of consulting an original document. Primary sources offer vital clues to how someone was feeling when they wrote their diary or letter. The crossings out, jottings in the margins, the pressure of their pen or pencil on the paper, the red rose preserved between the pages of a journal have all disappeared in an electronic age.

"Befriend an expert. No matter what your subject, chances are someone will have studied it"

Before you visit an archive try to establish in advance exactly what material it contains. Many have leaflets to help you navigate your way around their collection – for example the National Archives has research guides on subjects ranging from "hedgerows" to "Ireland: the Easter Rising 1916". Don't just turn up at the library or collection, in case it is closed for its annual stock take, or you need an appointment.

Ensure that your notes will be legible in a few years' time and that you know where to find a certain fact. This is particularly important if you decide to include footnotes. Record each piece of information and where it came from. You can buy a software package but a card index system works just as well. Remember to cross-reference topics. If you're writing about the first person to open a curry house in Britain you might have a card index on "curry house menu" cross-referenced to "general diet – Britain" to allow you to compare the dishes served in the restaurant with what most Britons were eating.

Source materials don't have to be dusty sheets of yellowing paper; people leave behind traces of themselves in a whole

Max Arthur on interviewing techniques

The basic rules of interview etiquette are dictated by common sense and courtesy. For example, it is important to be prompt.

Make sure your interviewee has understood in advance that you will be recording the interview, and take plenty of time to chat before you launch into the recording.

It's crucial to a good interview that your subject maintains confidence in you, and nothing diminishes that as quickly as a technical malfunction. Ensure that you have a high-quality tape recorder or DAT (Digital Audio Tape) machine, plenty of spare discs, a decent microphone and headphones, and check your equipment obsessively before you leave home.

Once the recording starts, make sure you've done your homework and can chat around the subject. Don't forget that you may well be the first person to whom they've told their story – a story that can sometimes be very painful for them to recall.

If you need to prompt them, make sure you ask open questions. For instance: "So, you were 18 when you went out to Spain?" may simply garner the answer: "Yes".

When interviewing people who are very old (the oldest I have interviewed was 110) you need to get in very close, and speak into whichever ear they feel is the stronger.

Once you've finished the interview and transcribed it, send them a copy: ask if there is anything they would like deleted in retrospect and, indeed, anything they would like to add. From experience, most do. Always remember you are recording history.

Max Arthur's most recent book is The Real Band of Brothers: First Hand Accounts from the Last British Survivors of the Spanish Civil War (Collins)

from the front line

Kathryn Hughes on how to find your way through the archives

When visiting a new (to you) archive, it's essential to develop an attitude that is both open and focussed. You don't want to be so certain of what you've come to find that you block out an important discovery which comes at you from left field. Nor, though, do you want to waste ages sifting through material that has no relevance. I go in with a series of questions written down – Why was he named after his uncle? Why was she buried 400 miles from home? – and try methodically to find the answers.

Since I'm both a fast touch-typist and physically chaotic, it makes sense to take all my notes on an ultra-portable laptop. But, whether you type or write, it's essential to make a clear record of which document you're using. Its description (or "descriptor" in archivese) – Letters from the Earl of Pembroke to his son – is far less important than the anonymous designation, which will be something like PT/Pem: 2, 50 DQ. It may not trip off the tongue, but it means you can identify the material easily if you need to check a detail several years later.

Do remember that the librarians and archivists who watch over this material are your best friends, so it pays to be nice to them. They'll be able to point you to the salient document within moments. Just don't expect them to take a personal interest in your research. I get embarrassed when I see punters boring on for Britain about their work to a librarian who is obviously itching to get on with her never-ending To Do list.

As for all those dreary rules about only using pencil and leaving your handbag in the cloakroom – sometimes I wonder why they don't insist on nude note-taking, just to ensure that you're not trying to smuggle out documents in your pants.

Kathryn Hughes' latest book is The Short Life and Long Times of Mrs Beeton (Harper Perennial)

from the front line

range of media. Old cine film will give you an idea how someone moved and how they related to other people. Many researchers find that they only really connect with their subject when they hear them speak – albeit against the hiss of an early sound recording – or catch a glimpse of them moving. The British Sound Archive has a wide selection of famous and not so famous voices.

Most biographers make pilgrimages to places that were significant to their subject. Antonia Fraser describes this as "optical research" and says it is as valuable as hours spent in archives. While she was researching both Charles II and the gunpowder plot she crammed herself into hidey holes constructed for forbidden Catholic priests, so that she could experience something of what they went through.

Bear in mind that a place may have changed dramatically. If your grandmother was a sales assistant in Peter Jones department store in London's Sloane Square don't assume that she worked in today's majestic glass-fronted shop. The modern frontage didn't appear until 1934 and your grandmother might have been used to the fussy Victorian building that preceded it.

Images
Photos can provide visual prompts for your story. Sebastian Junger uses a photo taken in 1963 of himself as a baby perched on his mother's lap with two workmen behind

Names
Write 500 words about your first name. Why did your parents choose it; is it a name that's been in your family for generations; were you named after anyone? Do you have any nicknames and do different people call you by different names – if so, how does each variation make you feel?

Taste, smell and sound

Answer the following questions in relation to your subject and the period in which they lived:

- What did it taste like? Tiffin or tandoori chicken?
- What did it smell like? The frangipani of Singapore or the burnt sugar of York?
- What did it sound like? Street vendors of Jaipur or organ grinders of Whitechapel?
- What did your subject read? Penny dreadfuls or Married Love by Marie Stopes?
- What did they wear? A flapper's dress or a twinset and pearls?
- How did they relax on a Saturday night? Embroidery or rolling back the carpet to dance to ragtime?

them as the starting point for his book, A Death in Belmont. One of the men is Albert DeSalvo, who later confessed to being the Boston Strangler – but did his crimes include the brutal murder of Junger's neighbour, Bessie Goldberg? The author re-examines the evidence in a way that makes the book part whodunit and part social history.

You can view thousands of images online at archives such as Hulton Getty, the Mary Evans Picture Library and the Imperial War Museum. Many collections, including the Science Museum and National Archives, include rare photos. The bigger agencies usually charge high fees for using their images and it's much cheaper if you can persuade family members or other people you interview to let you copy their photos. You are also more likely to find original images this way.

"Old cine film will give you an idea how someone moved and related to others"

Maps, diagrams, drawings, extracts from magazines or documents can be as visually arresting as photos. Guy Fawkes's two signatures – before and after torture – show more vividly than a description of his physical appearance how the ordeal affected him. The earlier signature is strong and firm, whereas the second is weak and tremulous.

Timeline

Draw up a timeline of the major events of the period you're writing about and put it in a file side by side with the timeline for the key happenings in your subject's life (see p78). Include in this second timeline events in the wider world – this might be the publication of Lady Chatterley's Lover, the Beatles performing their first gig, the election of a new prime minister.

Exercise

Getting to know the period

Immersing yourself in a period will help you to understand the context to your subject's life, their achievement and the difficulties they faced.

- Find a good biography of someone similar or of a prominent person of the day.
- Buy a general history of the period or topic.
- Read what your subject would have read. Study newspapers and magazines; look carefully at the adverts to see what people were eating and wearing. Read the popular novels and non-fiction of the period.
- Watch the films they would have seen: scan the TV listings for old movies or rent them on DVD.
- Listen to the music that was popular at the time. This will give you clues as to what people wore and how they moved (it would be difficult to Charleston in a crinoline).

Structure

The contents page of a biography or memoir will give you an idea of the structure the author has used. Chapters in biographies are usually around 6,000-8,000 words in length but there are no hard and fast rules. The occasional short chapter can bring variety to the pace of the book. Some authors punctuate their chapters with short asides in which they pause from the main narrative to expand a particular theme without interrupting the flow. Kathryn Hughes's The Short Life and Long Times of Mrs Beeton is laced with interludes in which she explores topics such as Mrs Beeton's awareness of the link between health and diet, and whether Mrs Beeton ruined British cooking. Each adds to the reader's knowledge of the period without causing the narrative drive to stall. Alternatively, you might prefer to weave themes into the central story.

Cradle to grave

A biography typically starts with the subject's birth (it's surprising how many begin with a description of the weather) and continues in a roughly chronological order until their death. The advantage of this approach, which could apply to the history of a family, is that it is easy to follow. The downside is that it can appear plodding – especially if you're writing about someone who had an action-packed early life but whose later days were tame. One solution is to condense your treatment of the less exciting years, but this can be difficult to achieve without making the book seem unbalanced. Alexander Masters turned the traditional form on its head in Stuart, A Life Backwards by telling the story in reverse chronological order.

A year in the life of ...

Another approach is to focus on a distinct period, as James Shapiro does in 1599, A Year in the Life of William Shakespeare. This was the year in which the playwright completed Henry V, wrote Julius Caesar and As You Like It and drafted Hamlet, but also a year of great excitement in England – an ageing Queen faced the threat of invasion by Catholic Spain, rebellion in Ireland and intrigue at court. Shapiro's book marries both threads together to create an intimate picture of what life must have been like for Shakespeare and the influences that fed into his writing. Shapiro starts with the winter of 1598 and refers to events before and after 1599 to illuminate a single year.

This could work equally well for family history. The year 1948, for example, is significant for many families as it marked the arrival of West Indian immigrants on the ship Empire Windrush. Andrea Levy, herself the daughter of Jamaican immigrants, focussed on this one momentous year in her novel, Small Island.

Richard Benson, a journalist with The Face, based his book, The Farm, on notebooks he kept during the few weeks when he helped his parents to prepare the family farm in Yorkshire for sale after they reluctantly decided they could no longer afford to live there. Although the book focuses on a distinct period in time, he widens its scope to reflect back on his childhood, and the importance of the farm in his life.

> "Writing about two or more people can give the reader more for less"

Group biographies and biographical pairings

Writing about two or more people whose lives have a natural symbiosis can give the reader more for less. The subjects might share a similar background and context, and the interaction between them will give the reader a deeper understanding of each.

This is especially true of family members and in particular siblings. James Fox's The Langhorne Sisters is both a group biography and a family history in which he uses letters and diaries to examine the lives of his great-aunts and grandmother who were born in Virginia, USA, but who made their mark on high society on both sides of the Atlantic.

One of the advantages of group biographies is that there is usually at least one figure who is more flamboyant than the others. He or she can sweep the story along, carrying other characters, who may be less compelling, with them. Nancy Astor, who became the first woman to take her seat in parliament, fills this role in The Langhorne Sisters.

In some instances the rivalry and tension between the biographical subjects add a sense of drama to a joint biography, whether the figures are Sylvia Plath and Ted Hughes or the cousins Elizabeth I and Mary Queen of Scots. Roland Huntford's joint biography of the polar explorers, Robert Scott and Roald Amundsen – The Last Place on Earth – opens with a short description (less than a page) of the two men embarking on their expeditions, before doubling back to outline earlier attempts to reach the South Pole and then jumping forward to look at Scott and Amundsen's biographical roots. His approach allows him to tell both their life stories at the same time as he recounts the race to the pole.

Another way of pulling together the lives of a group of people is to use a single event as a unifying theme. In A Night at the Majestic, Richard Davenport-Hines describes a famous dinner party at the Majestic Hotel in Paris in 1922 that was attended by Stravinsky, Joyce, Diaghilev, Picasso and Proust.

Lucky dip

The structure of Nigel Slater's memoir, Toast, appears to be little more than a bundle of headings, mostly connected to food and each evoking a 1960s childhood: "Spaghetti Bolognese", "Arctic Roll", "Butterscotch-Flavour Angel Delight" (which starts with a list of ingredients: "Sugar, Modified Starch, Hydrogenated Vegetable Oil, Emulsifiers ...)". Each is no more

Alexander Masters on structure

I'm rotten at planning books. Certainly I was with my first book, and I don't seem to have improved with the one I'm working on now. I write in blobs a possible chapter here, a couple of paragraphs there – and pray that sooner or later it'll all fit together.

With Stuart: A Life Backwards, I messed up royally on the first attempt. I used the old-fashioned, orderly biographical structure: begin before the beginning, dole out 20 pages of ancestors until the hero appears, meander on through school etc. Somewhere about page 50 the subject finally does something interesting. Stuart said the result was "bollocks boring", and he was right. It bored me to tears. That type of structure reflected nothing of his character. Stuart was the opposite of orderly: a chaotic, outrageous, alcoholic sociopath who spent much of his adult life on the streets or in jail.

Stuart discovered the solution. Tear up the first version and write the book the other way round, ie backwards, "like a murder mystery": start from the point when we first met, then work back to his childhood to find out "what murdered the boy I was". Not only did this structure offer a strong drive to the story, the telling of it became unpredictable and erratic again, and exciting to write. All that plodding preparation vanished. At last, the structure reflected the man.

Alexander Masters' Stuart: A Life Backwards won the Whitbread Award for biography in 2005

from the front line

than a few pages long. But, despite its apparent simplicity, the characters develop and the story unravels in a way that is far from haphazard.

Since Slater is a professional cook, recipes provide natural prompts but this is a format that could translate to other subjects. If your parents met through their shared passion for amateur dramatics you could use theatre programmes to tell their story. Or if you have a box full of old photos you could write commentaries to some of the pictures. As you progress you will find that themes start to emerge: the annual camping trip when your mother stayed at home, the different houses you lived in, or family celebrations.

Chapter breakdown

Once you've decided on a structure you will need a chapter breakdown outlining what you will cover in each chapter. This is a valuable way of helping you to organise your material and to assess the overall pace of your book. Are there sections that appear a little flat; where you might want to freshen up your writing with extra research so that you can inject some colour into the story? Or perhaps you need to move material around. Does one chapter contain too many facts or maybe you've revealed too much of the story too soon? Expect your chapter breakdown to change and evolve as your book takes shape. A publisher or literary agent will want to see it, together with at least one sample chapter, as part of your book proposal.

"A preface allows you to introduce your book and to tell the reader why you wrote it"

A preface allows you to introduce your book and to tell the reader its scope and why you've decided to write it. This can be useful if you want to explain to younger generations why you've chosen to write a family history. A prologue gives you the chance to write an introductory scene – perhaps from a dramatic moment in the life you're about to write. The aim is to hook the reader, but the danger in including a preface or prologue – or both – is that the reader doesn't quite know when the book proper has started.

Foreground versus background

Decide who the principal characters will be and the background
against which their story will be told. If you're writing the biography
of a famous fashion designer the background might include rival
designers, models, their partners and family. Their story might
switch between the East End of London (where they grew up), to
Carnaby Street (where they learnt their trade), to Paris (where they
worked) to New York (where they lived when they were famous).

Exercise

Finding your voice

Viewpoint

As you start to write your style will emerge. Before you begin
you should have some idea of how much of you will appear
in the book. If you're writing a memoir nearly all of it may
be written in the first person and yours may be the only
viewpoint that the reader sees. Margaret Forster makes this
change in emphasis explicit half way through her family
memoir, Hidden Lives. Just before this she has been telling
the story from her mother's point of view and describing her
concern about her precocious child. Then the tone changes:

"It was at this time, in 1943, when I was five, that my own
real memory begins, real in the sense that I can not only
recall actual events but can propel myself back into them, be
there again in my Aunt Jean's room-and-kitchen, standing by
the window at the back of the Buildings, staring out at the
outside staircase and the tops of the wash-houses, while
behind me Jean asks me what is the matter ... So I can stop
now, writing in the third person, stop retelling stories I
was told about the years before I was born, about when I
was under five, stop splicing oral history with local history
and start instead letting my own version of family lore
come into play. I am there, at the centre. What a difference it
makes, how dangerous it is." (page 132–133, pbk)

"I" is less common in a biography – unless you want to
incorporate a sense of a personal quest – but there is just
as much scope to write about a person's life from different

viewpoints. If you're writing about a singer you might describe how members of the band reacted to their decision to leave it or how a fan greeted the news.

Pace

Think of your subject's, or your family's, life as a series of dramatic peaks – such as when they went to war, moved to a new country or secured their first recording deal. Write in a way that builds up the momentum towards these peaks. Maybe your grandmother was a nurse tending wounded soldiers as they arrived at Dover following the evacuation of Dunkirk in the summer of 1940. At the same time, your grandfather may have been stranded on a French beach, unsure whether he would make it home. His rescue and reunion with your grandmother provide two obvious peaks. It's your job to lead the reader towards these peaks by setting the scene and describing the mounting tension.

Avoid historical hindsight – the reader knows the evacuation of Dunkirk saved thousands of lives, that the Nazis lost the war and that it ended in 1945, but people who lived through those events did not have such knowledge. Don't reveal too much too quickly. The sentence: "Grandmother arrived at the hospital where she would in two days' time be reunited with her future husband," robs your story of much of its tension.

Dealing with gaps

Most researchers hit a blank wall with at least one person who appears to have left few traces of their existence. Claire Tomalin wrote possibly her finest book about Nelly Ternan, the elusive mistress of Charles Dickens. In The Invisible Woman, Tomalin teases out the story of an actress who was effectively written out of history books. The hunt gives the book the edge of a detective story and one in which Tomalin is scrupulously honest with her readers:

"Choose a piece of furniture that has been in your family for a long time and tell its story"

"Nelly now disappears from view completely, conjured into thin air. For four years she remains invisible ... At a guess, she has been living in France. It is only a guess. This is to be a chapter of guesses and conjectures, and those who don't like them are warned ..."

Later on in the same chapter she adds: "We have seen that there is no hard evidence that Nelly had a child; but there is too much soft evidence to be brushed aside entirely."

How creative can I be?

It's useful to have a reader in mind, whether they're your grandson if you're writing a family history, or, if you're writing a biography, someone who enjoys the genre. Knowing your reader will help you to gauge the sort of language to use and what you will need to explain. To a teenager, for example, the "last war" might mean the Iraq War whereas an older person would assume you were referring to the second world war.

Just like a novelist, it's your task to paint a picture of events and to show, rather than tell. If your ancestors arrived in America by slave ship it's far more effective to show the reader what it felt like to be in the hold – to describe the heat, the smells and the noise in the cramped conditions – rather than simply to tell them that the slaves were transported by ship.

Very few biographers invent dialogue. Instead, they allow their subject's voice to emerge through letters, diaries or

Exercise

Story

Choose a piece of furniture, such as a kitchen table or chest of drawers, that has been in your family for a long time and write its story. If you're feeling imaginative, write it in the first person and from the furniture's point of view.

Tony Benn on how to write a diary

Those who write diaries use them in a number of ways: to record the day's events, to describe the people they have met, and to capture thoughts and emotions. An authentic diary tells the truth as the writer sees it at the moment when he or she writes.

Having written over 15m words since 1940 – a 68-year span – I know what a sweat it is to do it, and what pleasure it is to read it.

Experience has always been my greatest teacher and if I write at night I get two bites at that experience – when the pressure is off and I can describe what has happened in perspective. Then, when I read it, I get a third bite at my experience.

The daily diarist has a different job to the memoirist or the autobiographer: a good political diary must above all be contemporary, accurate and include mistakes. Published diaries are often selective by necessity, but misjudgements must be included and it must be accepted that nothing is altered after the event. Diarists follow different principles: some being famous for their wit, some for their sexy revelations, some as an expression of the diarist's style.

In the post-Blair era we have been treated to many accounts from those who have now retired from active politics and wish to intervene to put the record straight – as they see it.

Tony Benn's latest collection of diaries is More Time for Politics: Diaries 2001-2007 (Hutchinson)

from the front line

interviews. If you're writing a memoir or family history these sources may not exist, or you may want to supplement quotations with impressions of what you remember them saying. Often it is more effective to paraphrase or to describe how they spoke, rather than trying to invent convincing dialogue. In Unreliable Memoirs, for example, Clive James describes the agony he suffered as a small boy when his class faced their regular spelling test.

"I remember not being able to pronounce the word 'the'. I pronounced it 'ter-her'. The class had collective hysterics. They were rolling around on the floor with their knees up."

Dialogue should be a stylised form of real speech – chat with the dull bits left out. In this extract from Toast, entitled Pickled Walnuts, Nigel Slater uses comments from his Dad and stepmother, Joan, to increase the reader's knowledge of their personalities and their marriage.

"One weekend when we attended a fete in a field by the river, Dad came back with a jar of pickled walnuts as big as the jars of sherbet lemons that stood behind the sweet counter in the post office. 'It will last us a year or two,' he said, bringing them in from the boot of the car.

'I don't know how you can eat the filthy things,' shuddered Joan, screwing up her nose like he had just handed her a jar of preserved dog poo.'" (Toast, page 207)

In Peter Ackroyd's biography of Charles Dickens he not only makes up dialogue for his subject but invents a meeting between himself and Dickens. Making things up is a risky business and not every editor will appreciate your originality. The critics attacked Ackroyd for his audacity – but his biography was a bestseller.

Checklist

■ Does every fact deserve to be there?
By the time you're ready to write your memoir or biography
you will have gathered a mountain of material. The
temptation to put a fact in simply because you've gone to a
lot of trouble to find it can be overwhelming. Resist the urge.
Include only what is interesting or necessary to drive the
story forward.

■ Are my facts right?
A silly mistake or omission will make your reader doubt you.
Double-check figures, dates and place, and personal names.
Find an expert (probably someone who's already helped you)
to read the manuscript for factual errors.

■ Is there anything I don't understand?
It's easy to gloss over something you haven't quite grasped,
but, if you're confused, your reader will be mystified. If your
grandmother was a suffragette who was force fed but you're
not really sure what that involved, take time to find out.

■ Have I varied the pace?
Are there any sections where the narrative stalls or where the
tone is breathless? If one part feels a little tired pep it up with
new research – perhaps by visiting the area where that
particular scene took place. Consider ways of inserting
calmer descriptions into a sequence that might seem too
frantic.

▉ Is the writing as crisp as it could be?

Hunt down cliches and watch out for repetitions of phrases or facts. Do you have any pet words that you over-use? Vary your sentence length and how you begin paragraphs.

▉ Have I used too too much jargon?

If you're writing about a pioneering airwoman and describe her "checking her gudgeon pins and distributor points as part of the DI," your reader will soon be snoring. Some arcane terms, however, can help to create atmosphere, so long as you give the reader a full explanation.

What next?

Can't be bothered with publishers? As editor Vanessa Neuling explains, there is more than one way to see your book in print

Recent developments have made self-publishing a more viable choice than ever, but why would you choose to go it alone? You may have tired of mainstream publishers' rejections – the market for your book is too small, your profile not high enough – and decide not to let this stand in your way. It might also be that you wish to retain more control over the way your book is published, and are unwilling to compromise on editorial changes or cover decisions. Or it may even be that you are very confident in your book's sales potential and feel that you'll end up with a bigger slice of the profits this way.

Whatever the reason, self-publishing is unique in that it enables you as the author to see your book in print and to sell copies while retaining all rights to the content. You also keep ownership of the copies (as opposed to vanity publishing, where the company would have this control – never a recommended option). While in the past self-publishing was a costly business, available to only a limited number of writers, technological advances have already begun to revolutionise the industry. Gone are the days of misjudging a print run and ending up with hundreds of unsold books gathering dust in your attic. Print-on-demand means that books can be produced in tiny quantities – even a single copy – in response to firm sales. Bloggers, novelists and writers of specialist non-fiction are just some of the authors taking the advancements in desktop publishing as a cue to beat their own path, either laying the text out themselves, designing the cover and finding a printer, or using one of the many self-publishing companies out there to guide them on their way. These companies may also offer optional editing and proofreading services for an additional cost, and there are generally plenty of options in regard to cover design.

This route has its success stories – from books that have generated six-figure sales to the two self-published novels that made it on to the Booker shortlist. There have also been those books, the bestselling *The Celestine Prophecy* to name one, that have drawn attention in their self-published form and then been snapped up by mainstream publishers. Amazon have recently announced a new programme, AmazonEncore, that could give self-published titles a real boost, lifting well reviewed but low-selling titles and giving them a new marketing push. However, in spite of all this, a self-published book that really takes off is still very much a rare thing.

A key reason is that conventional publishing companies do more than just turn manuscripts into finished copies – from editorial and publicity to sales and distribution, there are various departments that work hard to ensure that the books they've invested in reach their sales potential. Replicating that effect in your one-person publishing enterprise is an immense challenge. If your wish is simply to have what you've written in print for those close to you to read, then once you've paid for that service your work is done. But if you have ambitions to make your money back or hope to break into the mainstream book trade, you will have to work hard.

Niche non-fiction can succeed if you know your market well and target your promotion, for instance by approaching local radio stations, sending out copies for review, giving talks at relevant events and reaching readers via websites. However, you are still likely to find that your book is treated very differently from those published through traditional channels. Your project has not had to go through the same filters to assess quality of writing and commercial appeal, and while it may be every bit as good, it is your job to convince people of that. While the stigma attached to self-publishing is lessening, it is a long way from having disappeared.

You will have to be outgoing, tireless in promoting your book and willing to enter financial, sales or marketing territory that may be unfamiliar. That said, if you're determined to see your writing in print, self-publishing is a more attractive option now than ever before.

Vanessa Neuling has worked at Virago and most recently as a commissioning editor at Random House

Journalism

Hot off the press

Are journalists born or made? According to Simon Jenkins, while the basics can be taught, first there has to be an intense curiosity about the world and a love of the written word

J ournalists are creatures of nature not nurture. The profession develops from instinct, from a peculiar way of seeing and describing the world. It may be objective in practice but it is subjective in motivation.

Journalism is expressed in the written or spoken word, but I have never regarded that as its essence. The technical skill is that of creating clear and succinct sentences, which any profession should inculcate. This can be taught and should be part of any core curriculum. Its absence from so much of written English nowadays, from users' manuals to student exam questions to government white papers, is deplorable. I sometimes think a well-produced newspaper is that last redoubt of clear English.

There is no talent for such technique. While some people pick it up quickly, it must be acquired, as must a skill at playing the piano. Like many ingénue journalists, I acquired it first in the trial and error of a student newsroom and then went on to a more formal training, in my case with the Times Newspapers.

The latter's Educational Supplement, then integrated with the main paper, possessed two invaluable bits of equipment. One was a source of stories, the politics of education, to which little harm could be done by my reporting. The other was a ferocious Irish subeditor. He would score through superfluous words, underline bad grammar and mercilessly spike articles, leaning back in his chair, removing his glasses and asking the classic question of any journalism teacher: "Now, what is it you are really trying to tell me." The style book was always open on his desk. Orwell, Gowers and Roget were his gods and the Times list of banned words was holy writ.

I absorbed his maxims like mother's milk. Never begin a paragraph with "it". Make every paragraph a single idea. Nouns and verbs are the workhorses of a sentence, never qualifiers. Delete every adjective and adverb from your story and reinsert only those that appear essential. Never use sloppy words such as supply, problem, accommodate and interesting and try to use concrete not abstract nouns. The best punctuation is a full stop.

I still shudder when I break these rules and hate seeing them broken by others. The best reporting rule is still: begin every story with who, what, when and where.

That training was a privilege greater than anything I acquired at school or university. It was the toolkit for a career, always to be kept oiled and polished. I watched colleagues floundering as they sought to fashion stories in ignorance of its framework. There are dozens of guides to clear English on the market. There is no excuse for not having bothered to read even one.

That said, these skills are necessary but not sufficient for journalism. They are instruments only. Beyond them lie talents of style and character that are less easy to instruct and without which skill is useless.

I used to ask aspiring journalists whether they kept a diary. What was their instinctive response to meeting an exciting person or visiting a beautiful place, to any highly charged emotion. Was it to phone a friend, dance round the park or just feel good – or did they write it down? Did they crave to communicate their experience through the written word? It is the best indicator I know of a natural reporter.

The qualities essential to journalism thus extend far beyond an ability to write. They are those of curiosity, an uninhibited

"He asked the classic question of any journalism teacher, 'what are you really trying to tell me?'"

mind, native cunning and an eagerness to communicate, summed up in the gift to narrate. Such is the raw material on which the story depends and without which there is nothing to say. There can be a story without journalism, but no journalism without a story.

Manipulating such material into print is the result of a sequence of skills, from page editor through reporter, to subeditor and designer, many of them unsung heroes of the craft. All are journalists. But there is no substitute for one of them, the person who saw it happen. The uniqueness of reportage lies in experience and the yearning to tell it to others.

My favourite cautionary tale is EM Forster's of the stone-age storyteller, the only member of the tribe who was excused hunting. The condition was that he told tales round the camp fire which never, ever sent them to sleep. If they fell asleep he was worthless. He was duly killed.

Simon Jenkins has edited the Times and the London Evening Standard. He writes a twice-weekly column for the Guardian

How journalists write

Journalism is about telling people what they didn't know, says your tutor Peter Cole, and making them want to know it

About your tutor

Peter Cole is professor of journalism at the University of Sheffield. Before re-entering higher education he was editor of the Sunday Correspondent, deputy editor and news editor of the Guardian, News Review editor of the Sunday Times and Londoner's Diary editor on the Evening Standard.

Journalists usually refer to what they write as stories. Not articles or reports, occasionally pieces, but stories. This does not apply only to reporters but to everybody in the editorial chain, from desk editors, copy editors, specialist and sports writers to the editor him or herself. Words published in newspapers, on air or online are stories.

Stories sound interesting; reports sound dull. To some, stories mean fiction: "Tell me a story, Mummy". Stories are tall and short, made up and true. True stories are about what happened. We tell stories in conversation, recounting experiences and events in which we took part or observed. The crucial thing about a story is that other people want to hear it, because it is interesting or entertaining. Otherwise the storyteller is a bore.

So journalists write stories for their readers to tell them what is going on, to inform them, engage them, entertain them, shock them, amuse them, disturb them, uplift them. The subject matter will vary according to the nature of the publication and the intended audience. The good newspaper editor will have a clear idea of the sort of people who are reading it, and cater to their interests and preoccupations, sometimes their prejudices. And the paper will include that vital ingredient serendipity – the story you didn't expect, the "just fancy that", the absurdities as well as the travails of the human condition.

Journalism is basically a simple game. It is about finding things out and telling other people about them. The finding out requires a variety of skills because those in power often prefer that we know only so much. Journalism is about holding such people to account, exposing their humbug and hypocrisy, the abuse of their power. This includes the control it gives them over the flow of information, the ability to bury the bad news, to spin and obfuscate. Good journalists must ask the awkward questions and question the answers, must dig to unearth and then explain, making comprehensible that which authority, by intent or verbal inadequacy, has left confused, incomplete or plain mendacious. Incomprehensible journalism is quite simply bad journalism, and therefore pointless.

Ultimately there is only one purpose: to make the reader read the story. If they don't, what was the point of finding it out and telling it? This booklet picks up the story when the reader has reached the stage of deciding to address the story. That is not the same as reading it, or even reading a certain amount of it. They have just reached the first word, perhaps attracted by the picture, the extracted quote, or any of the other presentational devices used to drag the reader to the story. We have reached the stage where the reader is going to subject the story to the final test, reading some or all of it. This is about writing.

Newspaper reading is different from reading a book. It is selective, does not involve commitment to the whole. Relatively little time is spent reading a daily newspaper. The newspaper reader, unlike the reader of the more literary novel, does not expect to invest effort in the endeavour. He or she will not read a sentence or paragraph a second time to be clear

"The average newspaper reader does not expect to invest effort in the endeavour"

about what is being said. Confusion, more often than not, will mean abandoning the story altogether and moving on. Many newspaper readers skim, sample or get a flavour of a story rather than reading it through.

So journalistic writing is different from creative writing. Many young people think they would like to be journalists because they have "always loved writing" or started writing poems when they were eight. It is certainly not enough and may well be a barrier to success in journalism. The late Nicholas Tomalin famously wrote that "the only qualities essential for real success in journalism are rat-like cunning, a plausible manner, and a little literary ability." He included writing, but he placed it third and prefaced it with a diminutive. The writing matters; but don't think of it as art. Think of it as working writing, writing doing a job, writing that puts across information in a way that makes readers want to absorb it.

At a time when the vast majority of entrants to journalism have degrees – welcome because journalism in a complex world is an intellectual pursuit – it is worth pointing out that writing for newspapers is also very different from the academic writing of student essays. No time to produce a route map for the essay and reach the point somewhere near the end; the journalist must grab the attention at once.

It is difficult to write simply and engagingly, so that readers will keep reading; to explain so that all the readers understand, and want to. This is the task the writing journalist has.

News writing

You've gathered the information, done the reporting. You've interviewed all the people involved, the eye witnesses to the explosion, the police, etc, etc. And now you have to write the story. You have pages in your notebook of facts, observations, quotes. You may have some agency copy, some material from other media. The first thing to do is stop and think. Do not start writing until you have a plan. Read through all your notes, marking the most important pieces of information and the quotes you want to use. The information you have gathered will not have entered your notebook in order of importance. You need to decide what is more important, what is less important, to establish a hierarchy of pieces of information. And this is where you must think about your audience. Not necessarily what interests you most, but what will interest them. It may not be the same thing, and this is where knowing, having a feeling for, understanding your audience is so important. As you stare at the blank screen try to imagine the reader.

It depends on the publication you are writing for, of course. You can assume more knowledge if you are writing for a specialist publication, or a specialist section of a newspaper. A cricket report or commentary can assume knowledge of the rules of cricket; an article for a motoring magazine can assume the reader knows what a supercar is. But some specialist publications set out to educate – computer magazines are a good example – and while interest can be assumed, knowledge of how to use specific pieces of software cannot. So understand the intentions of the publication you write for, or if you are a freelance you seek to sell to.

The market sector in which the newspaper is located is also relevant to how you write. You will find longer sentences and paragraphs and sometimes longer words in the more serious newspapers selling relatively small numbers of copies than in mass-selling newspapers with circulations 10 times as big. The reader of the Guardian will tend to be better educated and to have a larger vocabulary than the reader of the Sun. But do not, as a writer, show off your extensive vocabulary. It is never better, wherever you are writing, to prefer the less familiar word – "wordy" is always better than "prolix". Nobody is impressed by the use of a word they do not understand or would not use in everyday speech. The danger of talking down to the audience – assuming vocabulary as well as knowledge – is that it insults readers, makes them feel inadequate. And that turns them off and, worse, turns them away. They do not read on, and you have not communicated with them. The best writing for popular journalism is some of the best writing in journalism, and is hard to do. It is readily understandable, instantly readable and, if it is done well, makes you want to read on. Space is always the most precious commodity in a newspaper. Long words and sentences take up more space. Self-indulgent writing pleases nobody except perhaps the writer.

"You need to decide what is more and what is less important to your story"

Stephen King, who has sold more novels than most, reflected on his craft in On Writing, and drew a similar message: "One of the really bad things you can do to your writing is to dress up the vocabulary, looking for long words because you're maybe a little bit ashamed of your short ones. This is like dressing up a household pet in evening clothes. The pet is embarrassed and the person who committed this act of premeditated cuteness should be even more embarrassed."

So the overriding message in journalistic writing is: Keep It Simple. One of the greatest editors and journalists is Harold

Evans, who has written one of the best books on journalistic writing, Essential English for Journalists, Editors and Writers. He summed it up thus: "It is not enough to get the news. We must be able to put it across. Meaning must be unmistakable, and it must also be succinct. Readers have not the time and newspapers have not the space for elaborate reiteration. This imposes decisive requirements. In protecting the reader from incomprehension and boredom, the text editor has to insist on language which is specific, emphatic and concise. Every word must be understood by the ordinary reader, every sentence must be clear at one glance, and every story must say something about people. There must never be a doubt about its relevance to our daily life. There must be no abstractions."

Below are a series of tips for keeping things simple and encouraging the reader to read it. They are addressed at news writing, but most apply to all forms of journalistic writing.

The intro
This is the start of the story, the opening paragraph. The traditional news introductory paragraph, still the dominant form, has two related purposes: to engage the reader instantly and to summarise what the story is all about. The structure is known as the "inverted pyramid" and dates back to the days of hot metal when words on their way on to paper passed through a stage of being slugs of lead. It was always easier and faster to cut a story from the bottom, using a pair of tweezers. News stories always have to be cut because reporters write them too long, and the (imperfect) theory was that a well structured story could always be cut from the bottom so that in extremis (do not use – see later) if the intro was the only paragraph left it still made sense. The good intro depends on your judgment and decisiveness. It declares why the story is being published, what is the newest, most interesting, most important, most significant, most attention-grabbing aspect

of the story. It is not a summary of everything yet to come. The best intro will contain a maximum of two or three facts, maybe only one. In a popular tabloid it will consist of one sentence, probably no more than 25 words. The worst intro will be uncertain of what the story is all about and will contain several ideas. The best intro will demand that you read on. The worst will make it likely that you will move on.

As Tony Harcup puts it in his Journalism, Principles and Practice: "The intro is crucial because it sets the tone for what follows. A poorly written intro might confuse, mislead or simply bore the reader – a well-written intro will encourage the reader to stay with you on the strength of the information and angle you have started with."

Rest of the story
Once you've got the intro right, the second paragraph will be the most important you write. And so on. Holding the reader's interest does not stop until he or she has read to the end. You have already planned your structure, the hierarchy of information. After the intro you are amplifying the story, adding new, if subordinate, information, providing detail, explanation and quotes. And doing all this so that the story reads smoothly and seamlessly. News stories are about providing information, and there is nothing more frustrating for the reader that finishing a story with unanswered questions still hanging. Journalism students are taught about the five Ws: who, what, when, where and why. They are a useful tool to check you have covered all the bases, though not all will always apply. It is always difficult to detach yourself from your own prose when you read it through, but try. Try to put yourself in the place of the reader coming cold to the story, interested in it and asking the questions that will make it clear. Have you dealt with them? The subeditor, or text editor, will soon tell you if you haven't. There is always a problem over how much knowledge to assume, particularly

with a running story of which today's is another episode. You cannot always start from the beginning for the benefit of reader recently arrived from Mars, but you can include sufficient to ensure it is not meaningless. It is a matter of judgement.

Active not passive

Always prefer the active tense in news writing, and particularly in intros. The active tense is faster and more immediate; it also uses fewer words. "Arsenal were beaten by Manchester United last night ..." is slower than "Manchester United beat Arsenal ...", and if it is a London newspaper "Arsenal lost to Manchester United ..." is still preferable.

Positive even if it is negative

Not: "The government has decided not to introduce the planned tax increase on petrol and diesel this autumn." But: "The government has abandoned plans to raise fuel taxes this autumn." News is more engaging if it describes something that is happening, rather than something that is not.

"News stories always have to be cut because reporters write them too long"

Quotes

Long quotes bring a story grinding to a halt, particularly if they are from politicians, particularly local politicians, bureaucrats or bores. Short, incisive, direct quotes change the pace of a story, add colour and character, illustrate bald facts, and introduce personal experience. Journalists paraphrase speeches and reports to focus on the main points, and to make them shorter and more comprehensible. It is a vital skill, as is using indirect quotation. But a quote will add a different tone of voice, inject emotion or passion, answer the question "what was it like?", "how did you feel?", "what are you going to do next?", "what actually happened." Usually the reporter was not there and is gathering the information after the event. The direct quote provides actuality. And sometimes the quote has to be there to provide the precision, when the actual words used are crucial, and sometimes the story itself.

Never use a word other than "said" when attributing a quote. Affirmed, opined, exclaimed, interjected, asserted, declared, are all tacky synonyms which do nothing to help the flow of the story. When people speak they "say". On rare occasions it might be relevant to the story if they shout or scream; in which case break the rule.

Officialese

"People do not proceed; they walk. Police do not apprehend, they stop or arrest"

Language used in letters from bank managers, council officers, utilities and read from their notebooks by police officers giving evidence in court should always be avoided. People do not "proceed"; they walk. Police do not "apprehend"; they stop or arrest or detain. "At this point in time" is now.

George Orwell, in his essay Politics and the English Language, converts a passage from Ecclesiastes and turns it into officialese to make the point. Original: "I returned, and saw under the sun, that the race is not to the swift, not the battle to the strong, neither yet bread to the wise, nor yet riches to men of understanding, nor yet favour to men of skill; but time and chance happeneth to them all." Orwell's rewrite: "Objective consideration of contemporary phenomena compels the conclusion that success or failure in competitive activities exhibits no tendency to be commensurate with innate capacity, but that a considerable element of the unpredictable must invariably be taken into account."

Adjectives

Keith Waterhouse, the veteran Daily Mail and Daily Mirror columnist, wrote an irresistible book on journalistic writing called Newspaper Style. It was in fact an adaptation of the Mirror style book he had been commissioned to write. In it he warns of the dangers of adjectives thus: "Adjectives should not be allowed in newspapers unless they have something to say. An adjective should not raise questions in the reader's mind, it should answer them. Angry informs. Tall invites the question, how tall? The well-worn phrase: his expensive tastes ran to fast cars simply whets the appetite for examples of the expensive tastes and the makes and engine capacity of the fast cars."

This test should be applied to all adjectives used in journalistic writing. If they add relevantly to the information being provided, they can stay. If not, strike them. Too many writers believe adjectives add colour and style. Vague or general ones add nothing. "Use specific words (red and blue)," says Waterhouse, "not general ones (brightly coloured)."

Jargon, abbreviations, acronyms and know-all foreign phrases

All of us who work in organisations, professions, specific industries or bureaucracies are surrounded by jargon. We may regard it as shorthand to speed communication because we share the understanding of what it means, but, whether intentional or not, it is a protective shield that excludes those not in the know. That is the effect it has when used in newspaper writing. Those in the know understand; the rest do not. Anything readers do not understand makes them feel left out rather than included and turns them against the story. They may well stop reading. Medical, scientific and economic terms are a case in point. Avoid them or explain them. Price/earnings ratios and capitalisation mean nothing to the general reader. It is the same with abbreviations and acronyms. Today's students have no idea what CBI stands for; they are more likely to know FoI. A few could expand Nato, fewer the TUC. Many of the terms, although still in use, are generational. They need to be spelt out or explained, or another reader is lost. Just as long words speak down to those

"Pro bono, inter alia and in extremis usually mean the writer is showing off"

Acronyms

What do the following acronyms stand for? If you don't know instantly, then you can be sure there will be plenty of readers who don't. So do not use them without explanation.

Defra, Asbo, OECD, SEO; CBI; ISA; Fifa; PCT; Sats; FTSE

Answers:
Department for Environment, Food and Rural Affairs; Anti-Social Behaviour Order; Organisation for Economic Cooperation and Development; Search Engine Optimisation; Confederation of British Industry; Individual Savings Account; Fédération Internationale de Football Association; Primary Care Trust; Standard Assessment Tests; Financial Times Stock Exchange (used to describe stock market indices such as FTSE 100).

with a smaller vocabulary – and there is always a simpler, and less space consuming, alternative – so well-used Latin expressions mean nothing to those who have not learned that language, apart from lawyers who have had to mug up. Pro bono, inter alia and in extremis have no place in newspapers, and usually mean the writer is showing off.

Puns and cliches

Headline writers love puns and phrases from 60s pop lyrics and editors frequently have to restrain their use. They sit even less easily in copy, where only readers over 55 can identify. Again, the danger is excluding readers. Worst of all is the extended metaphor or pun. Like this (real) one: "Kingsbridge Silver Band has hit a high note with National Lottery chiefs to the tune of nearly £52,000. Tired old instruments struck a chord with the lottery board, which has drummed up enough cash for a complete new set, giving the band plenty to trumpet about." Yes, really.

Plain English

Rewrite the following two paragraphs in plain English suitable for publication in a newspaper or magazine. Remove unnecessary words, passive verbs, repetition, cliche, jargon and pompous or pretentious expression. Jot down some questions the story fails to answer.

"Joseph Foster and his sibling Kate were advancing cheerfully along Wesley Street when they were in minor collision with an HGV which unexpectedly mounted the pavement. It transpired later, when the multi-coloured Volvo truck driver who was transporting a container containing motor parts to Oxford was being interviewed by a local radio reporter, that the lorry veered to avoid a police car speeding towards him on the wrong side of the road. The spokesman at police headquarters told a different story. "But it was the children's lucky day as they escaped shocked but unscathed. A hospital spokesman at nearby Eddington hospital, run by the Barton NHS Foundation Trust, said the two children were lucky not to have been seriously injured. 'As it was,' declared Andrew Brown, 'they were examined in A and E and allowed to go home. Unfortunately Kate's buggy was beyond repair.'"

Exercise

Apostrophes

The printed word has done more to save the apostrophe than the whole of the teaching profession. Given the pace of newspaper and magazine production it is extraordinary that so few errors in spelling or punctuation appear, a tribute to the subeditors who prepare copy for publication. From advertising (shockingly, sometimes intentionally) to the greengrocer's board we are bombarded with mis- (and missing) punctuation, yet it is invariably correct in print, though seldom when it emerges from the home printer. If in doubt, and most people are, consult Lynne Truss (Eats, Shoots and Leaves). Often.

Features

Most of the news writing advice applies equally to features, although the intro and structure will be different. Feature is a broad term. Some news stories, even major front page stories, are written in the manner of a feature. This is usually called the narrative style. It is still story telling, but it is closer to the personal form of telling a child a story, building to a climax rather that giving it all away in the intro.

It represents the slow burn rather than putting the main point of interest in the intro. It is higher risk, because the golden rule of gaining and keeping the reader's attention paragraph by paragraph must still apply. The parody of the narrative story makes the point: "It was just another day for Sarah. Little did she know as she left the house that by the time she returned for tea her life would have changed for ever." Now read on; but few would.

"The main problem with celebrities is that you are given so little time"

The structure and the writing must demand that the reader wants to know what happened next, turning the narrative story into the newspaper equivalent of a page-turner. Extraneous or tedious information will make the reader lose interest and give up before finding out what the story is all about. The narrative works if there is narrative drive, and this demands more of the writer. The style can provide more atmosphere, more emotion, more colour. It can paint a picture and take the reader to the scene of events. It is emphatically not a chronological news story with more adjectives and more superfluous information that bores the reader and adds nothing to the story.

Features can be news backgrounders, fulfilling the explanatory role when there is not room for that in the main

Lynn Barber on interviewing celebrities

The main problem with interviewing celebrities today is that you are given so little time – one hour is considered generous. So any minute when the subject is not talking is a minute wasted. Questions should be short, clear, and specific rather than general. "What book did you last read?" is better than "Do you like reading?" because almost everyone will say they like reading, whereas if the last book they read was Heat magazine, you get a sharper idea of their reading habits. Never waste time asking for information that you could have found on Wikipedia. And do take a long list of questions, even if you don't stick to it – you are bound to need it occasionally as a prompt.

Always use a tape recorder, even if you also want to take notes, as libel insurance. That way, if the subject subsequently claims "I didn't say that", you have proof. And also, with a tape recording, you can reproduce their exact way of talking, not just the gist.

Be polite, pleasant, punctual. Always look interested, never shocked or disapproving. Let the reader do the disapproving – your job is to elicit the quotes.

There are various ways of presenting interviews but the one I prefer is the first person account that aims to answer the question, "What was it like to meet so and so?" This format does not pretend to any kind of omniscience, and for that reason I think it is the most honest.

Lynn Barber is an award-winning interviewer for the Observer

from the front line

news story. Increasingly, newspapers run packages, where news and background features – explanation, implications, case studies – are placed together in the newspaper. Features can also be away from the news: talking points, social trends, fads, fashions, arts and entertainment. They can explain

from the front line

Peter Bradshaw on how to write a review

In writing a review, your watchwords should be: simplicity, clarity and lightness of touch. You should always bear in mind a reader who, though, broadly acquainted with the sort of thing you are writing about, cannot be assumed to know all that much. He or she must be brought up to speed as quickly and fairly as possible about the matter at hand. Then you can start weighing in with all your subjective and provocative value judgments.

With film reviews, it is important to give some idea of the plot, but not to give too much away. Do this, and you are guilty of spoilerism. I have been an offender myself. One of the most difficult things is striking a balance between conveying the big picture about a film, and zooming in on the telling detail. You have to give what's happening on the screen your undivided attention and cultivate the art of remembering it. This means writing your review within a few hours of seeing the film.

Cliches? A wise editor of mine threatened to fine me £20 every time I used the word "darkly", rising to £50 if it was bolted to the word "funny" or "comic". By all means try to write funny reviews, though as Kingsley Amis said of novels: they don't have to be funny, but they can't afford to be unfunny.

Digression, riffing, going wildly off the point – it's all fine, as long as it's entertaining, and judging this comes with experience. You can annoy or enrage the readers as much as you like. Just don't bore them.

Peter Bradshaw is the Guardian's film critic

issues and add the human dimension to stories about statistics and medical conditions. They cover all the specialist areas, such as sport, education, environment, music, technology and travel. Features are not necessarily constrained by the journalistic obsessions with newness or exclusivity. They can deal with what is simply interesting, remarkable or amusing.

Features must be planned. Structure is paramount, the organisation of material gathered, from facts to quotes, description to context. The danger is for features to ramble or digress and then peter out. Whereas news stories are designed to be cut from the bottom (built in obsolescence at the end of the piece), the feature must have an end, a climax or a pay-off.

They will often have a prescribed length, which is both a luxury for the writer, and a challenge. No excuses if it doesn't flow. Nobody else to blame if vital facts are missing. The feature form allows for more expression by the writer because it is less formulaic than the traditional news story, but with that come pitfalls.

Features are the value-added part of the paper; you can keep up with the news without reading them. So they must maintain interest and be written in such a way that the reader keeps reading. That means changes of pace, lack of waffle, keeping to the point and ensuring that there is a narrative drive from beginning to end.

"With film reviews, it's important to give some idea of the plot but not to give it all away"

Columns

The great growth area in journalism, and a product of fatter newspapers. Columns, like features, come in many forms. They are defined by ownership; the column "belongs" to its author who has that ultimate journalistic luxury, a slot, guaranteed space over which he or she presides and has, in some cases, near total control over content. The assumption is that readers seek out the writer first rather than the subject matter, because they are interested in that writer's opinion, whether or not they agree with it. The so-called "me" columns, often dealing with no more than the everyday trivia and experiences of the writer are remarkably popular, providing a printed version of soap. It is a form of writing that seems to have translated effortlessly to the blog.

> "The so-called 'me' columns are popular, providing a printed version of soap"

Writing a column requires clarity of thought, the ability to communicate a message clearly and simply, and an engaging style. First comes the decision about the topic, which must lend itself to comment, ridicule, satire or whatever the nature of the column. It may be inspired by a particular quote from a public figure, a story in the news, a report, an unusual occurrence, a piece of bureaucratic absurdity, a domestic incident or a sporting controversy. The column must be planned so that the writer knows before he or she starts just what they are going to say. There must not be too many ideas (two or three will usually suffice), but plenty of opinions; the bland, obvious or fence-sitting must be ruthlessly expunged. Columns are there to get a reaction – agreement, disagreement, amusement, enlightenment. Intolerance is often a virtue. 'So what?' will not do. The column must sustain its theme, building towards a climax or "pay-off" line. If it wanders the reader will wander off.

Michael White on how to write a blog

Someone once said that the trick of doing radio is that it is a conversation between just two people, you and the listener you can't see.

It's the same with blogging. It's more like radio than it is like a newspaper column. The journalist's style must adapt to the different medium it is: more intimate, more informally conversational, more interactive. The writer can ask rhetorical questions – "Prince Charles is a plonker, isn't he?" – knowing that a dozen Royalists may leap to his defence.

Actually no, not in the Guardian. "Thread bores", as I sometimes hear them called, tend to lack deference; good for them. They may be right wing, though libertarian individualists is how I think of them in my kinder moments, but they are happy to kick anyone who ventures an ill-considered opinion or puts up facts which are wrong.

In the heyday of "dead tree" journalism (all that newsprint) error meant a postcard in green ink. Now it's a post to Comment is Free – sarcastic, abusive, mocking.

So a blogger must be careful with facts, even bad spelling can shatter the illusion of authority. He/she must be prepared to defend every fact and opinion – or apologise. Brevity is best, it always is. Beware the conceit (into which I fall) that the infinity of the blogosphere gives you the right to prattle on.

Above all, a blogger must have a thick skin. It's tough out there, but also fun. Among the hooligans there are clever, decent people who simply want to tell you things you didn't know.

Michael White writes the Guardian's Politics blog

from the front line

The good column will have a clear identity, so that the readers will feel they know the writer, his or her prejudices, enthusiasms and obsessions. The best columns inform the opinions of the readers; the best "me" columns are retold by their readers as though they are gossiping about friends.

Style

Competent, effective, functional, engaging journalistic writing can be learnt, and some advice has been provided in this section. Brilliant writing for newspapers has a plus factor which is hard to define and is not achieved by many. It comes down to style. Keith Waterhouse puts it this way: "What is this style? Why do some stories have it and others not? It would be fruitless to try to define it – as Fats Waller said when asked for a definition of jazz, 'Lady, if you have to ask, I can't tell you.' Obviously it demands flair, plus professionalism – two commodities that have never been in short supply in popular journalism. It demands experience, a quality that can be taken for granted in Fleet Street. For the rest, it consists simply of choosing a handful of words from the half million or so samples available, and arranging them in the best order."

Penultimate word to David Randall, whose Universal Journalist provides so much easily absorbed advice for the aspiring writer of journalism: "The pleasures of capturing something and pinning it down in words, your words, are immense. So too is the thrill of starting a piece with an assortment of disparate information and finding a pattern in it and new ideas about it as you write."

Last word to a much admired writer, who practises (daily in his parliamentary sketch) what he preaches, Simon Hoggart. Giving his own advice on writing in Writer's Market UK 2009, he says: "My advice would be to keep it simple. Dr Johnson said, about re-reading something you've written, 'Wherever you meet with a passage which you think is particularly

"The pleasures of capturing something and pinning it down in your words are immense"

fine, strike it out.' He was spot on. There is no substitute for clear, direct, straightforward writing. If you are Martin Amis you can get away with elaborate, stylised prose. If you aren't, you can't. The best journalism sounds like someone talking directly to you. It's not a school essay, so you don't need to begin with a long and ponderous introduction."

Hoggart provided two examples:

"Wrong: 'Philately has been described as the hobby for people who are too boring to be interested in beer mats. That is as may be. For me, it has always provided an agreeable and absorbing diversion.'

"Right: 'It was a second-hand shop in St Ives. I was leafing through the box of old postcards, and there it was: a 1932 Nyasaland Protectorate 2d yellow – without perforations. I thought my heart would stop ...'"

Write on!

Checklist

■ **Before you start**

Have I got a plan? Have I sorted through all the information I have gathered, rejected the unimportant and irrelevant, prioritised the most important and necessary? Have I sorted through the interviews and identified the people who must be quoted and the words I want to quote?

For features: have I sorted the facts, information and colour? Have I listed the biographical detail I need as well as the descriptive? Have I noted what she was wearing, what the room was like, books or CDs on the shelves?

■ **After you've finished**

Does the first paragraph set up the story and grab the reader?

"Does it hook the reader and set a scene the reader wants to explore?"

Read it out loud. Does it sound right? Does it sound punchy, urgent, interesting? Does it state clearly what the story is about and today's most important or attention grabbing development? Does it limit itself to one or two pieces of information, in one or two simple, active sentences? Does it whet the appetite for more?

For features: it may not be newsy, but does it hook the reader by providing a fact, an idea, an out of the ordinary human experience, or a talking point which leaves them wanting to know more? Does it set a scene the reader wants to explore? Or beg a question the reader wants answered?

■ **Have I used quotes sparingly but powerfully?**

Is there a quote high up the story, a strong, perhaps emotive, quote underlining or amplifying the thrust of the story as set out in the intro paragraph?

Is the quote short and does it reflect the person who said it?

Does it give a personal reaction to a situation? Does it describe feelings? Have I made sure it does not repeat information already provided more succinctly? Have I used other quotes to break up the story, change the pace and style, provide a break from description, or to add personal reactions and feelings?

■ **Is there anything in the story which is irrelevant or may not be understood?**

Have I used any words which some readers may not understand? If so substitute a simpler, better-known word. Have I written overlong sentences full of subordinate clauses likely to "lose" the reader along the way? Have I used an abbreviation or an acronym with which some readers may be unfamiliar? Have I used any adjectives gratuitously, rather than to provide more information? Have I used a vague adjective which begs a question rather than answering one? Would the story suffer if I cut this word?

■ **Have I read through the finished story?**

If no, start reading through the finished story. You will pick up mistakes, missing words, misspelt words, unnecessary words, rare words. If you are reading almost aloud you will hear how it sounds. Is there a rhythm or a monotony to your prose? Can you vary sentence length and construction to provide more flow and energy? And ask yourself, when you have finished reading through, whether you have left any questions unanswered, or begged some that were not there in the first place? Deal with them.

Further reading

- Essential English by Harold Evans (Pimlico)
- Journalism Principles and Practice by Tony Harcup (Sage)
- The Universal Journalist by David Randall (Pluto Press)
- Waterhouse on Newspaper Style by Keith Waterhouse (Viking)
  Out of print, but available second hand

What next?

Do you have the energy, flexibility and ambition it takes to be a journalist? Sean Dooley has some things you need to think about before beating a path to the editor's door

A dour regional daily editor once shared with me his infallible method for selecting trainee journalists. "At interview", he said, "I always ask for their second choice of career should they fail to get into newspapers. And anyone who replies social worker I immediately write off."

Most editors are not that precise in their phobias. But his approach did point up a valuable lesson for those wanting to join the media: take time to think through why you want to enlist.

It's useful advice for any career but particularly relevant to journalism: today's media offers a bewildering array of disciplines, and knowing which you want to pursue and why is a critical first step.

Once decided, the basic rules apply whether you're selling yourself or pitching freelance work at the local or national press. And no canon is more important than to exhaustively read and research your target publication.

Too many applicants and would-be contributors fail to do simple homework. At the very least an editor will look for candidate knowledge of circulation figures, sales area and target audience. Try also to buttonhole staff before interview about current culture on the editorial floor, and where needs are greatest.

Do be passionate about wanting to work specifically for the Daily Beast. Editors may themselves be cynical about what they can get out of their trainees, but very few are prepared to hire someone who shows little interest in anything other than how quickly they can be trained and move on to their next job.

Do be realistic about pay. Even in the good times my standard promise was to start juniors on a pathetic salary with the proviso that if they worked hard by the end of training it may have progressed to merely disgraceful. If anything, with the economic hurricane now blowing through the industry, rates have worsened.

Once hired, be honest in your ambition. Regional editors are fully reconciled to bright staff moving on, and most will help. If it's a national you want, there's no substitute for contacts. Day shifts are usually the first step and provide a good opportunity to taste the life and demonstrate your ability.

Be prepared to change your career ambitions. There will never be a better opportunity to experiment than in the climate of an under-staffed, all-hands-to-the-pump regional daily or local weekly. Many a would-be foreign correspondent has turned out a superb business editor simply because of an open mind.

If you want to freelance, think what you can offer that your target publication can't get elsewhere. Generic features are cheap and plentiful, so concentrate on ideas that a stretched newsdesk can't give staff time to chase.

Finally, remember that good working relationships are a two-way street. However desperate you may be for a start, ask every question imaginable on the quality and commitment to your in-house training. At the very least you'll impress the editor.

Sean Dooley edited regional daily newspapers for Northcliffe Media for 25 years until 2006. He now runs a consultancy, Workingthemedia, and is ombudsman for the National Council for the Training of Journalists.

"Regional editors are fully reconciled to bright staff moving on"

Plays and screenplays

Veering off script

Ronald Harwood explains the two distinct approaches required to write plays and screenplays. He also believes that although there are rules, they are best ignored

The golden rule in writing for the theatre or the screen is that there is no golden rule. Rules that have been made have always been broken. Throughout history, innovation and inspired ignorance have shattered long established guidelines and directives. For nearly a thousand years it was thought that in writing plays the three classical unities decreed by Aristotle had to be strictly applied for the piece to be thought properly structured. First, the unity of action: a play must have one plot and no sub-plots. Secondly, unity of place: the events should unfold in one physical space and there should be no attempt to represent more than one place on the stage. Thirdly, unity of time: the action should take place over a 24-hour period. It is certainly true that even today if these rules are adhered to, the result can have undeniable power.

It was Shakespeare who helped to overturn Aristotle's dicta. In Henry V he proclaims a revolutionary dramatic concept. "Suppose within the girdle of these walls," the chorus urges, "Are now confin'd two mighty monarchies", thus preparing the spectators for the shift of place. Later he warns the audience that it is their thoughts that must carry the characters "here and there; / jumping o'er times, / Turning the accomplishment of many years

/ Into an hour glass". Sub-plots abound and thus the classical unities were made redundant.

The cinema, too, has had its rules that seem to be ignored the moment they are made. For example, it used to be set down in celluloid that it was simply not possible to cut from one interior scene to another. Audiences, it was said, must know where they are and so it was thought that the exterior of a building, for example, had to be shown before seeing its interior, a formula by the way that television continues to employ. The under-estimating of the intelligence of the cinema-going public has been a curse on film makers.

Writing plays and screenplays cannot be taught. All that can be given is advice which may or may not be followed. There are gurus, especially in the cinema, who have decreed rules about plot structure, character arcs and God knows what else to be used as a scheme for all screenplays but it ought to be noted that these gurus have not had many, if any, of their own screenplays turned into movies.

"It is essential to recognise the chasm between theatre and cinema. The theatre is about language, the cinema about imagery"

Yet, for the beginner certain basic tenets need be understood. It is essential to recognise the chasm between theatre and cinema. The place where you sit to watch a play is called the auditorium which literally means a place where you listen. The theatre is about language, the cinema about imagery.

Plays demand that characters talk and so articulate emotions, attitudes and ideas. Simplistic though this may sound it is nevertheless the vital component of dramatic writing. No matter how realistic, economic or poetic, it is language that must reveal thoughts and feelings or, and most difficult of all, the thoughts and feelings that are being concealed.

In writing for the cinema, language takes second place. A look between two characters in close-up can reveal much more than pages of dialogue. Location, where a scene is set, is of vital importance to atmosphere and can be a way of intensifying story and plot. The pace at which a film unfolds, that subtle, almost indefinable rhythm, should be inherent in the screenplay.

What both writing for theatre and cinema have in common, however, is that the texts must be readable. This ideal is a little easier to achieve with a play because the need for intrusive technical directions are for the most part unnecessary. By contrast, the screenplay presents agonising difficulties.

Without doubt, the screenplay is the ugliest, most ungainly document imaginable, yet it is nevertheless essential to strive for making it easily comprehensible. Because the range of those who have to read covers a vast spectrum, from financiers and producers to director, actors and technicians, the objective must be simplicity. This means keeping technical directions to a minimum or removing them altogether. Many screenplays abound with instructions: close shot, long shot, camera moves in, out, dollies, cranes up, all of them inevitably ignored. If the writer requests a close shot, you may be sure the director will shoot from a mile away. Besides which these demands are insurmountable stumbling blocks in the reading process. It ought constantly to be remembered that screenplay is not the film. It is a guide, a blueprint for telling the story in the right order and for revealing the characters.

Every writer will have his or her own method of discovery. Some make detailed notes before commencing; others, like me, use the writing process itself to unravel the secrets of character, story and plot. As I said at the beginning, there are no rules. And if there are, break them.

Ronald Harwood is an Oscar-nominated scriptwriter and playwright. His adaptation of Jean Michel Dauby's The Diving Bell and the Butterfly won a Bafta in 2007.

Where to begin

Starting your first script may be daunting, but taking the right approach makes it far easier, explains your tutor Val Taylor

About your tutor

Val Taylor is a director, dramaturg, writer, development consultant for theatre, film, television and radio. She has directed the MA in Creative Writing: Scriptwriting at the University of East Anglia since 1998. She has also directed theatre productions on Broadway and in London's West End.

Scripts arise from thinking, feeling, daydreaming, remembering, reading, watching, listening, scribbling, abandoning and retrieving. Planning, writing and rewriting aren't doggedly linear; they require logical progressions, lateral, intuitive jumps and frequent retracing of steps. Script pages, if they are at all good, seem bare and incomplete until performed.

Scripts are better understood as organisms, not mechanisms; there are no rules or formulae you can follow. There are, however, observations you can make about recurring patterns, shapes and devices in stories, and ways of thinking you can use to prompt your writing. The following chapters suggest some of them.

Ideas and stories

Your idea will come from your experience of the world and your responses to it. Keep a notebook where you can record thoughts and observations, particularly of people, behaviour and situations you encounter.

Your idea may begin via a character or place, an event or theme, or perhaps an interest in a particular genre. It's not important where you start. What you are seeking is the germ of a dramatic story: a series of actions by, and between, characters that bring about changes in their circumstances, world, lives and possibly, their natures.

Six basic questions: Where? When? Who? Why? What? How?, serve as prompts to your imagination. Throughout, they help you organise information and assess how effectively your idea is communicated.

Where? Maps the "story world".

When? Locates us within a historical moment; orders the story chronology; maps the relationship between past, present and future; sets the duration (time bracket) of the action.

Who? Introduces the nature of characters and their relationships.

What? Shapes the events that happen to your characters, the decisions they make and their subsequent actions.

Why? Uncovers character and story motivation, enabling us to try to predict what might happen next and how characters might respond.

How? Tells the story through visual images, sound, music and language.

"Script pages, if they are at all good, seem bare and incomplete until performed"

Setting

L ocations, culture and society provide a recognisable context for your characters and story events. Whether naturalistic or fantastical, the world should operate according to a set of rules, to encourage our belief.

The world contains specific conflict arenas where the inhabitants act out their values according to the established systems.

"Create tension between what we can see onstage and what we know is offstage"

Your story world

- Is your story world urban, rural, village or wilderness? (For example, Manchester in Life on Mars.)
- What kinds of people inhabit it? Who are the insiders or outsiders? (Gene Hunt and his squad v Sam Tyler.)
- What are their values? Beliefs? Attitudes? Customs? What unites/divides them? (Policing methods divide, the concept of justice unites them.)
- How does their material environment reflect their values, attitudes, beliefs and prejudices? (The squad room; cars; cigarettes, alcohol.)
- How do they react to and arbitrate conflicts? (Gene thumps first, asks questions later; Sam uses forensics and psychological profiling.)
- What kinds of events are likely to occur there? (Criminal activities, arrests.)
- How does the period setting affect these answers? (1973 has limited crime-detection technology and different attitudes towards physical force.)

Your plot may unfold in multiple locations. It's useful to think in terms of contrasting spaces, such as:
- Interiors v exteriors;

– Private v public spaces;
– "Expansive" v "contracted" spaces, (Manchester streets v the police room);
– "Open" v "closed" worlds, (The squad is a closed world to Sam, but open to Gene.)

Ronan Bennett on how to write with a sense of place

Adventures in the Screen Trade by William Goldman, the Oscar-winning writer of Butch Cassidy and the Sundance Kid, Marathon Man and much more, is the only "how to" book on screenwriting I've read. Among the pearls of Goldman wisdom is his injunction to make the script "a reading experience". This is particularly important when it comes to the setting.

The setting is all about making the reader believe in the world you are trying to create. I emphasise reader because it's easy to forget that the screenplay's first audience is made up of readers – producers, script executives, development people, financiers, directors and actors.

I see a lot of scripts written in the minimalist Hollywood style. In the worst of these, stage directions are terse and make little effort to create the illusion that this world is real. For me, research is key. I want to know as much as I possibly can about the world my characters are going to inhabit.

When I was working on Public Enemies, about the bank robber John Dillinger, Michael Mann insisted that I not only visit the actual locations, but that I also spend a day driving vintage cars on a lot in LA. He didn't have to insist too hard.

The trick – not an easy one – is not to be a slave to your research, but to use it to give yourself the confidence to create vivid, compelling pictures in the reader's head.

Ronan Bennett's screenplays include Rebel Heart and Hamburg Cell

from the front line

Create tension between what we can see onstage/offscreen, and what we know is offstage/outside the frame. Keep us aware of the surrounding world via characters' entrances and exits; sound; and the structure of scene sequences, playing with our existing knowledge.

Write concise, vivid, descriptions of the story world. Think about (for example) colours, sounds, textures, smells, atmosphere, and iconic objects: what are the key features?

Character

I n naturalistic dramatic characters, we look for underlying motivations that provoke decisions and courses of action. To uncover these, we examine characters' outer and inner lives.

Outer life

A character's "outer life" is bound up with social roles and relationships: for example, parent/ child/ sibling; friend/ partner/ spouse; employer/employee. Complex story worlds create a spectrum of social roles: for example, legal systems offer clusters – law-makers, law-breakers, "thief-takers" and victims, the basis for crime or revenge thrillers, heists and capers, murder mysteries and television police or detective series.

Written or unwritten rules, expectations and taboos govern roles and relationships, prescribing (or challenging) public and private behaviour, and attributing high or low social status. Roles, relationships and status locate characters within their world, stipulating their everyday interactions. The story events cut across the everyday, generating conflicts within and between characters and situations.

For each character, consider:

- Sex and gender; race; ethnic origin; age; sexual orientation;
- Class; education; employment; financial circumstances; religion; political affiliation;
- Family and kinship groups; circles of friendship and affinity;
- Where on the high or low status axis would each of these categories place him?

Inner life

The "inner life" embraces his psychology (or pathology), emotional condition, and moral impulses. His outer life is his public face; the inner life, his private face. Effective characters experience harmony and conflict between outer and inner, public and private lives. This tension provides the source of his dilemma: the choice between courses of action leading to loss, gain and compromise.

Explore a character's internal "drives": desire, fear, need, and will. Ask:

- What does he want? Why? How badly? How strong is his will to acquire or achieve this?
- How far will he go in order to do this? What's stopping him from going further?
- What does he fear? How badly? Why? How strong is his will to avoid this?
- How far will he go to avoid this? What's stopping him from going further?
- What does he need? Why? How badly?
- How far will he go? And what, if anything, is stopping him from going further?
- Does he know he needs this? If not, why? And what has to happen to make him recognise it?

Create points of conflict between his desires, needs and fears: for example, to get what he needs, he'll have to face his worst fear; what he wants is the opposite of what he really needs. When need amplifies or opposes fear or desire, it raises the stakes.

A character lives in the present, but his past – his "backstory" – may dictate his emotional terrain and influence his actions. Strengths and weaknesses often lie there, providing 'ghosts' or 'cargo' (people, events) to haunt or drag down his present life. Root his present dilemma in the secrets, illusions or self-deceptions in his backstory; then compel him to confront the revelation of the truth.

Characterisation

Characters' outer and inner lives are revealed through:

- Physical type, body language and gesture: give each character a "tell" – a definitive, revealing gesture or movement. For example, in Ibsen's Hedda Gabler, Hedda plays with her late father's, General Gabler's, pair of pistols, taking casual pot-shots at an unwelcome visitor. This is a clue to her reckless, destructive nature.
- Costume and hair.
- Settings, particularly private spaces: think about how the objects, colours, sounds and textures reflect the character.
- Dialogue: how the character speaks, and what he speaks about.
- Actions: the decisions the character makes and carries out. In Hedda Gabler, when Lörborg is in despair at the loss of his precious book manuscript, Hedda doesn't reveal that she has got it; instead she gives him one of the pistols. After he leaves, she burns the book, page by page.

Pixar's film WALL.E is also an excellent case study in character creation and characterisation: the central characters WALL.E and EVE are anthropomorphised machines. Though their dialogue is mostly squeaks, beeps and chirps, their communication is clear and thoroughly rooted in character.

> "Effective characters experience harmony and conflict between outer and inner, public and private lives"

Character functions

The protagonist is the character who makes the most active decisions. The dramatic story tracks his progress, and may follow his point of view. He's not necessarily pleasant or good, but he is the character in whom we are invited to invest. Each character should have their own story, but the protagonist's should be the strongest.

The next strongest story belongs to the antagonist, generating conflict by disrupting and blocking the protagonist's progress. She is the force for change within the story. She must be capable of defeating – even destroying – him; if she's too thinly drawn, the story collapses. Build her outer and inner life, and backstory, in the same depth as the protagonist's. Use the characters' desires, fears and needs to set them in irreconcilable opposition.

The protagonist's may be a single character, a pair (love stories), or a group (for example, This Life). The antagonist may be any of the following:

- A character
- An opposing force, such as societal attitudes or changes
- Nature (the Asian tsunami, The Birds)
- Supernatural forces, or aliens
- Technology (HAL 9000 in 2001: A Space Odyssey)
- The protagonist can also be his own antagonist (Tom Ripley in The Talented Mr Ripley).

Secondary characters, as allies and opponents of the protagonist and antagonist, flesh out the main story. Allies and opponents can change sides or allegiances to help you create obstacles, setbacks and triumphs for your principals. Each secondary character should have a (lesser) story of his or her own, which provides comparison or contrast to the protagonist's story.

Story events

D ramatic stories build sequences of occurrences and actions: things that happen (such as monsoon rain; a flat tyre) and things that are done (such as sending messages; firing guns). Audiences' primary interest lies in characters' decisions and the ensuing consequences.

Story events rooted in human agency offer shape to scenes and sequences via familiar, culturally-specific behaviour patterns, routines and rituals. The skeleton shape may be confirmed through "proper performance" or disrupted by culture-clashes, misinterpretation or transgressive behaviour.

Working with event-types

What kinds of events are your characters likely to create within the story world? Does the genre imply particular events? What will audiences expect to see? Look for natural opposites, clusters and implied sequences between events. This indicative list suggests a few:

- Ceremony
- Celebration
- Reunion
- Meal
- Chase or pursuit
- Recruitment
- Seduction
- Interview or interrogation
- Investigation
- Game, competition or contest
- Test, trial or ordeal
- Deception

- Discovery or revelation
- Holiday
- Voyage or quest
- Arrival or departure (including birth and death), meeting or parting
- Argument or reconciliation
- Battle or negotiation.

Some event-types can frame the overall story. Combinations provide opportunities for conflict: Festen, for example, uses a family reunion to detonate explosive revelations around the table at a birthday celebration dinner.

Consider where each event belongs: its placing governs the unfolding of your theme. When you've found the story's climactic event, try reversing its position: what happens if it's the opening event, as in Harold Pinter's Betrayal?

Sequencing

Break down the event-type into sequences of incremental action. For example: Peace > Disagreement > Quarrel > Skirmish > Battle > War > Truce > Peace.

Here, the unvarying escalation becomes monotonous. Introduce reversals to create changes of direction: Peace > Disagreement > Quarrel > Reconciliation > Peace > Quarrel > Skirmish > Stand-off > Negotiation > Ceasefire > Skirmish > War > Truce > Peace.

The escalation breaks and reverses after the first quarrel, then renews. It reverses again when the skirmish reaches a stand-off and negotiation intervenes. The final reversal breaks the ceasefire, setting up the climactic escalation (war), ultimately resolved by truce and restoration of peace.

Understanding event sequences permits sophisticated plotting, where continuities of time and place can be fractured without losing the thread of the story, as in Memento, 21 Grams, or Michael Frayn's play Copenhagen.

"Once you've found the story's climatic event, try reversing its position"

Theme

Themes carry the emotional dimension, where we recognise a truthful observation about ourselves that transcends sentimentality, triteness or banality.

There may be several themes in the story, but it is the principal theme that governs the protagonist's decisions. He's unaware of this until the final sequence. Discernible in the degree of change he has undergone, the principal theme becomes clear in the final movement of the story.

Life on Mars had excellent features:
- An intriguing premise (modern-day policeman wakes up after an accident to find he's gone back in time to 1973).
- Engaging characters, led by Sam Tyler and Gene Hunt.
- Familiar police genre, with a sci-fi twist.
- Strong central conflict between Sam's and Gene's attitudes and methods.
- A good "hook": is Sam Tyler in a coma? Dreaming? Has he time-travelled? How can he get home?
- A strong goal: To get home, Sam first has to discover how and why he's been sent back in 1973.

The series had various themes: the nature of justice is an obvious example. But the principal theme carries the greatest emotional weight; to understand Life on Mars' principal theme, look at the climax of season two. Throughout seasons one and two, Sam has unwittingly been acquiring pieces of the puzzle about his own true self. When the last piece crystallises his internal need, his final choice – to be where he belongs – delivers a strong emotional charge.

Working with theme

Themes emerge as you write and rewrite; the principal theme won't be fully formed as you begin. This is the most personal part of your writing, so it's useful to approach it in a personal way.

– Why does your story attract you? Why do you care? What do you want to talk about, through your story?

– Your themes will respond to fears and needs, such as fear of death or the unknown; the desire for companionship, love or the society of peers. Express your early ideas as questions: ask "what does X have to overcome if she is to be redeemed?" Or "what is preventing X from achieving redemption?" As you explore the answers your investment in the story will become clearer to you and the principal theme will emerge.

– Use what you believe to be true about human behaviour and its motivations. Draw upon your own experience.

– Avoid judging your characters. Let them do what they do, say what they say, feel what they feel; allow yourself to be surprised, perhaps challenged, by their choices. David Simon (creator of The Wire) insists that characters' humanity should be explored in full, without moralising: "It's about making everybody whole."

"Theme is the most personal part of your writing. Why does your story attract you? Why do you care?"

Stakes

The stakes create jeopardy to motivate your characters. Don't over-pitch them at the outset; you need to escalate throughout ("rising action") without falling into repetitive, wearying, melodramatic action. Be wary, though, of under-pitching: insufficient risk means audiences won't invest in the characters.

Consider:
- What is at risk of loss or destruction? (At the extreme, death, or the end of the world.)
- Why? What is the threat? (Define the antagonist.)
- How severe is the risk? (Likelihood of occurrence increases audiences' engagement)
- When would the risk become irretrievable?
- What has to be done to avert it?
- What will it cost?
- What could be gained through confronting and overcoming it?
- Is passivity (or giving up) acceptable, or better? (These questions frame the protagonist's dilemma.)

Think about this in the story as a whole, then give yourself room to escalate; determine how little needs to happen to trigger the risk at the outset (the "inciting incident"). Use the questions to help plot the steps of rising action from scene to scene.

From "lack" to "gain"
These questions help to shape an event-driven story with cause and effect sequences (thrillers and mysteries, for

Frank Cottrell Boyce on set up and pay off

If you're making a generic film, you generally know what the ending is going to be: the crime will be solved, the lovers will kiss, the sequel will be suggested. But if you're writing away from the formula it's a lot harder to set up the ending. If you can come up with something in the last few minutes that makes the audience see the whole film in a new light, you're onto a winner.

In Sideways, Paul Giamatti's character carts his massive, unreadable novel around everywhere with him. It's a great running gag and a brilliant way of explaining what a loser he is. The ending of the film is that one person does read it. Just one. But the right one. It's very hard to set up something like that book without telegraphing it too obviously. The secret is not to try to write it in advance. Wait until you get to the end, then look back at what seems resonant or worth revisiting and chose that.

Another great example is the ending of Cinema Paradiso. Early in the film, the projectionist has the job of cutting out the steamy kisses from various movies. At the end, our grown-up, now cynical hero receives a reel of film. This turns out to be all the lost kisses. I don't even like the film, but that ending always pulverises me. It sends you back to the heart of the film, picks up what seemed like a throwaway joke and makes it into something that forces you to feel keenly the sense of loss that comes with growing up.

Frank Cottrell Boyce's screenplays include 24 Hour Party People *and* A Cock and Bull Story

example.) If you prefer character-driven stories, the stakes relate more to the characters' wellbeing and emotional condition. The questions can be rephrased:

– What does your protagonist lack, at the outset: for example, love, social status, economic stability, freedom?

- Why? (Explore her backstory and the story world.)
- What does she need to acquire to convert lack into gain: for example, knowledge, money, friends?
- What is stopping her? (Explore contradictions within your protagonist, and external circumstances.)
- What is at risk if she doesn't succeed? (Make the audience root for her.)
- What will it cost her? Why is it worth paying? (These two questions frame the protagonist's dilemma.)

Lack and gain can be ambiguous: for example, we regret loss of innocence; acquiring knowledge or experience is painful. Exploit such ambiguities in character-driven stories, such as romances, rites of passage.

"Be wary of under-pitching: insufficent risk means the audience won't invest in the characters"

Genre

Genres are categories of stories grouped according to shared, characteristic patterns of form, content and style. This grouping provides shorthand means of conveying to your audiences what kind of intellectual, emotional and physical experience to expect.

You may or may not want to write within genres; however, it's useful to understand how they function so that you can work within, across or outside them. Film and television employ genres extensively; commissioning discussions require you to be conversant with their functions. Theatre and radio employ genres more loosely, but a proper understanding remains valuable.

The UK Film Council reports that, in 2007, the most popular genres with UK cinema audiences were:
– Fantasy
– Comedy
– Thriller
– Drama
– Horror
– Crime
– Science fiction
– Romance
– War
– Action
– Adventure.

Television employs story genres within serial and series formats. Current schedules are anchored by "precinct dramas": groups or teams working within a tight-knit group of locations, often a workplace. Police and medical series are obvious examples: the station, laboratory, hospital or surgery provides the central location.

Mainstream UK theatre is dominated by musicals and comedy; subsidised or non-mainstream theatre draws on relationships, family and personal stories, social drama, and romance; radio does too.

Working with genre

Research the genre you're interested in: look at how key elements are used. I'll use horror as a model, with Alien, a horror/sci-fi hybrid, as an example:

- **Story world**: Are there characteristic locations? What are the rules of the story world? Horror uses places where the protagonist expects to feel safe or knows what the dangers are; they become traps once the antagonist appears. (The Nostromo spaceship.)
- **Stakes**: What is usually at risk? How are the stakes habitually raised? Is there a "ticking clock" timeline? Horror places the protagonist in mortal danger, closing off her escape routes as the antagonist draws near. (The Nostromo crew have to prevent the spaceship reaching Earth with the alien on board; Ripley barely escapes.)
- **Protagonist and antagonist**: What are the generic characteristics of the protagonist and antagonist? How is the audience aligned with them? The horror protagonist is a victim who must find extraordinary personal reserves to save herself. Our point of view is aligned with her; we share her terror. Horror antagonists are (literally or figuratively) monsters: superior in strength, malevolent in intent. (Ellen Ripley must turn implacable warrior to defeat the alien's speed and cunning.)
- **"Trigger" and resolution**: What are the events that trigger stories in this genre? How are they resolved? Horror triggers bring in the monster, sparking the protagonist's jeopardy. The resolution expects the monster to be

"Horror uses places where the protagonist expects to be safe, they become traps once the antagonist appears"

destroyed or expelled and the protagonist to escape. (Alien's trigger occurs when the crew members examine the alien eggs. It resolves when Ripley finally ejects the creature from the escape pod.)

- **The "expected scenes"**: What scenes would audiences expect to see? Horror establishes the protagonist's normal world before admitting the monster. There is a series of attacks which the protagonist at first tries to avoid, before being forced into a climactic battle: whether or not she wins is the writer's choice. (Alien begins with the routine schedule on the Nostromo, disrupted by the discovery of the alien eggs. The first attack takes place on the planet; the injured crewman unwittingly brings the alien onboard and it kills the crew. Ripley thinks she's escaped, but finding that the alien has hidden in her escape pod, she has to fight again.)

- **Style**: Does the genre employ characteristic visual and aural stylistic devices? Horror's usual tone is one of threat and unease, created by a close alignment with the protagonist's point of view. Strong contrasts of light and shadow are often used to conceal rather than reveal information. Periods of calm alternate with bursts of frantic action which grow longer as the action approaches its climax.

Familiarise yourself with the patterns of genre; use your notes to refine your decisions about the story world, characters, events, theme and stakes of your story.

Structure

Script structure creates a strong narrative framework that delivers your theme through the interaction of the story world, characters and events. It shapes audiences' experience of your story. Poor structure - or lack of a discernible structure - is the commonest weakness in scripts.

Three-act structure/Hero's journey/ 7 & 22 steps

Mainstream western cinema and television are dominated by three-act structure. This is a conflict-driven model, aligning audiences with the point of view of a protagonist who makes decisions and takes action to resolve a series of crises. Sequences are constructed in chains of cause and effect, progressively raising the stakes. Structural models such as the hero's journey (Christopher Vogler, following Joseph Campbell), and the 7 & 22 steps (John Truby) follow similar causal, goal-directed, conflict-based pathways.

Alternative models

The western independent sector and many national cinemas prefer more open structural models. These models use contrasting features: multiple protagonists and multiple plots; passive or powerless protagonists; no point of view alignment with the protagonist; narration; events linked by coincidence (such as time or location); an order of events that can be rearranged; ending, instead of resolution; the structure prevents audiences from empathy with characters. Examples of films using these kinds of structures would be Dogville, Intacto, and Magnolia.

Plays frequently choose less plot-driven alternatives, exploiting non-naturalistic devices and theatrical possibilities. Structures can be circular (Waiting for Godot); episodic (Top Girls); employ parallel action, echoes and associational links. Tom Stoppard (Arcadia, Rock'n'Roll), Michael Frayn (Copenhagen, Democracy) and Caryl Churchill (Far Away; Heart's Desire) all use open structures.

Working with structure

Look at your theme, characters and story.

– Is your theme best delivered through a single, goal-driven protagonist whose decisions and actions create change within himself and his world? (A)

– Does your theme address the effects of the story world upon one or more protagonists, whose actions cannot effect change internally or externally? (B)

– Should we be closely aligned with the protagonist's viewpoint? (A)

– Should we reflect on the characters' situations and actions, but not identify with them? (B)

Look at your story events in relation to your theme, characters and story world:

– Can you identify an event that would trigger a chain of cause and effect? An event that would finally resolve the chain? (A)

– Would these events, arranged into causal chains, support a main plot driven by the protagonist's decisions? (A)

– Are these events driven primarily by characters' decisions? (A)

– Are your events linked by time, location, characters or theme, not by cause and effect? (B)

– Would these events support multiple, smaller plots of equal importance? (B)

– Are these events driven primarily by factors outside characters' control? (B)

Mostly (A) answers could suggest using three- act structure, or the hero's journey, or the 7 & 22 steps. Mostly (B) answers could suggest alternative models.

Plotting

Structure organises the strategic release of narrative information. Many decisions will concern questions of knowledge:

– What does the audience already know?
– What does each character already know?
– To whom is each piece of information revealed? (Irony occurs when we know more than the characters.)
– How and when is it revealed?

Causal plots (A) are structured around obstacles, turning points and reversals. The trigger provokes the protagonist to formulate a goal, and to take steps to achieve it. Each step confronts him with a new obstacle to overcome. Each decision generates a turning point that takes the story in a new direction. Some turning points help him progress; others produce setbacks and reversals.

In three-act structure, each act pivots around a major turning point: act one's turning point comes from external events;. act two's turning point comes from an internal shift inside the protagonist; act three's turning point comes from the protagonist's final decisive action, and brings about the resolution.

Construct your scenes and sequences using this pattern: establish a situation, then disrupt it. Use turning points and reversals to provoke actions and reactions.

Alternative (B) structures also employ conflict, obstacles, turning points and reversals. The protagonist still makes decisions, but plot progression is driven externally. There may not actually be plot progression; the story describes the world and the characters, rather than engaging them in action, as in Waiting for Godot. In (B) structures, turning points often move us between parallel stories, or loop backwards and forwards between episodes in the story. In both (A) and (B) structures, try to build in echoes: images, sounds or lines that recur in different contexts; information that recurs in different ways. This process of foreshadowing operates as a form of prediction in (A) structures; in (B) structures, it binds together different threads of story, and carries your theme.

Exercise

Building a structure

Make at least four selections from each of the following lists of locations, characters and events, and work out the structure of a five-minute story.

Exterior: front doorstep; traffic intersection; garden.
Interior: bus; kitchen; department store display window.
Characters: cleaner; bus passenger; shop assistant; grandparent; school student; window-shopper.
Events: a text message is sent or received; a photograph is taken; a wallet is lost; a breakage occurs; a slap; a kiss.

Dialogue

Dialogue fulfils several key functions:

- **Characterisation:** Give everyone distinctive speech patterns, habits, vocabulary.
- **Communication between characters:** What they say, when, how and to whom, to propel the plot forward.
- **Exposition:** Key information should be shown, wherever possible, rather than spoken, in the visual media. Where it's revealed in dialogue, try to make the external situation, or an aspect of her inner life, provoke the character into giving information at that moment. Don't let characters tell each other what they already know as an early shortcut; it's often referred to as 'first act amnesia'.
- **Description:** Narration can create atmosphere, bring a detail into focus, or convey the speaker's response to unseen events.
- **Commentary:** Contextual perspective on character or story developments can be given. Greek drama employed the Chorus, contemporary drama sometimes uses a narrator.

"Poor structure – or lack of discernable structure – is the commonest weakness in scripts"

Writing dialogue

A character speaks for reasons arising from her nature, circumstances, inner life or goals. Why is she speaking? Is she seeking information, issuing an invitation, arguing, for example? Think about what she says versus what she means: could this be deception, evasion, intimacy or ignorance? When you're clear about the underlying intention, ensure the lines deliver it.

Silence is an eloquent component of dialogue, shaping speech rhythms. Silence points to emotional subtext, in conjunction with the character's gestures or body language,

Lucinda Coxon on how to write dialogue

Dialogue is the words characters speak to themselves, one another and an audience. And before that, of course, to the writer. When characters speak to the writer with tremendous urgency, that urgency translates into dialogue with real tension and immediacy.

Dialogue is also, of course, the words the characters do not speak. What is not said is always telling.

Audiences tend to assume that characters in plays and films are telling the truth. They trust them. It's imperative that the writer returns this compliment by trusting the characters also – even if they're pathological liars. Often you can hear the moments in the dialogue where the writer feels that they have a more important thing to say than the characters. This is rarely a good sign.

While dialogue can be informational, a way to develop character or reveal plot, it is emphatically not conversational, any more than war or sex or prayer is conversational. Dialogue is character, is plot. Above all, it is action.

The best exercise for writing dialogue is reading other people's. Read widely and read people who don't write like anyone else: Howard Barker, Caryl Churchill, Gregory Motton, Marguerite Duras. Read them (and your own work) aloud.

When the characters began to speak, the writer was really listening.

Lucinda Coxon's latest play, Happy Now?, premiered at the National Theatre in 2008

from the front line

which may confirm, amplify or contradict what she is saying.

Use dialogue economically and strategically. Plays employ more dialogue than screenplays, but you need less than you think. Characters should be succinct, though not necessarily direct: evasion, waffle or hedging may be appropriate. Save longer speeches for a genuine payoff: a revelation, or pivot point.

If your style is non-naturalistic, stylised speech may be appropriate, relying more on rhythm or metre, sentence structure, and imagery. The need for precision, economy and clarity is even greater, in this instance.

All dialogue needs to be read aloud to hear how it sounds, and recognise how much can be cut.

"All dialogue needs to be read aloud to hear how it sounds, and recognise how much can be cut"

Visual storytelling

Pixar's WALL.E begins with a skewed, futuristic city panorama: skyscrapers made from compacted rubbish, everywhere deserted. Closer in, a squat little robot busily collects and squashes rubbish for the next "trash tower". The robot is rusty, battered, but perky and inquisitive, sorting items for his collection. A stencilled acronym reveals his name: WALL.E. The story world, the protagonist and a major theme are introduced with visual style, charm and wit: no dialogue.

Llewellyn Moss hunts in baking Texas prairie in No Country for Old Men. He finds the aftermath of a shootout: bloody corpses, SUVs, guns. One man, dying, begs for water; Moss ignores him. He follows a blood trail, finds another corpse and a case full of dollar bills. Joel and Ethan Coen introduce the protagonist, story world and launch the plot through gripping images.

Sound plays a key role: dry desert rustling, rifle-shots, boots crunching, truck doors slamming, underscore the opening of No Country... As WALL.E works, he beeps and hums a tune from Hello Dolly! learned from a treasured videotape. Visual storytelling benefits from a well-chosen soundscape, which can include music and song, where appropriate.

Writing visually

- Images and dialogue should complement or contradict, without duplication. Juxtapose images within scenes and across sequences to create additional layers of meaning: for example, contrasting English and African locations, official buildings v villages; Tessa's bare skin and flamboyant clothing v the men's suits (The Constant Gardener).

- On screen, images narrate, dialogue should support. Where voiceover narration is used, it should establish an intimate, exclusive relationship with the audience (American Beauty), rather than give expositional information: use it for character purposes, not as a plotting shortcut.
- Give information visually, via (for example) labels, captions, advertising billboards, newspaper headlines, street and shop names.
- Clarify the scene's event-type: familiar events, such as meals, arrivals and departures, supply an existing, accessible visual grammar.
- In screenplays, visual montages can avoid repetition, compress time and reveal character: see WALL.E's faithful protection of EVE as she awaits her recall to the spaceship Axiom.
- Gestures, movements and expressions provide characterisation and plot information. Psychological gestures can reveal emotional truths, secrets, or subtext: consider how Chigurh's life-or-death coin-tosses reveal his psychopathic nature (No Country...).
- Where dialogue slows the tempo unnecessarily, cut it: make sure the transitions from image to image generate pace and rhythm.

"Visual montages can avoid repetition, compress time and reveal character"

Create a scene

Write a three-minute visual scene or sequence based around a ceremony (wedding or funeral; launching a ship; official 'robing' or investiture; parade) in which the protagonist is involved. Sound, including music and song, can be used, but no more than 10 words of dialogue.

Exercise

Stage plays do require visual writing: we are looking as well as listening. Locations are fewer: make them work harder – exploit the tension between onstage/offstage. Psychological gestures are particularly valuable in naturalistic plays: in The Seafarer, alcoholic Sharky refuses to join in the heroic drinking bouts, until he believes his soul is forfeit to the sinister Lockhart. Then he fatalistically downs glass after glass of poteen.

Stage images carry significant metaphoric weight (Max's armchair, placed dead centre in The Homecoming), and hint at plot or character revelations (the burn scars on Mag's arm and the chip pan on the cooker in The Beauty Queen of Leenane).

Layout and formats

Script formatting is highly conventionalised, so you need to acquaint yourself with the correct format; this will differ for theatre, cinema, television or radio.

Published scripts don't always reflect the required conventions; many are reformatted for publication.

Internet sites offer downloadable original screenplay drafts: some are free, others for purchase. Good sites include: screenwriterstore.co.uk; script-o-rama.com; iscriptdb.com (a search resource for locating free screenplay downloads.) The BBC Writersroom (bbc.co.uk/writersroom) supplies radio scripts and television episodes. Stage plays aren't online, but published scripts often retain original formatting conventions.

Scriptwriting software packages (for PCs and Macs) can be very expensive but, particularly for screenplays, are a better option than trying to construct your own formatting templates. Final Draft is widely used within the screen industries.

There are also free software packages: Celtx (celtx.com) has good online support. The BBC Writersroom offers ScriptSmart, for screenplays, but there is no online support. The website also has sample formats for theatre, film, radio and studio-based television, for reference.

Formatting conventions stipulate layout, including spacing: Courier New is a standard font; use font size 12. The conventions allow for approximate conversion of pages to performance running time: one page of A4 script, properly formatted, converts to approximately one minute, across a full-length script. They also allow the reader to distinguish quickly between character cues, dialogue and stage/ scene directions.

"Your script will go through several drafts; much of your task will be rewriting and editing"

The average feature film running time is 90-120 minutes. Television formats dictate running time: 30-minute episodes are usually the minimum, with many drama series using episode lengths of 50-60 minutes. Radio scripts also work in format lengths: 45-minute and 60-minute single plays; 5-part x 15-minute serials; two-part x 60-minute classic adaptations. Stage plays vary widely, anywhere between 75 (without an interval) to 120 minutes (including interval).

In your script, focus on the story and characters. Keep description to a minimum, and avoid trying to direct the actors and the camera. In stage/ scene directions, avoid "purple" vocabulary, but do ensure that you paint the picture vividly. Your script will go through several drafts; much of your task will be rewriting and editing, so it's OK to overwrite the first draft, to some extent. Remember: it's easier to cut than to add, without the script seeming "patched".

What next? Screenplays

Want to get your script into the hands of a
Hollywood producer? Nothing is impossible, says
Debra Hayward, as long as you do your homework

There are no easy options when presenting yourself or
your screenplay for the first time, but your first
objective is to ensure that it is read by as many
influential people as possible. There are a number of
avenues you can pursue simultaneously, but before getting your
screenplay out there, make sure you do your homework.

If you have written a comedy for instance, identify producers
who specialise or have had success in this genre. If you're not
sure, don't be afraid to call up and ask what sort of material
they are looking for. Research and enter screenwriting
competitions and schemes (there are many reputable ones) for
which your screenplay might be suitable. Shortlisted screenplays
on these types of initiatives often get into circulation and are
read by producers and executives in film and TV companies.
Network – attend seminars, forums and festivals about
screenwriting. Meeting people at these kinds of events offer up
opportunities to get your work noticed, or at the very least
provide useful advice.

Read the trade press. Keeping up to date with what's going
on in the industry generally might help you identify gaps in the
market or potential buyers. Get yourself an agent. Most
producers here, or in the US, won't accept unsolicited material,

so it helps to have an agent who can get your screenplay read by decision-makers. They will also help you be realistic about whether your screenplay will sell or should be considered as a "writing sample" for possible future commissions.

"Most producers won't accept unsolicited material, so it helps to have an agent"

Getting an agent can be tough, so be persistent. Identify one who shares your sensibilities and can help you grow as writer – a good relationship with your agent can be the bedrock of a successful writing career.

When sending out your screenplay, don't underestimate the importance of the presentation. Don't use gimmicks. Professional screenwriters don't use coloured pages, fancy fonts, ring binders, illustrations or any visual aids. No amount of customising will improve your submission; in fact it usually has the opposite effect. The people reading your screenplay read hundreds and you need to make the reading experience as painless as possible. Invest in a screenwriting programme such as Final Draft and let the writing speak for itself.

Finally, be realistic about the challenges you face in getting your work produced and even read by the right people. While you wait for responses, don't stop writing. Get on with the next outline or screenplay, build up your bank of ideas for the future.

Debra Hayward is an executive producer at Working Title Films

What next? Plays

West End theatres receive thousands of scripts a year. The Royal Court's Dominic Cooke explains how to make sure your play gets read

There are several guidelines worth following before you submit your play to a theatre. The crucial starting point is to find out as much information as possible about a theatre, whether it produces new plays and, if they do, what processes they use for reading unsolicited scripts. Also, be clear on how the theatre in question likes to receive scripts and who exactly you should write to. In the larger theatres it is likely to be the literary manager. Theatre literary offices are very busy places – at the Royal Court we receive up to 3,000 scripts a year – so make it as easy as possible for the theatre to read your work by following their guidelines for submission meticulously.

Make sure that what you are submitting is a stage play. This may sound ridiculous but at the Royal Court we frequently receive film scripts or tarted-up TV ideas. If it is a film script and you fancy seeing it on stage, you need to reconceive it for the stage and rewrite it accordingly before sending it in.

Ensure that the play is as complete as possible before sending. It's not a good idea to submit a first draft that hasn't been read by anyone but you. Ask appropriate friends or family to give feedback. You'll only have one shot with each script, so it's really worth submitting the work at its best. Remember that a theatre is not a reading service. If it receives unsolicited scripts it will be serious about evaluating the script in terms of its suitability for production, but is under no obligation to give detailed feedback. There are reading services such as The Writer's Room who will give you that kind of advice.

Crucially, acquaint yourself with the theatre's taste and previous programming. There's no point submitting, for example, an absurdist slasher monologue to a producer of West End musicals. Also, avoid bombarding every theatre in the country. If the play is accepted by more than one theatre at the same time, you'll annoy at least one of the potential producers.

Another route you might want to go down is that of finding an agent. Most produced writers have agents, although often agents don't pick up writers until after they've been accepted for production. There's no denying, however, that a play submitted by a reputable agent will be read more quickly by a theatre than a play coming from an unknown source. And the agent will be an invaluable source of advice on the suitability of a given theatre for your play. Again, it's important to do your homework. Find out who represents the playwrights you admire, or whose work is close to yours in feel. You can do this by checking the front of the writer's published playtexts. There will be an agent's name and address under the heading "Application for Performance by Professionals".

Finally, if you face rejection, take "no" for an answer and move on. If a theatre or agent passes, maybe the relationship is not for you anyway. Remember that most leading playwrights had early plays rejected.

Dominic Cooke is the artistic director of the Royal Court Theatre

> "You'll only have one shot with each script, so it's really worth submitting the work at its best"

Comedy

Joke's on you

After years of self-confessed bad writing habits and a few near-disaster experiences, Catherine Tate has found a way to write that works for her. Here she offers her advice for navigating the troubled waters of writing funny stuff

'Writing' always means 'not writing' to me, because I will do anything to put it off. I think this is mainly because writing anything down and then handing it over to a third party – especially in comedy – is such an exposing act that you naturally want to delay the process.

Also, the control required to get ideas out of my head and into some tangible form that I can present to others doesn't come easily to me. I will quite simply do anything other than sit down in front of a blank screen and begin. I just can't do it, or more accurately, won't. The irony is that once I have stopped colour coding my tea towels and leaving messages for people I haven't spoken to in years, I do get into the flow of it and, dare I say it, enjoy writing. But it's the getting started.

I remember writing (or not writing) my first show for the Edinburgh festival. I had to literally drag that show out of me word by painful word. Being a deadline junkie, I went right up to the wire and had to cancel all the London previews as a consequence. I had half an idea about doing some characters: an old lady, a highly sexed Irish nurse, a drunk bride. But I had nothing concrete and certainly nothing written down.

When I arrived at the Pleasance, the venue where I was performing, the stage manager asked me for a copy of the script so she could plot the lighting and sound cues. Busted. It dawned on me just how little prepared I was and I mumbled something about "not really working like that" as I felt a wave of panic rise up and threaten to choke me. We agreed to go with visual cues for the sound and light.

Few things focus the mind like fear. That night – the opening night – the show somehow went well. It was part-improvised and entirely raw, being the first time I'd performed any of it in front of anyone, let alone a paying crowd. But I had enough of a skeleton of the material in my head to get through it, and I came off stage with relief pouring out of me. I still feel grateful that my fledgling comedy career didn't crash and burn during those 50 minutes. The first thing I did was ask if anyone remembered what I'd said. Finally it was time to write things down.

"Don't take criticism personally, take from it what's useful. Apply it and move on to something better."

I went to an internet cafe and typed up everything I could remember saying and although it wasn't word for word, by about 2am I had a fairly decent-sized document that, once it had been printed out and bound in a cellophane folder, looked dangerously like a script. The sense of achievement was immense. But it didn't have to be that stressful.

Over the next 30 odd times I performed that August the show changed dramatically. Every night things would be added and improved upon; it was a moveable feast that became the basis of my TV show a few years later. That Edinburgh show was a steep learning curve for me and the most important thing I learnt (aside from it being helpful to write a show before you perform it) was how valuable an audience is. When we came to recording the first series of my show, almost every sketch had been tried out in front of a live crowd and was all the better for it.

So I suppose what I'm saying is I don't feel in a position to give advice about writing because, technically, I don't consider myself a writer. I've just fallen into bad habits, habits that have now become the way I work and so far no one's asked for their money back. But if I can offer up a few random things it's these:

Trust yourself. You have to start with what you think is funny before you can have the confidence to write to anyone else's brief. Give a gag three chances to work, if after three (separate) attempts they're still not laughing, bin it. It's not them. It's you. Don't take criticism personally, take from it what's useful. Apply it and move on to something better. And be brave. No one got anywhere by being too scared to open their mouth in case nobody laughed. Good luck! Oh and this for the writer-performers: never cancel your previews.

Catherine Tate is a comedian and the creator of the award-winning the Catherine Tate Show. As an actress she has appeared, among other things, as the Doctor's companion Donna Noble in Dr Who.

Funny ideas

Forget careful composition, says Richard Herring, often the best material comes from a flash of insane inspiration

"Analysing comedy is like dissecting a frog. Nobody laughs and the frog dies."

So claims the legendary Barry Cryer. Indeed, there is nothing more damaging to a joke than trying to explain it. It's like revealing how the lady is sawn in half or telling someone who hasn't seen The Sixth Sense that Bruce Willis is a ghost (sorry). But even in a cursory examination of writing comedy, I'm afraid some frogs are going to die.

There are comedic rules and formulae and, while these tenets should be respected, especially by a newcomer, perversely you can still succeed by openly contradicting them. Because comedy is about breaking the rules. Even its own rules. Though, as with many disciplines, it is wise to master the basics before you attempt to subvert them.

Comedy is also so subjective that a script that reduces one audience to tears of laughter, can leave another staring at you in threatening silence.

So how do you even come up with a joke? Richard Pryor gave the excellent advice, "Be truthful and funny will come." Though of course veracity is not enough on its own, it can often be extremely boring or depressing. Conversely many comics make a great living telling downright lies.

Often ideas come from a subconscious flash of inspiration. Dara O'Briain discusses how Douglas Adams described how Arthur Dent learned to fly: "apparently the way to do it is to fall and then get distracted. At which point you forget you've just fallen and take off. That essentially is the best description

About your tutor

Richard Herring is a comedian, writer and one half of Lee and Herring, from the cult BBC2 sketch shows Fist of Fun and This Morning With Richard Not Judy. He also wrote and starred in ITV1's You Can Choose Your Friends.

of writing jokes, you trigger yourself to not think about something and then something comes out."

This epiphany can come from the collision of two idle thoughts, the juxtaposition of unlikely events, questioning conventional wisdom or by viewing society without preconceptions. It's why children so often say funny things, because they have not yet learnt about conformity and notice the hypocrisy that adults are too jaded to spot. So you always have to be primed to see the humour in the everyday life, but perversely not desperately be searching for it.

How can you hurry the comedy along? Some writers use artificial stimulants such as alcohol or drugs. As a younger man I felt I wrote better after consuming a dangerous cocktail of chocolate and diet coke. Though booze can sometimes help you relax a little and hallucinogens can alter your perspective, on the whole you're better off staying clean. If logic breaks down, comedy doesn't usually follow. We all know that what appears funny when you're inebriated can seem embarrassing the morning after.

"I like leaving things to the last minute, then letting blind panic be my stimulus"

A comic's mind usually retains some childishness (and not always in a pejorative sense). Perhaps there's some insanity in there too, but the comedian (usually) has control over their madness.

Personally I find that deadlines are the best inspiration. I like leaving things to the last possible minute, then letting blind panic be my stimulus.

Wasting time is part of the process. For me genius is "1% inspiration and 99% procrastination." Graham Linehan says, "It's the nature of writing, that you procrastinate and procrastinate until it gets to 4 o'clock and ... and then it's tea time." I will do anything but sit at my desk, but all the time, ideas are ruminating around in the back of my mind and then suddenly after six hours of Guitar Hero, something concrete emerges from the void.

How to write a joke

Most jokes are based on surprise. They take advantage of a confusion of language, or a twist in logic, or a contradiction of some perceived truth, or sometimes just saying something so shocking and offensive that the audience will gasp and then (hopefully) guffaw.

As with all comedy laws, however, the opposite is also true. Some comedians make a marvellous living doing material that is completely predictable, that reminds people of things that they already know or jokes that they are already familiar with.

But go back to even the most simple gag and you will see that "surprise" is at the heart of it.

Man 1: *My dog has no nose.*
Man 2: *How does he smell?*
Man 1: *Terrible.*

Man 1 reveals he is the owner of a canine, who, for whatever reason, has an absence of the olfactory organ. Man 2, our brain logically assumes, wishes to know how a noseless hound can discern aroma. However, Man 1 believes the enquiry is about the mutt's hygiene and answers accordingly. For a moment we are confused, then our brain shifts to encompass the other, less likely definition. We laugh.

Except that this is such an old joke and so familiar to everyone but the tiniest child that we know full well what the punchline will be, so the only chance of getting a genuine response is by subverting it:

Man 1: *My dog has no nose.*
Man 2: *How does he smell?*
Man 1: *He can't. He doesn't have a nose.*

How will you know if your joke is funny? The terrifying thing is that you can't really be certain until you try it in front of other people. Even professionals are never sure until they hear the reassuring sound of laughter. Or don't.

Tips
- Train your brain to be looking for possible material everywhere and start small. The better you get at observation, the better you will be as a writer.
- Always carry a notebook with you. Write down anything that strikes you as even slightly amusing. It might come in useful.

"If you are totally blocked then choose a topic at random. It can be anything."

Defamiliarisation

Use people's expectation of the familiar. Look through a dictionary of proverbs, find a well-known saying and see if you can come up with an alternative and amusing second line. Here are two of mine:

To be or not to be....
That is the first and only question on the University of Bee Keeping entrance exam.

What walks on four legs in the morning, two legs in the afternoon and three legs in the evening?
Paul McCartney and his wives.

Exercise

- Write with a partner. Not only will they let you know if your idea is funny, but you should also be able to spark off each other, if you have the requisite chemistry.
- Read as much as you can: newspapers, books, pamphlets you find on the train. A news story might provide a plot for a sitcom, or something to satirise in a sketch or just be funny enough to read out verbatim on stage. Or just get you thinking about something you had never considered before.
- If you are totally blocked then choose a topic at random. It can be anything: cheese, ghosts, Guy Fawkes, love. Then try and think of something funny about it. Do some proper research. I found out that on discovery with his gunpowder, Guy Fawkes had claimed he was called John Johnson, surely the most unimaginative pseudonym ever. There was a sketch in that obscure fact.
- Have a conversation with a child. Their unfettered imagination might inspire you or take an idea in an unexpected direction.

Honing a joke

There is more to this than simply having a "crazy idea". If you cannot express it then all is lost.

There is a rhythm to a good joke, a certain pacing. You will require a command of language, an ability to select the right word and phrasing, with economy usually, but always precision.

You can learn more about the technical side of things by listening to and watching the professionals. Like many nerdy youngsters I spent much of my childhood listening to Monty Python records, learning them verbatim, fittingly parroting them.

You may well start off by unintentionally imitating the style and intonation of someone you admire, but it's important to discover your own voice.

As a novice it is best to try and distil your ideas down into the fewest possible words, but more experienced comedians can stretch and explore one idea thoroughly over several minutes. Check out George Carlin or Stewart Lee, who are rarely brief, yet demonstrate exquisite mastery of the English language.

It is rare for a joke to emerge fully formed and it is worth grafting away until it is absolutely right. Though perversely too much work, too much thought, can destroy a gag completely.

There is no correct path. Sometimes it is good to create a tension before a punchline by dragging out the preamble, other times you will find it more effective to cut straight to the chase. A variety of tone and rhythm and speed will make it easier to wrong-foot an audience, but sometimes monotony can become infectiously hilarious.

> "It is rare for a joke to emerge fully formed and it is worth grafting away until it is right"

A beautifully chosen, unexpected adjective can transform a comedy routine into poetry, while the banal repetition of a commonplace noun can make that word, and consequently all language, suddenly appear ridiculous.

If you are a stand-up you can hone your material over successive performances, based on the audience response. Changing a single word or altering the pace or emphasis can make a previously failed witticism work.

You might be saying too much. Let the audience discover the consequences of a comedic notion themselves. A pause can be as effective as a paragraph of exposition.

Finally, remember that you will learn the most through trial and error.

Exercise

Editing a joke

Take the joke that you wrote in the previous section and take it apart. Do you need every word? Are they in the right order? Use a thesaurus to see if a well-chosen synonym can make the joke funnier. Make a note of any word that is new to you or amuses you. It may come in useful on another occasion.

Writing sketches

You may be tempted to crack straight on with a sitcom, but start small. Containing an idea in a two-minute sketch will teach you about structure, establishing characters and how to write pithy, economical dialogue.

It is easy to put on a sketch show at your college, pub or on the internet. A producer will be happier to read a page or two rather than a whole script and there are radio and TV shows which are looking for shorter sketch material, which means you have a much better chance of selling your work.

I started my professional career writing topical sketches for the now defunct Radio 4 show Weekending. I actually pretty much loathed the programme, as it was rather formulaic and rarely biting. Yet I stayed for a year, serving an apprenticeship that taught me many skills: from the mundane business of how to format a script (for this and further advice see bbc. co.uk/writersroom/) to technical tricks such as how to avoid clunky exposition like:

FX: *Knock on door*
MAN: *You asked to see me Prime Minister!*

This opening establishes location and characters artlessly. You need to look for more subtle ways to inform the listener or you will lose their interest and respect. Don't treat them like they're stupid.

"You can set up your own sketch group and take a show to the Edinburgh Fringe or film it."

from the front line

Mitchell and Webb on writing sketches

Make sure you have an idea before you start. It's no use sitting in front of a blank screen saying "right, it could be anything." "Anything" isn't a brief, it's a mental wilderness. You need to decide what you're going to write before you write it, and this is best done away from the winking cursor.

A sketch needs a premise, a core funny idea that is its reason to exist. As soon as a sketch begins, the audience looks for this premise and it needs to be apparent. Presenting a character? Make sure the funny thing about them is expressed early. Taking the piss out of some element of modern life? Present it at the beginning and quickly undermine it.

You need the element of surprise in comedy but, before that, you need to make people comfortable with where you are. There needs to be, to quote the protesting philosophers from the Hitchhiker's Guide to the Galaxy, "rigidly defined areas of doubt and uncertainty". So establish the setting first, make it clear why it's funny, throw in a surprise and get out. Ideally the last joke, or punchline, should be the best but the sad fact is there are more premises than punchlines. It's a great argument against intelligent design.

Sketch comedy doesn't benefit from the audience's loyalty to characters, it's only as funny as its last joke. But its advantage is that it can embrace any setting, subject or situation. Use these strengths by having lots of short and contrasting items. That way, if the audience doesn't like one sketch, you soon get the chance to win them over with something else.

David Mitchell and Robert Webb are the creators of TV series That Mitchell and Webb Look.

I soon learned that even though we were paid by the minute, it was foolish to write a five-minute sketches. The show was only 25 minutes, so longer skits would be binned, while lightning gags might fill a gap. It was economical to be economical.

Now I prefer to stretch an idea as far as it will go, then a little further. If you can learn to write a blistering 60-second skit with four laughs, a beginning, a middle and an end, then everything else will be easy.

While Weekending is no more, there are plenty of sketch shows on radio and TV that invite outside contributions. If there are lots of writers' names in the credits, write a couple of sketches in an appropriate style (even if it's not your particular sense of humour), send them to the producer and you will probably get feedback.

Or you can set up your own sketch group and take a show to the Edinburgh Fringe or film it for YouTube. Try to make your own material as original as possible. When Stewart Lee and I began writing together at university, we set rules about things we wouldn't write about: celebrities, parodies of TV shows, political satire, all of which were in vogue. By limiting ourselves we came up with a lot of unusual ideas and created our own voice.

Character comedy

Watch a whole morning of daytime telly. Look out for an interesting character and then try and write a sketch about them. Don't try to parody the shows you have watched, just try to find a persona and then put them into a real life situation. Many of the Little Britain characters were created this way.

Exercise

Sketch writing tips

- Keep an eye out for interesting real life characters. My driving instructor seemed overly critical of my inability to drive, given that that was the reason I was employing him, so I wrote a sketch about an instructor who berates his pupils for being non-driving idiots.
- Don't start with a catchphrase. It will seem forced and probably end up with you creating a one joke persona. Create the character, write some sketches and a catchphrase might present itself. Look at Al Murray the Pub Landlord. It's a multi-layered persona and the catchphrases "I was never confused", "rules is rules" and "glass of white wine for the lady" come out of the character rather than vice versa.
- Starting with a simple premise and exploring the consequences can be better than trying to conceive something outlandish. Monty Python's dead parrot sketch begins with the premise of a pet shop owner selling a customer a deceased bird. The genius is in the execution.

Writing for stand-up

I n the early 90s I met Jimmy Tarbuck backstage at a show. I told him I was a struggling comic. "Good luck!" he said as he puffed on his cigar, "Comedy is the hardest job in the world!"

I don't agree with Tarbuck. It's not as hard as being a fireman or a brain surgeon or in the SAS or (given that you work for 20 minutes a night and then get drunk), as hard as working in an office. Still, most people would rather eat their own liver with some fava beans and a nice Chianti than perform stand-up comedy.

At its best, stand-up comedy is the purest and most immediate medium for comedy and possibly even self-expression. What other outlet allows you to have an idea in the afternoon and then try it out that evening to an actual audience?

The jokes, although important, are not in themselves enough. You need to be able to appear relaxed and confident, control the room, think on your feet, involve the audience without letting them steal focus from you, and adapt your style and material to dozens of different, difficult scenarios. The only way to gain these skills is to get up on stage and do gigs. As many nights a week as you can. Probably for at least five years.

All those things will come to you, if you have the right stuff. So if you're starting out, then what you need to concentrate on is your material. Most clubs have an open spot where an unpaid wannabe can do five minutes. The audience will be

> "At its best stand-up comedy is the purest and most immediate medium for comedy."

from the front line

Josie Long on writing for stand-up

If you want to start writing stand-up, try not to feel like there are any conventions you have to subscribe to. There are no established rules as to what your show should contain.

Try to find your own voice. Think about what you find funny and what you would want to see if you were watching. It's not helpful to second-guess the audience's tastes in advance. It's better to take risks and perform material that may not work if it is something you genuinely think is hilarious. Everyone has bad gigs and through them you will develop and evolve as a performer.

All of that having been said, it's good to be economical with your material. Only use things you feel are essential. It's not just about enjoying yourself onstage, but about finding a way of conveying your sense of humour to other people.

Try as many different ways of writing as you can, and try to write as much and as often as possible. Don't decide against trying a joke because it doesn't fit the style you've chosen for yourself. Include any ideas for jokes you have.

Write at home on paper, steal your best conversations, do specific research, write by speaking out loud on your own, play writing games, take good ideas onstage then bat them around and improvise, note down things you see or are struck by... you never know what will develop into a longer routine or piece.

Josie Long won the Edinburgh Festival's best newcomer award in 2006

quick to judge you and you're trying to get booked, so start small. Write a five-minute script (don't overrun), with a punchline every 30 seconds, with your best three jokes at the start and another belter at the end. Make sure that the jokes are original. Make sure you know exactly what you're going to say. Practice and be prepared for failure.

Once you feel comfortable on stage you might have the confidence to try out stories or even to reveal your personal secrets. Be truthful and funny will come.

You will also find that you do a lot of your "writing" on stage. When you are in the zone you find you can leave behind the script and just chat. Inspiration strikes and you discover new avenues, even in well trodden routines.

The comedian's toolbox

Comedic formulae must be used carefully and subtly, because the more they are used the more familiar and predictable they become and thus the less effective. You will need the misdirectional skills of a magician to hide the approaching gag.

Rule of three
Grouping items into threes can provide a satisfying pay off. The first thing in the list introduces the idea, the second thing reinforces it, but then the third thing (using the comedic law of surprise) deviates from what is expected.

Here's Woody Allen: "By love, of course, I refer to romantic love – the love between man and woman, rather that between mother and child, or a boy and his dog, or two head waiters."

Pull back and reveal
A term derived from the TV practice of panning out from a close-up to discover a humorous situation. Essentially you are holding back a piece of pertinent information until the end of the story.

In the wrong hands this is a hackneyed and predictable technique, with cliched punchlines including, "then I got off the bus," and "that was just the teachers!" But used with skill it can be sublime, as with this opener from the visually startling, dishevelled Michael Redmond, "People often say to me... get out of my garden."

Puns

It is difficult to get away with too much word play in a stand-up set, as most puns are fairly corny or obvious , though if you are relentless and unashamed it can be quite infectious. Discovering a new pun can be very impressive. This from the brilliant Milton Jones:

"While I was in Australia I learnt some Aboriginal words like 'boo', which means to 'return' – cos when you throw an ordinary meringue... "

"It is difficult to get away with too much word play in a stand-up set, as most puns are corny"

Observational comedy

Observational comedy essentially involves saying "Did you ever notice?" and then recounting something that will hopefully be universally familiar, but that won't necessarily have been consciously noted by your audience. If it's too obvious an observation it won't be funny (Have you ever noticed how buses always come in threes? Yes.) and if it's too oblique then it won't hit home. Jerry Seinfeld is the master: "Did you ever notice when you blow in a dog's face he gets mad at you? But when you take him in a car he sticks his head out the window."

Character comedy

It's tempting to try and hide behind a false persona on stage. But creating a character that will work in a stand-up situation is a lot more difficult than just being yourself. For every Alan Partridge and John Shuttleworth, there are a thousand men in funny hats and long coats, trying and failing to be E L Wisty. It is a better idea, when starting out, to make your persona merely a slightly funnier or exaggerated version of yourself. But if you really want to go down the character route then make sure you are capable of stepping outside of the script and engaging the audience. Then do a lot of work on creating a persona that is three-dimensional and original.

Saying the unsayable

Performers such as Chris Morris and Brendon Burns challenge an audience's preconceptions by shocking them. One of the functions of comedy is to act as a release valve. When we laugh at something sick or horrendous it takes away some of our anxiety, even if it is only for a few minutes.

But even in the hands of an experienced comic, joking about such topics as paedophilia, racism, rape or cancer can go horribly awry. It is best avoided completely as a novice, but if you insist on trying then do not be offensive just for the sake of it, try to make some kind of point. And know what that point is, so you are able to justify your material.

> "The chances are that the heckler is much drunker and far less funny than you"

from the front line

Jo Caulfield on how to write a joke in 10 steps

1. Choose your subject (for example, vacuous celebrity culture)
2. Define your attitude. How does the subject make you feel? Happy? Sad? Angry? A passionate point of view makes a joke stronger.
3. Write as much as you can about your chosen subject. Use similes, oxymorons, cliches, proverbs, double entendres, whatever you want. Make lists of people, places and things associated with the subject (eg Jordan, Kerry Katona, Big Brother, Paris Hilton, Heat magazine, BBC3, Lily Allen, Pete Doherty, her with the rats maze hairdo and tattoos, Heather Mills buying a shoe).
4. Cast your eye over what you've written and the funniest bits will stick out. Those are the bits you want.
5. Edit, edit, edit. Cut away as much as possible. Your mildly amusing two-page story can become a fantastic one-line joke.

from the front line

6. Misdirection. Inflate the balloon. Lead the audience as far away from the joke as you can: "Me and my friend Allison (*) have been invited to a fancy dress party ... we're going as Paris Hilton and Jodie Marsh."

7. Time for a PAUSE. What you don't say is just as important. The audience thinks quicker than you can speak so let them conjure up their own pictures of a fancy dress party.

8. Quickly spin them in the opposite direction and burst the balloon. "I'm getting a lobotomy and Allison is having her vagina widened." Almost there.

9. Listen to the audience. Audiences will help you write the joke. Originally Allison and I were going to be John Leslie and Ulrika Jonsson, then we were going to be Lembit Opik and Abi Titmuss. It was the British public who, after much trial and error, chose "Paris Hilton and Jodie Marsh".

(*) I'm aware that it should be "My friend Allison and I..." but ...
10. Jokes don't obey no rules of English grammar, baby.

PS: Always put the punchline at the end, don't laugh at your own jokes, don't get them wet, keep them out of strong sunlight and never feed them after midnight.

Jo Caulfield was a gag writer on all five series of the BAFTA award-winning show So Graham Norton.

Dealing with hecklers

This is usually easier than it appears, though occasionally nothing you do will make a persistent drunk shut up (put "Richard Herring heckler" into YouTube to see me struggling with such a sot). There are some useful stock lines which you can employ:

"This is what happens when cousins marry."

"I remember when I had my first drink."

"It's annoying isn't it? You start up a really good conversation and someone builds a comedy club around you."

But in most cases you're actually better off if you just calmly respond to whatever is being shouted at you with the first thing that comes into your head. Audiences are much more impressed with improvisation than with prepared put-downs, and the chances are that the heckler is much drunker and far less funny than you.

Most importantly, try not to lose control of the situation. In the YouTube exchange you can see that I am furious about the guy wrecking my act, but I just about manage to stay in command.

Comedy blogging

Write a blog. Take one amusing thing that happened in your day and try to describe it. You will normally really struggle to think of anything and be forced to examine the minutiae of your life, but you might recall something that passed you by at the time.

If you are stuck write about something mundane and look for the ridiculousness in something you take for granted. I have been writing a blog daily for six years (richardherring.com/warmingup) and have generated a huge amount of material for stand-up. One unpromising sounding entry about a checkout girl commenting on my purchase of nine yoghurts developed into a 40-minute routine.

Exercise

Writing sitcom

Creating a successful sitcom is almost impossibly difficult. Not only do you have to find a compelling enough situation, but you need to create characters who will continue to entertain and divert an audience in possibly a hundred episodes' time. Then you have to convince a broadcaster to make it, usually based on one script.

If you can think of a unique situation then that might give you a head start, but the heart of any sitcom is the characters. So while the Home Guard was a brilliant setting, it was Captain Mainwaring's misplaced self-importance that made the show a classic. Plus the intricate relationships between all the old men reluctantly forced together.

You need conflict between characters, but also some reason why they are forced to spend time together. Are they tied together by blood like Steptoe and Son, by marriage like Basil and Sybil Fawlty, by their job like Tim and Gareth from The Office or are they literally incarcerated like Fletcher and Godber in Porridge?

You need to work on your characters and get to know them before you start. Write down what they do, their philosophies, their back history. Plenty of extra detail will be added once you start the script, but the more prepared you are, the better. You need to establish their basic character almost instantly in the first episode, but then you have time to release nuggets of new information. The deeper and more engaging the characters

"You need to establish basic character almost instantly in the first episode"

are, the less you have to rely on gimmicky, outlandish plots, like Fonzie waterskiing over that shark.

There are outlandish sitcoms that work brilliantly, like Father Ted, Reggie Perrin and Arrested Development, but these still have a solid foundation of brilliant, recognisable, yet original characters.

Group dynamics

Exercise

Take a group of people that you have known personally: work colleagues, family, friends, whatever. Consider the situation that you were in and the dynamics of the group, what people's funny attributes were, where the conflict came and see if you can turn it into a sitcom. Even if you change characteristics to make things more interesting, starting from a real situation can be informative and might even lead to a useable script.

If you want to create something great and memorable then don't rely on the formulaic gags and stereotypes which give the genre a bad name ("there's no way in a million years you will ever get me to go to the opera!" CUT TO...).

I read a TV critic who described a game that they played while watching My Family where they paused the action after a feedline and tried to guess the punchline. They correctly predicted it or improved it, nearly every time. This is one of the most watched sitcoms in the country, showing that some people want familiarity from comedy. But would you be happy if someone was able to play that game with something you had written? It's possible to be popular and comedically excellent.

Look at the Simpsons. And note that the most successful episodes are the ones that focus on the minutiae of family life. But with honesty and charm.

> "However much time you spend crafting on paper cuts and changes will leap out at you when you hear it"

David Nobbs on writing a sitcom

There are just two vital elements to writing successful situation comedy: you need good and amusing characters, and you need, as the title of the genre suggests, a good and amusing situation. A man running a bad hotel wouldn't excite anyone as an idea. Basil Fawlty in a mental home wouldn't excite anyone. But Basil Fawlty running a bad hotel ... character and situation come together to make an irresistible series.

The first great sitcom writers were Simpson and Galton. Not all the Hancock episodes work today. We can't accept him as a judge or pilot, because sitcom, as it developed, came to need reality. In their masterpiece, Steptoe and Son, situation and character fit perfectly. Father and son trapped in a junkyard, hating each other, needing each other, son longing to escape, never will.

A sitcom can be fantastic, futuristic, surreal, but if it isn't true to its own reality, and if the characters do not behave believably, it will fail. Most of the best sitcoms are very real indeed: Only Fools and Horses, Dad's Army, Rising Damp with the brilliant Leonard Rossiter.

Sitcoms are not about "gags". It's bad sitcoms that are full of jokes. Think of one of the funniest lines ever penned: 'Don't tell him, Pike.' Nothing funny in that, character and situation make it hilarious.

Take a crazy medical unit. Put them in the middle of a really serious war, and you have my favourite of them all, MASH.

David Nobbs is the creator of The Fall and Rise of Reginald Perrin.

from the front line

Tips

- Be brutal in the editing to keep pace and focus. Often you will find taking out the scene that you think is funniest will actually improve the episode as a whole.
- Some writers like to plot everything out. They will work out exactly how the episode will end and then work backwards to make their hilarious denouement come to

pass. But why not try writing an episode chronologically, without any idea of where you are going? Then any twists and turns can surprise you as much as anyone else and things will not be as contrived. It may not work, but it's an interesting exercise and a good way to avoid being predictable.

"Don't sit back and wait for TV executives to knock on the door. You have to take the plunge."

- Get the script read out by actors or friends. However much time you spend crafting the script on paper, it will be astounding how many cuts and changes leap out at you once you hear it. Also, as always, you will get useful feedback as to which bits are actually funny.

- Get inside the heads of your characters. Work out what motivates them, what makes them who they are, and make them human and three-dimensional, however small a part they have to play. The peripheral characters in "The Office: an American Workplace" are especially well observed and

from the front line

Caroline Raphael on how to write comedy for radio

This is the serious side of the business. Most people who try to get a comedy script accepted will have their heart broken at some stage. It doesn't mean they can't write, it's just that they're incompatible.

Listen to the station, get the names of the producers whose shows intrigue you, and target them. But woo, don't stalk them!

If you're a newbie, your calling card is a finished script. You have to demonstrate you can complete one and then, before it gets commissioned, you need to prove you can rewrite. The rewrite is often when the relationship between writer and producer wobbles. You'll be worrying the producer is trying to call it all off and they'll be fretting that you are a one-draft wonder. For your first script, don't fuss about what it looks like on the page, or getting all the technical details right. We can help you with that.

from the front line

Radio is not theatre. It's not TV either, although it's closer to TV than theatre. Just without the pictures. And there's the rub. Can you convey everything the listener needs to know through dialogue? Can you make each character so distinct that we can follow it even if you forget to indicate which line belongs to which character?

A few jokes would also be nice. If we can't hear the studio audience laugh, then why should we at home be laughing?

All work has to have a producer attached before it can be commissioned. The newly smitten producer will then discuss it with the commissioner. Even if you have delivered an excellent first script, the relationship might need to slow down, the gap between a good 30-minute script and a six-part series is massive. The producer may suggest you do some sketch work. If they do, grab the opportunity and don't feel too wounded. Just get your stuff on air. There are a host of writers now working steadily on BBC Radio 4 who started this way.

All the above assumes you're a writer and not a writer/performer. The comedy world is fuelled by the latter nowadays. If truth be told, most of them are better writers than performers and you can see the panic in their eyes on stage. Some of them are performers, who have glamour and stage presence, but goodness me, they need some material. A few, very few, can do both.

Caroline Raphael is commissioning editor for comedy and entertainment at Radio 4

give a depth to the series. Be especially vigilant with unsympathetic characters. They have to have a reason for behaving as they do. From their own point of view they must think that they are justified in the way they behave.

- Make sure your script is properly laid out. It is worth investing in a software package to give your work a professional appearance. Final Draft is simple, and extensively used in the industry.

What next?

Once you've finished writing, the hard graft begins – getting your break into the business and your work seen and heard

S o you've got a routine or a collection of sketches or a sitcom script, but where do you take it? How do you get it on TV or radio?

My advice is to not be too impatient. Old school comics would constantly reiterate the importance of "learning your craft" and they were right. TV can eat up and spit out comics who have only a year or two's experience and a 20-minute set. If you work your way up gradually then you will have a much better chance of long-term success.

Don't sit back and just wait for TV executives to knock on the door. You have to take the plunge. Increasingly there are more and more outlets to get your work seen. There are thousands of comedy clubs with open spots, dozens of sketch shows looking for writers, many broadcasters desperate for the next hit sitcom. You can write a blog or do a podcast. The more you do, the better you'll get and the more chance you have of someone sitting up and taking notice.

If you're making people laugh then agents and producers will begin to take notice. But you have to keep chipping away at it, keep sending in your scripts and don't get disheartened if it doesn't happen overnight.

Be prepared to accept that perhaps you are not as funny as you think you are. The comics with the most self belief are always the very best and the very worst. Most of the rest of us are floundering in a pit of insecurity, but the genii and the talentless seem to have unfailing faith in their ability.

With comedy, unlike any other art form, there is a great way of gauging your success. Laughter tells you how you're doing. A lack of laughter tells you that what you're doing isn't working, or you're doing it to the wrong people. Set yourself a time limit. If no one is laughing after five years, then it might be time to move on.

But plenty of successful writers have taken years before they get their break. It took the general public a long time to tune into the Mighty Boosh, but they never compromised and kept going.

Don't run before you can walk. The best place to start, I think, is by submitting stuff to the radio and trying to build up a relationship with producers there. Chances are that they too will be new to the job and be hungry to discover something fresh.

I wish you good luck. You'll need it. Comedy is the hardest job in the world. Now back to Guitar Hero.

A guide to good style

Do not put statements in the negative form. And don't start sentences with a conjunction. If you reread your work, you will find on rereading that a great deal of repetition can be avoided by rereading and editing. Never use a long word when a diminutive one will do. Unqualified superlatives are the worst of all. De-accession euphemisms. If any word is improper at the end of a sentence, a linking verb is. Avoid trendy locutions that sound flaky. Last, but not least, avoid cliches like the plague

William Safire

Introduction

Oh for the good old days, when children were taught grammar and everyone could parse and precis, when nary a mistake appeared in the newspapers, when even greengrocers knew how to use the apostrophe ...

This is, of course, nonsense.

Since at least the 18th century, self-appointed experts from Jonathan Swift to the Daily Mail have railed against declining standards of English, typically placing the golden age a decade or two before they started spouting about it.

Guardian readers, a liberal and well-informed bunch, are not immune to this. "In a piece in today's paper, you use the word 'wuss', not once but twice," reads a recent letter. "There is no explanation. Obviously a trendy term which has become modish in recent times, not used when yours was a proper newspaper, the Manchester Guardian."

Here is a verbatim extract from one of our attempts, as a "proper newspaper", to cover American politics in the 1960s:

"Mr Nion was looking towards Washington, but the committee was liiking at Mr Nixon. He would have to oick the candidate, and if he oicked another man, eho lost, the party would be loth to nominate for the Preidency a national leader whose influence could not carry his own state in a state election. Yet, if Mr Noxon ran himself and won, he would practiclly forsweat the presidency; for, like allaspiring governors, he has been bocal and bitter about men who use the governor's mansion as a springboard int the White House."

The "Grauniad" nickname, once well-earned, has been hard to shake off, but we do better today – computerisation and the internet have opened up a new world of resources, although one with its own set of pitfalls (see the "spellchecker" entry).

What follows is a condensed version of Guardian Style, which began life 80 years ago as a manual of house style for our journalists but has found a wider audience since going on sale to the public.

The first "Style-book of the Manchester Guardian" (as it then was), appeared in 1928 when the great CP Scott was well into his sixth decade as editor. That version survived until 1950 and subsequent editions followed at approximately 10-year intervals, with an online version since 2000 (guardian.co.uk/styleguide).

The hundreds of entries in the full guide, and in this book, may be broadly divided into the following categories:

- **Grammar and punctuation** (which have their own section): to paraphrase Shakespeare, "nouns, verbs and other abominable words", with advice on such matters as semicolons (good) and split infinitives (also, it may surprise you to hear, good).

- **Words:** easily confused, frequently misspelt, or regularly misused (or all three) – avoid those embarrassing "did I just write infer when I meant imply?" moments.

- **Good writing:** cliches to avoid like the plague; how (should you fall on hard times and be forced to seek employment as a subeditor) to write a good headline.

- **Facts:** from the Chatham House rule to the Geneva conventions, from Occam's razor to the Teletubbies, this book is a mine of information that may actually prove useful.

- **Values:** why Guardian writers – and, we hope, you – do not use such terms as "air hostess", "illegal asylum seeker", "mentally handicapped" and "wheelchair-bound". (And "politically correct".)

What you won't find here is a list of prescriptive rules. Language changes, and some traditional rules are arbitrary or baseless. We want the language we use to be clear, contemporary and consistent, reflecting what we stand for and according respect to those we write about. And that is ultimately what this guide is about: using English to communicate effectively.

David Marsh and Amelia Hodsdon

Grammar and punctuation

A preschooler's tacit knowledge of grammar is
more sophisticated than the thickest style manual

Steven Pinker

Ambrose Bierce defined grammar as "a system of pitfalls
thoughtfully prepared for the feet of the self-made man". He had a
point. Generations of schoolchildren were taught grammar as an
arbitrary set of dos and don'ts laid down by people who knew, or
thought they knew, best.

Nowadays, grammar may be more helpfully defined as the
set of rules followed by speakers of a language. The aim is to
communicate effectively, not to feel superior to other people
because you know what a gerund is.

Rather than encourage readers to, say, protest outside cinemas
carrying placards drawing attention to Hollywood's perceived
syntactical shortcomings, this section is designed to give them a
practical guide to some common points of grammar, punctuation
and English usage

apostrophes
Apostrophes are used to indicate a missing letter or letters (can't,
we'd) or a possessive (David's book).

Don't let anyone tell you that apostrophes don't matter and
we'd be better off without them. Consider these four phrases, each
of which means something different:
- my sister's friend's investments (refers to one sister and her
  friend).
- my sister's friends' investments (one sister with lots of friends).
- my sisters' friend's investments (more than one sister, and
  their friend).

- my sisters' friends' investments (more than one sister, and their friends).

The possessive in words and names ending in S normally takes an apostrophe followed by a second S (Jones's, James's), but be guided by pronunciation and use the plural apostrophe where it helps: Mephistopheles', Waters', Hedges' rather than Mephistopheles's, Waters's, Hedges's.

Plural nouns that do not end in S take an apostrophe and S in the possessive: children's games, men's magazines, people's republic, etc.

Phrases such as butcher's knife, collector's item, cow's milk, goat's cheese, pig's blood, hangman's noose, writer's cramp, etc are treated as singular.

Use apostrophes in phrases such as two days' time, 12 years' imprisonment and six weeks' holiday, where the time period (two days) modifies a noun (time), but not in nine months pregnant or three weeks old, where the time period is adverbial (modifying an adjective such as pregnant or old) – if in doubt, test with a singular such as one day's time, one month pregnant.

Some shops use an apostrophe, wrongly, to indicate a plural ("pea's"), but will generally omit the apostrophe when one is actually required ("new seasons asparagus"), a phenomenon sometimes referred to as the greengrocer's (or grocer's) apostrophe. Try to avoid this

brackets
If a sentence is logically and grammatically complete without the information contained within the parentheses (round brackets), the punctuation stays outside the brackets.

(A complete sentence that stands alone in parentheses starts with a capital letter and ends with a stop.)

"Square brackets," the grammarian said, "are used in direct quotes when an interpolation [a note from the writer or editor, not uttered by the speaker] is added to provide essential information"

collective nouns
Nouns such as committee, family, government, jury and squad take a singular verb or pronoun when thought of as a single unit, but a plural verb or pronoun when thought of as

a collection of individuals:
• The committee gave its unanimous approval to the plans;
The committee enjoyed biscuits with their tea
• The family can trace its history back to the middle ages;
The family were sitting down, scratching their heads

colons

Use between two sentences, or parts of sentences, where the first introduces a proposition that is resolved by the second, eg "Fowler put it like this: to deliver the goods invoiced in the preceding words."

A colon should also be used (rather than a comma) to introduce a quotation: "He was an expert on punctuation," or to precede a list – "He was an expert on the following: the colon, the comma and the full stop."

We are in danger of losing the distinction between colon and semicolon; many writers seem to think they are interchangeable but to make it clear: they are not

commas

"The editor, Alan Rusbridger, is a man of great vision" – correct (commas) if there is only one editor.

"The subeditor Amelia Hodsdon is all style and no substance" – correct (no commas) if there is more than one subeditor.

A misplaced comma can sabotage a sentence, as in this example from the paper: "Neocon economists often claim a large, black economy turbo-powers growth ... " (the writer was talking about a big black economy, not a big and black one, which is not the same at all)

compare to or with?

The former means liken to, the latter means make a comparison: so unless you are specifically likening someone or something to someone or something else (eg Nothing Compares 2 U), use compare with.

The lord chancellor compared himself to Cardinal Wolsey because he believed he was like Wolsey; I might compare him with Wolsey to assess their relative merits

dangling participles

Avoid constructions such as "having died, they buried him"; the pitfalls are nicely highlighted in Mark Lawson's novel Going Out Live, in which a TV critic writes: "Dreary, repetitive and well past the sell-by date, I switched off the new series of Fleming Faces."

A particularly exotic example of this that somehow found its way into the Guardian: "Though long-legged and possessing a lovely smile, gentleman journalists aren't looking up her skirt and wouldn't even if she weren't gay ... "

hyphens

Our style, which reflects a widespread trend in English, is to use one word wherever possible. Hyphens tend to clutter up text (particularly when a computer breaks already hyphenated words at the end of lines).

Inventions, ideas and new concepts often begin life as two words, then become hyphenated, before finally becoming accepted as one word. Why wait? "Wire-less" and "down-stairs" were once hyphenated.

There is no need to use hyphens with most compound adjectives, where the meaning is clear and unambiguous without: civil rights movement, financial services sector, work inspection powers etc. Hyphens should, however, be used to form short compound adjectives, eg two-tonne vessel, stand-up comedian, three-year deal, 19th-century artist, etc.

Also use hyphens where not using one would be ambiguous, eg to distinguish "black-cab drivers come under attack" from "black cab-drivers come under attack".

Do not use hyphens after adverbs ending in -ly, eg a hotly disputed penalty, a constantly evolving newspaper, genetically modified food, etc; but hyphens are needed with short and common adverbs, eg ever-forgiving family, much-loved character. When an adverb can also be an adjective (eg hard), the hyphen is required to avoid ambiguity – it's not a hard, pressed person, but a hard-pressed one

it's or its?

it's shortened form of it is or has: it's a big dog, it's been ages since I saw her; **its** possessive form of it: the dog is eating its bone

like or as if?

Using the former to mean the latter is, at best, inelegant: say "it looks as if he's finished" not "it looks like he's finished"

like or such as?

"like" excludes; "such as" includes: "Cities like Manchester are wonderful" suggests the writer has in mind, say, Sheffield or Birmingham; she actually means "cities such as Manchester".

Do not, however, automatically change "like" to "such as" – the following gaffe appeared in the paper: "He is not a celebrity, such as Jesse Ventura, the former wrestler ... "

may or might?

The subtle distinctions between these (and between other so-called modal verbs) are gradually disappearing, but they still matter to many of our readers and can be useful.

May implies that the possibility remains open: "The Mies van der Rohe tower may have changed the face of British architecture forever" (it has been built); might suggests that the possibility remains open no longer: "The Mies tower might have changed the face of architecture forever" (if only they had built it). Similarly, "they may have played tennis, or they may have gone boating" suggests I don't know what they did; "they might have played tennis if the weather had been dry" means they didn't, because it wasn't.

May also has the meaning of "having permission", so be careful: does "Megawatt Corp may bid for TransElectric Inc" mean that it is considering a bid, or that the competition authorities have allowed it to bid?

metaphor

Traditionally defined as the application to one thing of a name belonging to another, eg bowling blitz, economic meltdown, "every language is a temple in which the soul of those who speak it is enshrined" (Oliver Wendell Holmes)

none

It is a (very persistent) myth that "none" has to take a singular verb: plural is acceptable and often sounds more natural, eg "none of the current squad are good enough to play in the Premier League", "none of the issues have been resolved"

one in six, one in 10, etc
Should be treated as plural, eg "more than one in six Japanese are 65 or older" – not "more than one in six Japanese is 65 or older". "One in six" means one-sixth on average over the whole group, and a plural verb better reflects this

only
Can be ambiguous if not placed next to the word or phrase modified: "I have only one ambition" is clearer than "I only have one ambition"; however, be sensible: no need to change the song lyric to I Have Eyes Only for You

prepositions
You appeal or protest against something, not "appeal the sentence", "protest the verdict", etc.

Schoolchildren used to be told (by English teachers unduly influenced by Latin) that it was ungrammatical to end sentences with a preposition, a fallacy satirised by Churchill's "this is the sort of English up with which I will not put" and HW Fowler's (beautifully grammatical) "What did you bring me that book to be read to out of for?"

quotation marks
Use double quotes at the start and end of a quoted section, with single quotes for quoted words within that section. Place full points and commas inside the quotes for a complete quoted sentence; otherwise the point comes outside – "Anna said: 'Your style guide needs updating,' and I said: 'I agree.'" but: "Anna said updating the guide was 'a difficult and time-consuming task'."

When beginning a quote with a sentence fragment that is followed by a full sentence, punctuate according to the final part of the quote, eg The minister called the allegations "blatant lies. But in a position such as mine, it is only to be expected."

Headlines, etc take single quote marks

reported speech

When a comment in the present tense is reported, use past tense: "She said: 'I like chocolate'" (present tense) becomes in reported speech "she said she liked chocolate" (not "she said she likes chocolate").

When a comment in the past tense is reported, use "had" (past perfect tense): "She said: 'I ate too much chocolate'" (past tense) becomes in reported speech "she said she had eaten too much chocolate" (not "she said she ate too much chocolate").

Once it has been established who is speaking, there is no need to keep attributing, so long as you stick to the past tense: "Alex said he would vote Labour. There was no alternative. It was the only truly progressive party," etc

semicolons

Used correctly (which occasionally we do), the semicolon is a very elegant compromise between a full stop (too much) and a comma (not enough). This sentence, from a column by David McKie, illustrates beautifully how it's done: "Some reporters were brilliant; others were less so"

split infinitives

"The English-speaking world may be divided into (1) those who neither know nor care what a split infinitive is; (2) those who do not know, but care very much; (3) those who know and condemn; (4) those who know and distinguish. Those who neither know nor care are the vast majority, and are happy folk, to be envied." (HW Fowler, Modern English Usage, 1926)

It is perfectly acceptable, and often desirable, to sensibly split infinitives – "to boldly go" is an elegant and effective phrase – and stubbornly to resist doing so can sound pompous and awkward ("the economic precipice on which they claim perpetually to be poised") or ambiguous: "he even offered personally to guarantee the loan that the Clintons needed to buy their house" raises the question of whether the offer, or the guarantee, was personal.

George Bernard Shaw got it about right after an editor tinkered with his infinitives: "I don't care if he is made to go quickly, or to quickly go – but go he must!"

subjunctive
The author Somerset Maugham noted more than 50 years ago:
"The subjunctive mood is in its death throes, and the best thing to
do is put it out of its misery as soon as possible." Would that that
were so.

Most commonly, it is a third person singular form of the verb
expressing hypothesis, typically something demanded, proposed,
imagined: he demanded that she resign at once, I propose that she
be sacked, she insisted Jane sit down.

The subjunctive is particularly common in American English
and in formal or poetic contexts: If I were a rich man, etc. It can
sound hyper-correct or pretentious, so use common sense; Fowler
notes that is is "seldom obligatory"

syntax
Beware of ambiguous or incongruous sentence structure – the
following appeared in a column in the paper: "This argument,
says a middle-aged lady in a business suit called Marion, is just
more London stuff … " (What were her other outfits called?)

tenses
We've Only Just Begun was playing on the radio. He began to
drink; in fact he drank so much, he was drunk in no time at all.
He sank into depression, knowing that all his hopes had been
sunk. Finally, he sneaked away. Or perhaps snuck away (according
to Pinker, the most recent irregular verb to enter the language)

that
Do not use automatically after the word "said", but it can be
useful: you tend to read a sentence such as "he said nothing by
way of an explanation would be forthcoming' as "he said nothing
by way of an explanation" and then realise that it does not say
that at all; "he said that nothing by way of an explanation would
be forthcoming" is much clearer

that or which?
"that" defines, "which" gives extra information (often in a clause
enclosed by commas):
· this is the house that Jack built, but this house, which John
  built, is falling down;

- the Guardian, which I read every day, is the paper that I admire above all others.

Note that in such examples the sentence remains grammatical without "that", but not without "which"

who or whom?

From a Guardian report: "The US kept up the pressure by naming nine Yugoslav military leaders operating in Kosovo whom it said were committing war crimes." The "whom" should have been "who". That one was caught by the subeditor, but it is a common mistake.

If in doubt, ask yourself how the clause beginning who/whom would read in the form of a sentence giving he, him, she, her, they or them instead: if the who/whom person turns into he/she/they, then "who" is right; if it becomes him/her/them, then it should be "whom".

In the story above, "they" were allegedly committing the crimes, so it should be "who".

In this example: "Brown was criticised for attacking Cameron, whom he despised" – "whom" is correct because he despised "him". But in "Brown attacked Cameron, who he thought was wrong" – "who" is correct, because it is "he" not "him" who is considered wrong.

Use of "whom" has all but disappeared from spoken English, and seems to be going the same way in most forms of written English too. If you are not sure, it is much better to use "who" when "whom" would traditionally have been required than to use "whom" incorrectly for "who", which will make you look not just wrong but wrong and pompous

A-Z of
style terms

Aa

> "He's supposed to have a particularly high-class style:
> 'Feather-footed through the plashy fen passes the
> questing vole' ... would that be it?"
> "Yes," said the Managing Editor. "That must be good
> style. At least it doesn't sound like anything else to me."
>
> **Evelyn Waugh, Scoop**

a or an?

Use an before a silent H: an hour, an heir, an honourable man, an
honest woman; a hero, a hotel, a historian (but don't change a
direct quote if the speaker says, for example, "an historic")

abbreviations and acronyms

Do not use full points in abbreviations, or spaces between initials:
US, mph, eg, 4am, lbw, No 10, PJ O'Rourke, WH Smith, etc.

Use all capitals if an abbreviation is pronounced as the
individual letters: BBC, VAT, etc; if it is an acronym (pronounced as
a word) spell out with initial capital, eg Nasa, Nato, unless it can
be considered to have entered the language as an everyday word,
such as awol, laser and, more recently, asbo, pin number and sim
card.

If an abbreviation or acronym that readers may not
immediately recognise is to be used more than once, put it in
brackets at first mention. However, it is not necessary to spell out
well-known ones, such as EU, UN, CIA, FBI, CD, etc.

Cap up single letters in such expressions as C-list, F-word, "the
word assassin contains four Ss", etc

accents
Use on French, German, Spanish and Irish Gaelic words (but not anglicised French words such as cafe, apart from exposé, résumé, roué). People's names, in whatever language, should also be given appropriate accents; this may be tricky in the case of some languages but we have had complaints from readers that it is disrespectful to foreign readers to, in effect, misspell their names

Aa

actor for both male and female actors; do not use actress except when in name of award, eg Oscar for best actress; one 27-year-old actor contacted the Guardian to say "actress" has acquired a faintly pejorative tinge and she wants people to call her actor (except for her agent, who should call her often)

admit take care when using this subtly judgmental word

adoption
Mention that children are adopted only when relevant to the story: a reader points out that "explicitly calling attention to adoptions in this way suggests that adoption is not as good, and not as real a relationship, as having a child normally". So say biological father, biological family rather than "real father", "real family", etc

Adrenalin trademark; a brand of adrenaline; **adrenaline** hormone that increases heart rate and blood pressure, extracted from animals or synthesised for medical uses

aeroplane or plane, not "airplane", despite what you may have read in other versions of this guide

affect or effect? exhortations in the style guide had no effect (noun) on the number of mistakes; the level of mistakes was not affected (verb) by exhortations in the style guide; we hope to effect (verb) a change in this

African American but **African-Caribbean** (not Afro-Caribbean)

aggravate to make worse, not to annoy

aggro despite the once-popular terrace chant "A, G, A-G-R, A-G-R-O: agro!"

ahead of avoid; use before or in advance of

Aids acquired immune deficiency syndrome, but normally no need to spell out.
   Don't use such terms as "Aids victims" or someone "suffering from Aids", language that in the words of one reader is "crass, inaccurate and reinforces stigma", implying helplessness and inviting pity; "people with Aids" (or "living with Aids") is preferable. Also to be avoided: "full-blown Aids" (it does not have various stages)

alibi being somewhere else; not synonymous with excuse

A-list etc, but to refer to "C-list celebrities" and its variations has become tedious. An edition of G2 referred to "D-list celebrities" and, less than hilariously, in a separate piece about the same reality TV show, "Z-list celebrities"

all mouth and trousers not "all mouth and no trousers"

all right is right; alright is not all right (but note the Who song, much loved by generations of headline writers, was The Kids Are Alright)

alter ego we have been known to spell it "altar ego" (to be used only as a headline on a story about an arrogant bishop)

America, Americans
Although like most people we use these to mean the United States and its citizens, we should remember that America includes all of North and South America

amid not amidst

amok not amuck

among not amongst

Aa

among or between?
Contrary to popular myth, between is not limited to two parties. It is appropriate when the relationship is essentially reciprocal: fighting between the many peoples of Yugoslavia, treaties between European countries. Among belongs to distributive relationships: shared among, etc

ancestors precede descendants; we frequently manage to get them the wrong way round

antenna (insect) plural **antennae**; (radio) plural **antennas**

anticipate take action in expectation of; not synonymous with expect

antisemitic

apostrofly "an insect that lands at random on the printed page, depositing an apostrophe wherever it lands", according to the Guardian's former readers' editor

apples lc: cox's orange pippin, golden delicious, granny smith, etc

appraise to evaluate; **apprise** to inform

Arab
Both a noun and an adjective, and the preferred adjective when referring to Arab things in general, eg Arab history, Arab traditions. Arabic usually refers to the language and literature: "the Arabic press" means newspapers written in Arabic, while "the Arab press" would include newspapers produced by Arabs in other languages

Arabic names
Though Arabic has only three vowels – a, i and u – it has several consonants that have no equivalent in the Roman alphabet. For instance, there are two kinds of s, d and t. There are also two glottal sounds. This means there are at least 32 ways of writing the Libyan leader Muammar Gadafy's name in English, and

a reasonable argument can be made for adopting almost any of them. With no standard approach to transliteration agreed by the western media, we must try to balance consistency, comprehensibility and familiarity – which often puts a strain on all three.

Where a particular spelling has become widely accepted through usage we should retain it. Where an individual has clearly adopted a particular western spelling of his or her own name, we should respect that. For breaking news and stories using names for which the Guardian has no established style, we follow the lead given by Reuters wire copy

arguably unarguably one of the most overused words in the language

arms akimbo hands on hips, elbows out; it is surprising how often the phrase "legs akimbo" turns up in the paper, "suggesting that such a posture exists, but lacks a word to define it", as David McKie wrote

arranged marriages are a traditional and perfectly acceptable form of wedlock across southern Asia and within the Asian community in Britain; they should not be confused with forced marriages, which are arranged without the consent of one or both partners, and have been widely criticised

arse British English; **ass** American English

as or since? "as" is causal: I cannot check the online style guide as the connection is down; "since" is temporal: Luckily, I have had the stylebook on my desk since it was published

assassin, assassination the murder of prominent political figures rather than, say, celebrities

asylum seeker
Someone seeking refugee status or humanitarian protection; there is no such thing as an "illegal asylum seeker", a term the Press Complaints Commission ruled in breach of its code of

practice.

Refugees are people who have fled their home countries in fear for their lives, and may have been granted asylum under the 1951 refugee convention or qualify for humanitarian protection or discretionary leave, or have been granted exceptional leave to remain in Britain.

An asylum seeker can become an illegal immigrant only if he or she remains in Britain after having failed to respond to a removal notice

auger used to make holes; **augur** predict or presage

autism neurological disorder, to be used only when referring to the condition, not as a term of abuse, or in producing such witticisms as "mindless moral autism" and "Star Wars is a form of male autism", both of which have appeared in the paper

average, mean and median

Although we loosely refer to the "average" in many contexts (eg pay), there are two useful averages worth distinguishing.

What is commonly known as the average is the mean: everyone's wages are added up and divided by the number of wage earners. The median is described as "the value below which 50% of employees fall", ie it is the wage earned by the middle person when everyone's wages are lined up from smallest to largest. (For even numbers there are two middle people, but you calculate the mean average of their two wages.)

The median is often a more useful guide than the mean, which can be distorted by figures at one extreme or the other

awards, prizes, medals are generally lc, eg Guardian first book award, Nobel peace prize, Fields medal (exceptions: the Academy Awards, Victoria Cross); note that categories are lc, eg "he took the best actor Oscar at the awards"

awopbopaloobop alopbamboom

Bb

At last – a book that tells everyone the difference between balk and baulk

Ronnie O'Sullivan

bachelor now has a slightly old-fashioned ring to it, so probably better to say (if relevant) unmarried man; "confirmed bachelor" should definitely be avoided, as should "bachelor girl" (unless writing about swinging 60s movies)

backbench newspaper or politics

bacteria plural of bacterium, so don't write "the bacteria is"; even more important, don't confuse with viruses

balk obstruct, pull up, stop short; **baulk** area of a snooker table

band names lower-case "the": the Beatles, the Black Eyed Peas, the The; but upper-case equivalents in other languages, eg Les Négresses Vertes, Los Lobos.
    Bands that do not take the definite article (though they are often erroneously given it) include Arctic Monkeys, Pet Shop Boys and Ramones; most bands have their own website, or at least webpage, where this can be easily checked.
    Bands take a plural verb: Editors are overrated, Iron Butterfly were the loudest band of the 60s, etc.
    Try to include diacritical marks if bands use them, no matter how absurd: Maxïmo Park, Mötley Crüe, Motörhead, etc

banlieue French for suburbia, not suburb: strictly singular, but a French reader points out that the Petit Robert dictionary listed *les banlieues* among its "nouveaux mots" in 2006; the French for suburb is *faubourg* (literally, "false town")

Bb

Baron Cohen, Sacha the man behind Ali G and Borat

Baron-Cohen, Simon a professor of developmental psychopathology at Cambridge University and cousin of Sacha

barons, baronesses are lords and ladies in the Guardian, even at first mention: Lord Adonis, Lady Scotland, Lady Thatcher, etc; do not use first names with title ("Lady Patricia Scotland")

Base jumping extreme sport; the acronym stands for four categories of object from which you can jump, if so inclined: building, antenna, span and earth

basically this word is unnecessary, basically

bebop, hard bop, post-bop

because can be ambiguous: "I didn't go to the party because Mary was there" might mean that Mary's presence dissuaded me from going or that I went for some other reason

Becket, Thomas (1118-70) the murdered Archbishop of Canterbury, not Thomas à Becket

begs the question is best avoided as it is almost invariably misused: it means assuming a proposition that, in reality, involves the conclusion. An example would be to say that parallel lines will never meet, because they are parallel, assuming as a fact the thing you are professing to prove. What it does not mean is "raises the question"

beleaguered overused, even when we spell it correctly

bellwether sheep that leads the herd; customarily misspelt, misused, or both

berks and wankers

Kingsley Amis identified two principal groups in debates over use of language: "Berks are careless, coarse, crass, gross and of what anybody would agree is a lower social class than one's own; wankers are prissy, fussy, priggish, prim and of what they would probably misrepresent as a higher social class than one's own"

betting odds

These are meaningless to many readers, and we frequently get them wrong. But here's a brief explanation: long odds (eg 100-1 against, normally expressed as 100-1) mean something is unlikely; shorter odds (eg 10-1) still mean it's unlikely, but less unlikely; odds on (eg 2-1 on, sometimes expressed as 1-2) means it is likely, so if you were betting £2 you would win only £1 plus the stake

between 15 and 20 not "between 15 to 20" or "between 15-20"

biannual twice a year; **biennial** every two years; biannual is almost always misused, so to avoid confusion stick with the alternative twice-yearly; an alternative to biennial is two-yearly

Bible cap up if referring to Old or New Testament; lc in such sentences as "the Guardian stylebook is my bible", the adjective biblical is always lc

biblical quotations

Use a modern translation, not the Authorised Version. From a reader: "Peradventure the editor hath no copy of Holy Writ in the office, save the King James Version only. Howbeit the great multitude of believers knoweth this translation not. And he (or she) who quoteth the words of Jesus in ancient form, sheweth plainly that he (or she) considereth them to be out of date. Wherefore let them be quoted in such manner that the people may understand"

biceps singular and plural (there is no such thing as a bicep)

bid use only in a financial or sporting sense, eg Royal Bank of Scotland has made a bid for ABN Amro, Barcelona have put in a bid for Rooney, etc; or when writing about an auction. Say "in an effort to" rather than "in a bid to"

Bb

big usually preferable to major, massive, giant, mammoth, behemoth, etc, particularly in news copy

billion one thousand million; in copy use bn for sums of money, quantities or inanimate objects: £10bn, 1bn litres of water; otherwise billion: 6 billion people, etc; use bn in headlines

birdwatchers also known as birders, not "twitchers"; they go birdwatching or birding, not "twitching"

Biro trademark; say ballpoint pen if in doubt

blackberry fruit; plural **blackberries; BlackBerry** handheld wireless email device; plural **BlackBerrys**

Blackpool pleasure beach a giant funfair, not a beach, so do not illustrate with a picture of donkeys on the sand

Blade Runner not Bladerunner

bleeper pager; not to be confused with beeper, a thing that goes "beep" (eg on a microwave)

blog (noun) collection of articles, (verb) action of publishing an article to a blog: "I just blogged about that"

blond adjective and male noun; **blonde** female noun: the woman is a blonde, because she has blond hair; the man has blond hair and is, if you insist, a blond

Bluffer's Guide trademark; beware of using phrases such as "a bluffer's guide to crimewriting", a headline that led to a legal complaint

Blu-Tack trademark

Boddingtons popularly known as Boddies, it remains the cream of Manchester, despite the closure of the Strangeways brewery

bon vivant not bon viveur

bored with, bored by not bored of, although usage seems to be changing, particularly among younger people

borstals named after a village in Kent, these institutions were replaced by youth custody centres in 1982, four years after being immortalised by the Sham 69 single Borstal Breakout

both unnecessary in most phrases that contain "and"; "both men and women" says no more than "men and women", takes longer, and can also be ambiguous

Boudicca not Boadicea

brickbat use only if you know what a brickbat is

Britain, UK
These terms are synonymous: Britain is the official short form of United Kingdom of Great Britain and Northern Ireland. Used as adjectives, therefore, British and UK mean the same. Great Britain, however, refers only to England, Wales and Scotland.
 Take care not to write Britain when you might mean only England and Wales, for example when referring to the education system

Broadmoor a secure psychiatric hospital, not a prison

Brontë Charlotte, Emily, Anne and their brother Branwell; they grew up at Haworth (not Howarth) in what is now West Yorkshire

brutalise render brutal, not treat brutally; so soldiers may be brutalised by the experience of war

budget, the lc noun and adj, eg budget talks, budget measures, mini-budget, pre-budget report, etc

bumf not bumph

Bb

burgeon means to bud or sprout, so you can have someone with burgeoning talent; often misused to describe anything that is growing or expanding, especially population

burned or burnt? burned is the past tense form (he burned the cakes); burnt is the participle, an "adjectival" form of the verb ("the cakes are burnt")

businessman, businesswoman but say business people or the business community rather than "businessmen", which still finds its way into the paper occasionally

but, however often redundant, and increasingly wrongly used to connect two compatible statements; "in contrast, however, ... " is tautologous

Cc

I am a poet. I distrust anything that starts with a capital letter

Antjie Krog

cabin attendant, flight attendant, cabin crew, cabin staff not air hostess, stewardess

caddie golf; **caddy** tea

caesar salad

Caesars Palace no apostrophe

Californian a person; the adjective is California, or Brian Wilson would have written about "Californian Girls"; the same rule applies to other US states, so a "Texan drilling for Texas tea" is an oilman

call girl old-fashioned term best left to the Sunday tabloids

Canary Wharf the whole development, not the main tower, which is No 1 Canada Square

cannabis people smoke cannabis rather than "experiment" with it, despite what politicians and young members of the royal family might claim

canon cleric, decree, principle, body of writings, type of music; **cannon** something you fire

Canute (c994-1035) Danish king of England, Denmark and Norway who commanded the tide to turn back, so the legend says – not in a vain attempt to exercise power over nature, but to prove to his toadying courtiers that he was not all-powerful

canvas tent, painting; **canvass** solicit votes

---

capitals

Times have changed since the days of medieval manuscripts with elaborate hand-illuminated capital letters, or Victorian documents in which not just proper names, but virtually all nouns, were given initial caps (a Tradition valiantly maintained to this day by Estate Agents).

The tendency towards lower case, which in part reflects a less formal, less deferential society, has been accelerated by the explosion of the internet: some net companies, and many email users, have dispensed with capitals altogether. Our style reflects these developments. We aim for coherence and consistency, but not at the expense of clarity.

To quote the 1950 edition of the Manchester Guardian stylebook: "The general principle is, when in doubt, keep down"

jobs all lc, eg prime minister, chancellor of the exchequer, US secretary of state, editor of the Guardian, readers' editor

titles cap up titles, but not job description, eg the Archbishop of Canterbury, the Most Rev Rowan Williams, at first mention, thereafter Williams or the archbishop; President George Bush (but the US president, George Bush, and Bush on subsequent mention); the Duke of Westminster (the duke at second mention); the Pope; the Queen

British government departments of state initial caps, eg Home Office, Foreign Office, Ministry of Justice; other countries lc, eg US state department, Russian foreign ministry

government agencies, commissions, public bodies, quangos, etc initial caps, eg Commission for Equality and Human Rights, Crown Prosecution Service, Heritage Lottery Fund, Revenue & Customs

acts of parliament initial caps (but bills lc), eg Official Secrets Act, Criminal Justice Act 1992

parliamentary committees, reports and inquiries all lc, eg trade and industry select committee, Lawrence report, royal commission on electoral reform

airports, bridges cap the name but lc the generic part (if necessary at all), eg Heathrow, Gatwick (no need for "airport"), Liverpool John Lennon airport, Golden Gate bridge, Waterloo bridge, etc

art and culture initial caps for names of institutions, etc, eg British Museum, National Gallery, Royal Albert Hall, Tate Modern; art movements are lc (eg art nouveau, surrealism), but note Modern British, Romantic

churches, hospitals and schools cap up the proper or placename, lc the rest eg St Peter's church, Great Ormond Street children's hospital, Ripon grammar school, Vernon county primary school

councils lc, eg Kent county council, London borough of Bromley, West Berkshire council

courts lc, eg court of appeal, high court, European court of human rights, supreme court

dogs and cats lc, alsatian, doberman, rottweiler, siamese, yorkshire terrier; but Irish setter, old English sheepdog

festivals lc, whether artistic or sporting: Cannes film festival, Cheltenham festival, Edinburgh Fringe festival, Reading festival, etc

food and wine mostly lc, eg brussels sprouts, champagne, chardonnay, cheddar cheese , cornish pasty, yorkshire pudding; exceptions include Parma ham, Worcestershire sauce

geographical features lc, eg river Thames, Sydney harbour, Monterey peninsula, Bondi beach, Solsbury hill (but Mount Everest).

Cc

universities and colleges of further and higher education caps for institution, lc for departments, eg Sheffield University department of medieval and modern history, Oregon State University, Free University of Berlin, University of Queensland school of journalism, London College of Communication

wars lc, eg civil war, cold war, hundred years' war

words and phrases based on proper names that have largely lost connection with their origins are normally lc, eg balaclava, cardigan, french windows, wellington boots

---

careen to sway or keel over to one side; **career** to rush along

career girl, career woman these labels are banned

carer an unpaid family member, partner or friend who helps a disabled or frail person with the activities of daily living; not someone who works in a caring job or profession

cashmere fabric; **Kashmir** place

caster sugar, wheels on a sofa; **castor** oil

casualties includes dead and injured, so not a synonym for deaths

catch-22 lc unless specifically referring to Joseph Heller's novel Catch-22

CD, CDs, CD-Rom a CD is a disc, not a disk

celibate, celibacy strictly refer to being unmarried (especially for religious reasons), but it is now acceptable to use them to mean abstaining from sexual intercourse

Celtic not Glasgow Celtic

censor prevent publication; **censure** criticise severely

central belt the swath across Scotland, containing Glasgow and Edinburgh, where population density is highest. It is in the south, not the centre of the country

centre on or in; **revolve** around

chair acceptable in place of chairman or chairwoman, being nowadays widely used in the public sector and by organisations such as the Labour party and trade unions (though not the Conservative party, which had a "chairman" in kitten heels)

chaos theory not a synonym for chaos. It describes the behaviour of dynamic systems that are sensitively dependent on their initial conditions. An example is the weather: under the "butterfly effect", the flap of a butterfly's wing in Brazil can in principle result in a tornado in Texas

Chatham House rule often mistakenly called "rules". There is just one, namely: "When a meeting, or part thereof, is held under the Chatham House rule, participants are free to use the information received, but neither the identity nor the affiliation of the speaker(s), nor that of any other participant, may be revealed."
   Chatham House is more formally known as the Royal Institute of International Affairs, based at Chatham House in London

chatroom, chatshow

checkout noun, adjective; **check out** verb

Cheshire cat but **cheshire cheese**

chicken tikka masala Britain's favourite dish; note that there is also an Italian dish called chicken marsala

child trust fund colloquially known as baby bonds

Chloé (fashion) not Chloë

choose for some strange reason this often appears as "chose", its past tense

chords musical; **cords** vocal

christened, christening use only when referring to a Christian baptism: don't talk about a boat being christened or a football club christening a new stadium; named is fine

Christian name use first name, forename or given name (in many cultures, it comes after the family name)

chronic means lasting for a long time or constantly recurring, too often misused when acute (short but severe) is meant

church lc for the established church, eg "the church is no longer relevant today"; Catholic church, Anglican church, etc, but Church of England

cineaste someone who enjoys films; but note that, in France, a *cinéaste* is someone who makes them

civil partnership rather than gay marriage, but gay wedding is fine and does not need quotation marks

CJD Creutzfeldt-Jakob disease, not normally necessary to spell it out; it is acceptable to refer to variant CJD as the human form of BSE, but not "the human form of mad cow disease"

cliches
Overused words and phrases to be avoided, some of which merit their own ignominious entry in this book, include: back burner, boost (massive or otherwise), bouquets and brickbats, but hey ... , count 'em, debt mountain, drop-dead gorgeous, elephant in the room, fit for purpose, insisted, key, major, massive, meanwhile, politically correct, raft of measures, special, to die for, upsurge; verbs overused in headlines include: bid, boost, fuel, hike, signal, spiral, target, set to.
   A survey by the Plain English Campaign found that the most irritating phrase in the language was at the end of the day, followed

by (in order of annoyance): at this moment in time, like (as in, like, this), with all due respect, to be perfectly honest with you, touch base, I hear what you're saying, going forward, absolutely, and blue sky thinking; other words and phrases that upset people included 24/7, ballpark figure, bottom line, diamond geezer, it's not rocket science, ongoing, prioritise, pushing the envelope, singing from the same hymn sheet, and thinking outside the box

Close, Glenn two Ns (as in bunny boiler)

collectible

Colombia South American country that we frequently misspell as "Columbia"

Columbia as in District of Columbia (Washington DC) and Columbia University (New York)

comedian male and female; do not use comedienne

commented "said" is normally adequate

Commons, House of Commons but **the house**, not the House

Commons committees lc, home affairs select committee, public accounts committee, etc

common sense noun; **commonsense** adjective: "William Hague's 'commonsense revolution' showed little common sense"

company names
A difficult area, as so many companies these days have adopted unconventional typography and other devices that, in some cases, turn their names into logos. In general, we use the names that companies use themselves: c2c, Capgemini, easyJet, eBay, ebookers, iSoft Group, etc.
    Exceptions include Adidas (not adidas), ABN Amro (not ABN AMRO), BAE Systems (not BAE SYSTEMS), BhS (no italicised H), Toys R Us (do not attempt to turn the R backwards), Yahoo (no exclamation mark)

Cc

compass points lc for regions: the north, the south of England, the south-west, north-east Scotland, south Wales; the same applies to geopolitical areas: the west, western Europe, the far east, south-east Asia, central America, etc; cap up, however, when part of the name of a county (West Sussex, East Riding of Yorkshire) or province (East Java, North Sulawesi, etc); note the following: East End, West End (London), Middle East, Latin America, North America, South America

complement or compliment? to complement is to make complete: the two strikers complemented each other; to compliment is to praise; a complimentary copy is free

comprise to consist of; "comprise of" is wrong

conjoined twins not Siamese twins

contemporary of the same period, though often wrongly used to mean modern; a performance of Shakespeare in contemporary dress would involve Elizabethan costume, not 21st-century clothes

continent, the mainland Europe is preferable

continual refers to things that happen repeatedly but not constantly; **continuous** indicates an unbroken sequence

controversial overused, typically to show that the writer disapproves of something ("the government's controversial academy schools scheme"); as with "famous", it can normally be safely removed from copy to allow readers to make up their own minds

convince or persuade? having convinced someone of the facts, you might persuade them to do something

cooperate, coordinate no hyphen

coruscating means sparkling, or emitting flashes of light; people seem to think, wrongly, that it means the same as excoriating, censuring severely, eg "a coruscating attack on Brown's advisers"

cosmetic surgery is not the same as plastic surgery, which should be reserved for people treated for deformity or illness

court martial plural **courts martial**

crescendo a gradual increase in loudness or intensity; musically or figuratively, it is the build-up to a climax, not the climax itself (we frequently get this wrong)

cripple, crippled offensive and outdated; do not use

crucifix not synonymous with cross: a crucifix depicts the body of Christ on the cross

Cub scouts boys (and now girls) aged from eight to 10, organised in packs but no longer known as "Wolf Cubs"; avoid dated "Dyb Dyb Dyb, Dob Dob Dob" jokes but if relevant, it is spelt thus (it stands for "do your best" and we will "do our best"), and not "Dib"

cull means pick or choose as in "culled from the best authors". It doesn't mean killed, axed or massacred (though you cull sheep in order to kill them). So a jobs cull does not mean the same as mass sackings

Cummings, EE US poet (1894-1962) who, despite what many people think, used capitals in his signature

currently "now" is usually preferable, if needed at all

cusp a place where two points touch (eg "on the cusp of Manchester and Salford", "on the cusp of Taurus and Gemini"), which may be extended metaphorically to a place or time where two things or groups of things come into contact, as in this elegant example from the Review: "It was a world caught on the cusp between postwar recession, stasis and a dying moral code, and the colour, mobility and licence of the 60s."
   Writers who use cusp under the impression that it is a clever way to say on the brink of or about to ("on the cusp of adolescence", "on the cusp of the final", "the garlic was on the cusp of bursting into a constellation of white stars") are, sadly, mistaken

Dd

"Leave the rooster story alone – that's human interest!"
Ben Hecht and Charles MacArthur, The Front Page

Dad or dad? I'll ask Dad, then you can check with your dad

Dáil Éireann lower house of parliament in the Irish Republic, normally just the Dáil

dark ages

dashes
Beware sentences – such as this one – that dash about all over the place – commas (or even, very occasionally, brackets) are often better; semicolons also have their uses

data takes a singular verb (like agenda); though strictly a plural, no one ever uses "agendum" or "datum"

dates
Our style is July 21 2008 (no commas), and has been since the first issue of the Manchester Guardian on May 5 1821 (it is occasionally alleged that putting month before date in this way is an "Americanisation")

daughter of, son of
Think twice before using these terms. Often only the person's father is described and such descriptions can smack of snobbery as well as sexism

Dd

Day-Glo trademark

D-day

deaf ears
Avoid or say "closed ears": the phrase is not just a rather lazy cliche but offensive to many deaf people; for the same reason, do not use "dialogue of the deaf": most deaf people are perfectly capable of conducing a dialogue using BSL and other sign languages

debacle no accents; like farce and fiasco, to be used sparingly in news reporting

decades
1950s, etc; use figures if you abbreviate: roaring 20s, swinging 60s, a woman in her 70s, the first reader's email of the 00s

decimate nowadays used to mean destroy

deep south of the US

defuse render harmless; **diffuse** spread about

degrees like this: my sons all got firsts, but I only got a second – although it was a 2:1 – and I did go on to a master's

delusion or illusion? "That the sun moves round the Earth was once a delusion, and is still an illusion"(Fowler)

Democratic party not "Democrat party", despite attempts by some Republicans to call it this

Dench, Dame Judi not Judy

dependant noun; **dependent** adjective; **dependence**

deprecate express disapproval; **depreciate** reduce in value

de rigueur the two Us are de rigueur

Derry not Londonderry

Dd

descendants come after ancestors; you wouldn't think the Guardian would get this simple thing wrong as often as we do

desiccated not dessicated

dessert pudding, but **just deserts**

developing countries use this term in preference to third world

dialects cockney, estuary English, geordie, scouse

dietitian must be trained and qualified in dietetics, and registered with the Health Professionals Council; not the same as a nutritionist, a less precise term (although some nutritionists are also registered dietitians)

different from or **different to**, not different than

direct speech
People we write about are allowed to speak in their own, not necessarily the Guardian's, style, but be sensitive: do not, for example, expose someone to ridicule for dialect or grammatical errors. Do not attempt facetious phonetic renditions such as "oop north", "fooking" and "booger" when interviewing someone from the north, or "dahn sarf" when writing about south London

disabled people, not "the disabled"
Use positive language about disability, avoiding outdated terms that stereotype or stigmatise. Terms to avoid, with acceptable alternatives in brackets, include victim of, suffering from, afflicted by, crippled by (prefer person who has, person with); wheelchair-bound, in a wheelchair (uses a wheelchair); invalid (disabled person); mentally handicapped, backward, retarded, slow (person with learning difficulties); the disabled, the handicapped, the blind, the deaf (disabled people, blind people, deaf people); deaf and dumb (deaf and speech-impaired, hearing and speech-impaired)

disc rotating optical disc: CD, CD-Rom, DVD etc; **disk** rotating magnetic disc: disk drive, floppy disk

Dd

discomfit thwart, readily confused with **discomfort**, make uncomfortable

discreet circumspect; **discrete** separate

disinterested means free from bias, objective (the negative form of interested as in "interested party"); often used incorrectly instead of **uninterested**, not taking an interest (the negative form of interested as in "interested in football")

D notices issued by the defence, press and broadcasting advisory committee, "suggesting" that the media do not publish sensitive information

Doctor Who the title of the series; the character's name is the Doctor, and it should never be abbreviated to Dr Who

D'oh! as Homer Simpson would say (note the apostrophe)

Domesday Book but **doomsday scenario**

doner kebab; **donor** gives money

dos and don'ts

dotcom

downplay play down is preferable

Down's syndrome say (if relevant) a baby with Down's syndrome, not "a Down's syndrome baby" – we wouldn't say "a cerebral palsy baby". The diagnosis is not the person

down under don't use to refer to Australia or New Zealand

Dr use at first mention for medical and scientific doctors and doctors of divinity (not, for example, a politician who happens to have a PhD in history); thereafter, just use surname

dreamed not dreamt

drink past tense **drank**, past participle **drunk**: he drinks, he drank, he has drunk

Dd

drone honeybee whose function is to mate with the queen, and by extension therefore someone who lives off the work of others (the worker bees); it seems to be used increasingly to mean something like an obedient, unimaginative worker ("office drone")

drug use a more accurate and less judgmental term than "drug abuse" or "misuse" (often all three terms have been scattered randomly through the same reports)

dub avoid such tabloidese as "they have been dubbed the nation's leading experts on English language" (even if true)

duct tape not duck tape

due to
Traditionalists argue that rent may be due to the landlord, but unless it is the complement of the verb "to be", "due to" should otherwise be replaced by "because of"; thus:
"The train was late due to leaves on the line" is wrong;
"The train was late because of leaves on the line" is correct;
"The train's late arrival was due to leaves on the line" is also correct.
   A rough and ready test is that "due to" is fine if it can be replaced by "caused by", but not when it can be replaced by "because of".
   This distinction, once routinely taught in primary schools but now assailed on all sides, especially by train and tube announcers, is being lost

dumb do not use: say speech-impaired

dwarves plural of dwarf (not dwarfs); but the verb is to dwarf, eg 1 Canada Square dwarfs the surrounding buildings

Dynamo football teams from the former Soviet Union are Dynamo; teams from Romania are **Dinamo**

dyslexia write "Paul has dyslexia" rather than labelling him "a dyslexic" or saying he "suffers from" dyslexia

Ee

Say all you have to say in the fewest possible words, or your reader will be sure to skip them; and in the plainest possible words, or he will certainly misunderstand them

John Ruskin

earlier often redundant: "they met this week" is preferable to "they met earlier this week" and will save space; "earlier this month" occurs almost every time we publish a paper on the first of the month, when it should, of course, be "last month"

Earth in an astronomical or science fiction context; but moon, sun

east Asia or **south-east Asia** rather than far east

East End inner east London north of the river (the equivalent district south of the Thames is south-east London)

EastEnders TV soap

Easter Day not Easter Sunday

easyJet

eBay

ecohome, ecosystem, ecotown, ecowarrior

Ee

effectively is not a synonym for in effect: "the Brown campaign was effectively launched in 2007" means the launch was official and its intended effect was achieved; "the Brown campaign was in effect launched in 1997" means this was not the official launch, but events at the time described did have the effect of launching it, whether intended or not.

The word is almost invariably misused, and can often be omitted

effete does not mean effeminate or foppish, but "weak, ineffectual or decadent as a result of over-refinement ... exhausted, worn out, spent" (Collins)

elderly do not use to describe anyone under 70, and say elderly people (or even better, older people), never "the elderly"

El Dorado fabled city of gold; **Eldorado** fabled flop of a soap

electrocution death by electric shock, so don't say survivors of torture were "electrocuted" during their ordeal – rather that they were given electric shocks

elephant in the room
This cliche appeared in the Guardian 38 times in one year; elephants in the room have included trade figures, policy, lack of policy, climate change, Iraq, the US, Europe, anti-Americanism, men, women, single women, a new French football league, race, religion, Islam, Catholicism, Tessa Jowell, Andrew Neil, Jimmy Greaves, fatness, thinness, Stalinism, Hitler and Tony Blair's departure from office.

Mercifully, this tedious expression now seems to be on its way to the elephants' graveyard

email

empathic not empathetic

employment tribunal not industrial tribunal

England, English take care not to offend readers from other parts of the UK by saying England or English when you mean Britain or British, and vice versa (we published a map of England's best beaches, with the headline "Britain's best beaches"); *see Scotland*

enormity something monstrous or wicked; not synonymous with large

en suite two words, whatever estate agents might claim

epicentre the point on the earth's surface directly above the focus of an earthquake or underground explosion; frequently misused to mean the centre or focus itself

epilepsy we do not define people by their medical condition: seizures are epileptic, people are not; so say (if relevant) "Smith, who has epilepsy" not "Smith, an epileptic"

ere long not e'er long

escapers not escapees, despite the apparently unstoppable advance of the -ee suffix (can it be long before Guardian readers become "readees"?)

Eskimo is a language spoken in Greenland, Canada, Alaska and Siberia. Note that it has no more words for snow than does English for rain. The people are Inuit (singular Inuk), not "Eskimos"

Eta Basque separatists; **ETA** estimated time of arrival

ethnic never say ethnic when you mean ethnic minority, which leads to such nonsense as "the constituency has a small ethnic population"

ethnic cleansing do not use as a euphemism for genocide unless in quotation marks

Ee

EU European Union (no need to spell out at first mention); formerly EC (European Community); before that EEC (European Economic Community)

euro currency; plural euros and cents

Europe includes Britain, so don't say, for example, something is common "in Europe" unless it is common in Britain as well; to distinguish between Britain and the rest of Europe the phrase "continental Europe" may be useful; central Europe, eastern Europe, western Europe

European court of human rights nothing to do with the EU: it is a Council of Europe body

Eurosceptic one word, capped: they are sceptics about the EU, not just the euro

every day noun and adverb: it happens every day; **everyday** adjective: an everyday mistake

every parent's nightmare avoid this cliche

exclamation marks do not use!

exclusive term used by tabloid newspapers to denote a story that is in all of them

execution the carrying out of a death sentence by lawful authority, so a terrorist, for example, does not "execute" someone

expat, expatriate not ex-pat or expatriot; this is "ex" meaning "out of" (as in export, extract), not "ex-" meaning "former" (as in ex-husband)

explained "said" is normally sufficient

eyewitness one word, but witness is preferable, except in the Guardian's Eyewitness picture spread

Ff

Trying to determine what is going on in the world by reading newspapers is like trying to tell the time by watching the second hand of a clock

Ben Hecht

factoid not a trivial fact, but a mistaken assumption repeated so often that it is believed to be true (a word coined by Norman Mailer, who defined it as "something that everyone knows is true, except it ain't!")

FA Cup the Cup (the cap C is hallowed by convention); all other cups lc at second mention

Fairtrade
The Fairtrade mark is a certification system run by the Fairtrade Foundation; products are entitled to be called Fairtrade (cap F) if they meet the following criteria: a price that covers producers' costs, a premium for producers to invest in their communities, and long-term and more direct trading relations

fair trade refers to the movement as a whole, eg only fair trade will enable farmers in developing countries to become self-sufficient

famous, famously overused and often unnecessary

far, farther, farthest of distances, otherwise **further, furthest**

Ff

far away adverb; **faraway** adjective: she moved to a faraway place, and now lives far away

farrago a hotchpotch or jumbled mixture, not synonymous with fiasco (a humiliating failure)

fatality use death

fat cats use sparingly, unless writing about overweight moggies

father of two, mother of two etc (no hyphens); only describe people in this way if relevant

fatwa an edict, not necessarily a death sentence

fazed overwhelmed; **phased** staged

fed up with not fed up of

female not "woman" or "women" in such phrases as female home secretary, female voters

female genital mutilation rather than "female circumcision"

ferris wheel do not cap up

fewer or less? fewer means smaller in number, eg fewer coins; less means smaller in quantity, eg less money

fiance male; **fiancee** female; but note divorcee is male and female

fiasco like debacle and farce, overused in news stories: who says it's a fiasco?

figures spell out from one to nine; numerals from 10 to 999,999; thereafter 1m, 3.2bn (except for people and animals, eg 2 million viewers, 8 billion cattle)

fine-tooth comb

Finnegans Wake

firing line the people who do the firing; if they are aiming at you, you are in the line of fire not in the firing line

first name, forename not Christian name

fit for purpose a recent cliche that quickly proved itself unfit for the purpose of good writing

flammable rather than inflammable (although, curiously, they mean the same thing); the negative is non-flammable

flaunt or flout? to flaunt is to make a display of something, as in flaunting wealth; to flout is to show disregard for something, as in flouting the seatbelt law

flounder or founder? to flounder is to perform a task badly, like someone stuck in mud; to founder is to fail: a business might be foundering because its bosses are floundering

following prefer after, eg Leeds United went to pieces after yet another relegation

footie abbreviation for football, but in Australia (particularly Victoria), **footy** is what they call Australian rules football

forbear abstain; **forebear** ancestor

foreign placenames
We opt for locally used names, with these main exceptions (the list is not exhaustive, apply common sense):
Archangel, Basle, Berne, Brittany, Cologne, Dunkirk, Florence, Fribourg, Genoa, Gothenburg, Hanover, Kiev, Lombardy, Milan, Munich, Naples, Normandy, Nuremberg, Padua, Piedmont, Rome, Sardinia, Seville, Sicily, Syracuse, Turin, Tuscany, Venice, Zurich.
And the next time someone says we should call Burma "Myanmar" because that's what it calls itself, point out that

Ff

Muammar Gadafy renamed Libya "The Great Socialist People's Libyan Arab Jamahiriyya"

foreign words and phrases
Italicise, with roman translation in brackets, if it really is a foreign word or phrase and not an anglicised one, in which case it is roman with no accents (exceptions: exposé, résumé, roué). Remember Orwell: do not use a foreign word where a suitable English equivalent exists

forensic belonging to the courts; does not mean scientific

forego go before; **forgo** go without

forever continually: he is forever changing his mind; **for ever** for always: I will love you for ever

formula plural **formulas**, but **formulae** in scientific context

formula one motor racing

fortuitous by chance, not (as most people seem to think) by good fortune; if we manage to use the word correctly, it is entirely fortuitous

french fries, horn, kiss, letter, polish, window

Freud, Lucian British artist, not Lucien

friendly fire no quotation marks necessary

Frisbee trademark; if in doubt, call it a flying disc

fulsome
Another example of a word that is almost never used correctly, it means "cloying, excessive, disgusting by excess" (and is not, as some appear to believe, a clever word for full); so "fulsome praise" should not be used in a complimentary sense

Gg

I have made this letter longer only because I have not had the time to make it shorter

Blaise Pascal

Gadafy, Muammar Libyan leader rather than president (he holds no government office and is generally known in Libya as "leader of the revolution"); Col Gadafy on second mention

gaff hook or spar, also slang for house; **blow the gaff** give away a secret; **gaffe** blunder

gambit an opening strategy that involves some sacrifice or concession; so to talk of an opening gambit is tautologous – an opening ploy might be better

gay use as an adjective rather than a noun: a gay man, gay people, gay men and lesbians not "gays and lesbians"

Gb gigabits; **GB** gigabytes

gender issues

Our use of language reflects Guardian values, as well as changes in society. Phrases such as career girl or career woman, for example, are outdated (more women have careers than men) and patronising (there is no male equivalent): never use them.

Gg

actor, comedian: covers men and women; not actress, comedienne (but waiter and waitress are acceptable – at least for the moment). Firefighter, not fireman; PC, not WPC (police forces have abandoned the distinction), postal workers, not postmen.

Avoid terms such as businessmen, housewives, male nurse, woman pilot, woman (lady!) doctor, etc, which reinforce outdated stereotypes. If you need to use an adjective, it is female and not "woman" in such phrases as female MPs, female president.

Never say "his" to cover men and women: use his or her, or a different construction; in sentences such as "a teacher who beats his/her pupils is not fit to do the job", there is usually a way round the problem – in this case, "teachers who beat their pupils ... "

Geneva conventions (not convention)
Four treaties, last revised and ratified in 1949, which with three more recently adopted protocols set out international standards for the humanitarian treatment of prisoners of war and civilians caught up in war

geography distinct areas are capped up: Black Country, East Anglia, Lake District, Midlands, Peak District, West Country; but areas defined by compass points are lc: the north, the south-east, the south-west, etc

geriatrics branch of medicine dealing with elderly people, not an amusing way to describe them in an attempt to make yourself sound cool

ghoti George Bernard Shaw's proposed spelling of the word "fish" (gh as in trough, o as in women, ti as in nation)

gift not a verb (unless, perhaps, directly quoting a football manager or player: "We gifted Spurs their second goal")

girl female under 18

girlie noun (only when quoting someone); **girly** adjective (eg girly clothes); girlish behaviour

Giuseppe regularly misspelt as Guiseppe; this is sloppy

Gg

GLA

A mistake we repeat ad nauseam is the assumption that GLA stands for "Greater London assembly". There is no such thing. The Greater London authority comprises the mayor, who runs it, and the London assembly, which holds the mayor to account

God

Google cap up, even when used as a verb ("I Googled myself"); named after googol, the number 1 followed by 100 zeros or 10^{100}

Goths (uc) Germanic tribe that invaded the Roman empire; **goths** (lc) Sisters of Mercy fans who invaded the Shepherd's Bush Empire

---

government departments

British government ministries (but not ministers) take initial caps, as follows:

Cabinet Office (but the cabinet)
Home Office
Foreign Office (abbreviate to FCO – for Foreign and Commonwealth Office – after first mention)
Treasury
Department for Business, Enterprise and Regulatory Reform (BERR)
Department for Children, Schools and Families (DCFS)
Communities and Local Government
Department for Culture, Media and Sport (DCMS)
Department for Environment, Food and Rural Affairs (Defra)
Department for Innovation, Universities and Skills (Dius)
Department for International Development (DfID)
Department for Transport (DfT)
Department for Work and Pensions (DWP)
Department of Health (DH)
Ministry of Defence (MoD)
Ministry of Justice (MoJ)
Office of the Leader of the House of Commons
Northern Ireland Office
Scotland Office not Scottish Office

Wales Office not Welsh Office

Gg

Use the abbreviations in brackets sparingly, especially the clumsy ones: culture and sport department, innovation and skills department, and so on are fine, or just the department, the ministry, etc.

The rebranded Communities and Local Government is tricky, having decided to drop "Department" from its name: if we say, for example, "Communities and Local Government yesterday announced a shakeup in council tax" it makes us sound equally silly, so best to call it the communities and local government department (lc) or just communities department or local government department, depending on the story.

Departments and ministries of other countries are lc, eg US state department, Iraqi foreign ministry

---

government lc in all contexts and all countries; resist the awful trend to say such things as "Lord Browne fended off accusations of being too close to government" – it should be **the government**

grandparent
Mention this status only when relevant: leave "battling grannies" and similar examples of ageism and sexism to the tabloids; in particular we should avoid such patronising drivel as "How this 55-year-old granny came to earn $25m a year"

Great Britain England, Wales and Scotland; if you want to include Northern Ireland, use Britain or the UK

grisly gruesome; **grizzly** bear

Ground Zero caps for former site of World Trade Centre in New York, lc for referring to the exact location of explosions, eg at Hiroshima in 1945

Guides not "Girl Guides"; the organisation is Girlguiding UK

guineas
Younger readers may not be aware that a guinea was worth £1 1s (£1.05) unless they buy or sell racehorses (the buyer still pays the auction house in guineas, and the auction house then gives the vendor the same number of pounds, thus netting the auctioneer his 5% commission)

Gulf, the not the Persian or Arabian Gulf

Gypsies recognised as an ethnic group under the Race Relations Act, as are Irish Travellers, hence capped up

Would you convey my compliments to the purist who reads your proofs and tell him or her that I write in a sort of broken-down patois which is something like the way a Swiss waiter talks, and that when I split an infinitive, God damn it, I split it so it will stay split

Raymond Chandler

Häagen-Dazs American ice-cream; despite appearances, the name was made up to give a European cachet to a product emanating from the Bronx in New York City

haemorrhaging is best avoided, even if you manage to spell it correctly, as it has become a cliche – in expressions such as "haemorrhaging cash" – and completely wrong as an adjective meaning big, eg "in the face of haemorrhaging financial losses"

Haiti is not an island: Haiti and the Dominican Republic make up the Caribbean island of Hispaniola

Hamilton Academical not Academicals, nickname the Accies

handicapped do not use to refer to people with disabilities or learning difficulties

hara-kiri known less vulgarly in Japan as *seppuku*

hardcore one word, whether noun or adjective and whether you are talking about music, rubble, a hardcore of rebels or hardcore pornography

hare lip never use: say cleft lip or cleft palate

Haverfordwest in south-west Wales, not "Haverford West" as we managed to say

hazard or risk?
Scientists use hazard to mean a potential for harm and risk to mean the actual probability of harm occurring; though headline writers may feel more at home with risk than hazard, the distinction is worth bearing in mind

---

headlines
What makes a great, or at least memorable, headline? They can be historic ("Man walks on Moon"), campaigning ("A liar and a cheat"), classical ("Between Cilla and Charybdis"), subtle ("Flo quiets the Dons"), funny ("Super Caley go ballistic – Celtic are atrocious"), notorious ("Gotcha!"), or downright absurd ("Freddie Starr ate my hamster"). There is no magic formula but here are a few guidelines.

Use active verbs where possible, particularly in news headlines: "Editor updates style guidelines" is much better than "Style guidelines updated". Avoid tabloid cliches such as bid, brand, dub and slam, and their broadsheet counterparts such as insist, signal and target. Imagining that you are describing an event, in words, to real people, is a good antidote to journalese: no one in a pub says "Do you think that Miliband will dramatically oust Brown in a shock power bid?"

Just as we would in copy, we need to take care with words such as debacle, farce and fiasco, especially when combined, which we contrived to do in the headline "Hips fiasco descends into farce"– the fact that "Hips farce descends into fiasco" would work just as well tells you something is probably wrong here.

Strive to be fresh: tired plays on the phrase "Mind the gap", heard only occasionally these days by passengers on the London underground, have become tedious, as well as either baffling or infuriating to readers who do not happen to live in the capital.

Take care over ambiguity: "Landmine claims dog UK arms firm", which appeared in the paper, contains so many successive nouns, some of which may or may not be verbs, that you have to read it several times to work out what it means.

Exclamation marks – look, I've written something funny! – should never be used. Question marks are also to be avoided, as are quotation marks, unless essential to signify a quote or for legal reasons.

Puns are fine – "Where there's muck there's bras", about a farmer's wife who started a lingerie business from a barn, was voted headline of the year – but do not overuse, or resort to tired puns such as "flushed with success" (this story has got a plumber in it). It is possible to try just a little too hard ("To baldly grow where no mane's grown before").

Unexpected twists, or subtle plays on words and phrases, show the craft at its best: a power failure in a theatre became, in the Guardian, "Bad lights stop play". A light touch can work beautifully: "Drop dead, gorgeous", on a story about office jealousy, added one comma to a well-known film title to create the perfect headline. When Tate Modern exhibited a giant sun, to create its own indoor climate, the beautiful Guardian headline – "But is it weather?" (a rare example of a question mark being required) – deserved to be framed and exhibited in a gallery in its own right.

Be careful when making references to popular culture: "Mrs Culpepper's lonely hearts club banned" works, because most people are familiar with the Beatles' Sgt Pepper album, but allusions to your favourite obscure prog-rock LP are likely to pass over most readers' heads. "Book lack in Ongar", about a shortage of resources in Essex libraries, remains one of the all-time great headlines, but it only works if you get the reference to John Osborne's 1956 play Look Back in Anger (or at least it did until Oasis helpfully recorded a song called Don't Look Back in Anger).

It's time for some formulaic headlines to be given a decent burial, or at least a long rest. "The kids are alright" (based on a song by the Who, and subsequently a film) crops up, with minor variations, on a weekly and sometimes daily basis in British newspapers. Even more ubiquitous are "Size isn't everything" and its close relative "Size doesn't matter", used to refer to a car (in two different newspapers), school uniforms, the actor Simon

Hh

Callow's height, a hotel in Turkey, new houses, national economies, motorbikes, a footballer, the gallery following a golf tournament, and – once – penis size.

The ever-popular "Brighton rocks" and its variations are an allusion, still common, to the Graham Greene novel and subsequent film, both more than 50 years old. How many people still understand the reference? "So lucky, lucky, lucky", a recent headline we used above a photograph of Kylie Minogue, quoted lyrics from a hit she had nearly 20 years ago.

The important thing is to think of the readers and remember that we are writing headlines for their benefit, not for our own amusement or to show how clever we are

---

headteacher one word, not headmaster, headmistress

Heathrow airport or simply Heathrow; not "London's Heathrow"

help help to decide or help decide; not "help and decide"

here generally avoid if what you mean is "in Britain"

high street lc in retail spending stories: "the recession is making an impact in the high street"; capped only in the proper name: "I went shopping in Cheltenham High Street"

hijack of movable objects only, not of schools, embassies, etc

hike a walk, not an increase in interest rates; "Motorists face new petrol hike" (not one of our better headlines) suggested a long walk to a garage rather than simply a price rise

hip-hop

HIV a virus, not a disease, but do not call HIV "the Aids virus" or an HIV test an "Aids test"; an HIV-positive man (hyphen) is HIV positive (no hyphen)

Hizbullah not Hezbollah; it means "party of God"

hoard or horde? a hoard of treasure; a horde (or hordes) of tourists

Hobson's choice a "choice" between taking what is offered and nothing at all

hoi polloi common people, the masses; "the hoi polloi" is acceptable, even for speakers of ancient Greek

Holocaust do not trivialise by comparing piles of cattle during the foot-and-mouth outbreak to the Holocaust, or through phrases such as "Belsen-skinny" which, incredibly, found its way into a story about Kate Winslet

homogeneous uniform, of the same kind; **homogenous** (biology) having a common descent; the latter is often misused for the former

honorary knights are not given titles, so it is still plain "Geldof" rather than "Sir Bob"

honorifics

Use just surname after first mention, eg Gordon Brown at first mention, thereafter Brown; Sir Richard Branson at first mention, thereafter Branson; Lord Adonis at first mention, subsequently Adonis.

As always, use common sense: in a story where two people have the same name (eg a court case about a husband and wife or brothers), it may be necessary to use Mr and Mrs or Ms, or forenames.

Follow traditional Guardian style in leading articles (but not other comment pieces and columns on leader pages): use honorifics after first mention, unless writing about an artist, author, journalist, musician, criminal or dead person; use Ms for women on second mention unless they have expressed a preference for Miss or Mrs

"honour" killings always use quotes; as a reader says: "There is no honour involved in these murders and calling them honour killings belittles the victims and plays down the crime"

hoodie a hooded top, as well as someone who wears one

Hoover trademark; say vacuum cleaner unless you are sure it is a Hoover (uc); but lc for figurative hoovering up (eg "the Guardian website hoovered up all the awards")

hopefully like many other adverbs, such as frankly, happily, honestly and sadly, hopefully can be used as a "sentence adverb" indicating the writer's view of events – "hopefully, we will reach the summit" – or as a "manner adverb" modifying a verb: "we set off hopefully for the summit". Why some people are upset by "hopefully we will win" and not "sadly we lost" is a mystery

househusband, housewife use with care; avoid sexist stereotyping such as lower food prices being "good news for housewives" (it's good news for shoppers)

Human Genome Project

humanity, humankind not mankind, a word that, as one of our readers points out, "alienates half the population from their own history"

hummus you eat it; **humus** you put it on the garden

hyperbole don't overegg stories: strive instead for straight and accurate reporting – Guardian readers prefer the unvarnished truth

"Iraq or Iran – what's our style?"
Freelance subeditor (not at the Guardian)

iconic in danger of losing all meaning after more than 1,000 appearances in the Guardian in one year, employed to describe anything vaguely memorable or well-known – from Weetabix, Dr Martens boots and the Ferrero Rocher TV ads to Jimi Hendrix's final gigs, a plinth in Trafalgar Square and drains

if not can be ambiguous: does "it is the most beautiful castle in France, if not the whole of Europe" mean "and maybe in the whole of Europe" or "but not in the whole of Europe"?

illegitimate do not use to refer to children born outside marriage (unless in a historical context, eg "the illegitimate son of Charles the Good")

immaculate conception nothing to do with the birth of Jesus: it is the doctrine that Mary herself was conceived by her mother (St Anne) without the stain of original sin. The virgin birth is the doctrine of Christ's birth without a human father. This is one of our most frequent errors

impact a noun, not a verb

impracticable impossible, it cannot be done; **impractical** possible in theory but not workable at the moment

inchoate just beginning or undeveloped, not chaotic or disorderly

Ii

index plural **indexes**, except for scientific and economic **indices**

Indian placenames the former Bombay is now known as Mumbai, Madras is now Chennai, Calcutta is now Kolkata and Bangalore is now Bengalooru

indie music, films, etc; **Indy** short for the Independent, a newspaper

infer or imply? to infer is to deduce something from evidence; to imply is to hint at something (and wait for someone to infer it)

initials no spaces or points, whether businesses or individuals, eg WH Smith, PCR Tufnell

inner city noun two words, adjective hyphenated: inner-city blues made Marvin Gaye wanna holler

inquiry not enquiry

insisted overused, especially in political stories; said should normally suffice

insure against risk; **assure** life; **ensure** make certain

interned imprisoned; **interred** buried (yes, we have got them confused)

into or in to? one word if you go into a room, but two words in such sentences as I called in to complain, I listened in to their conversation and I went in to see my friend; **on to** two words

invalid means not valid or of no worth; do not use to refer to disabled or ill people

invariable, **invariably** unchanging; often used wrongly to mean hardly ever changing

ironic, ironically do not use when what you mean is strange, coincidental, paradoxical or amusing (if you mean them say so, or leave it up to the reader to decide). There are times when ironic is right but too often it is misused, as in this typical example from the paper: "Tottenham won 2-0 at Nottingham Forest, ironic really with the north London club having a big interest in Forest's Republic of Ireland midfielder Andy Reid ... " (not that sport are the only, or biggest, offenders).

As Kingsley Amis put it: "The slightest and most banal coincidence or point of resemblance, or even just-perceptible absence of one, unworthy of a single grunt of interest, gets called 'ironical'." The idiotic "post-ironic", which Amis would be glad he did not live to see, is banned

-ise not -ize at end of word, eg maximise, synthesise (exception: capsize)

issue not a synonym for problem ("she has stylebook issues")

italics
Use roman for titles of books, films etc; the only exception is the Review, which by special dispensation is allowed to ignore the generally sound advice of George Bernard Shaw:
    "1 I was reading The Merchant of Venice.
    2 I was reading 'The Merchant of Venice'.
    3 I was reading *The Merchant of Venice*.
The man who cannot see that No 1 is the best looking, as well as the sufficient and sensible form, should print or write nothing but advertisements for lost dogs or ironmongers' catalogues: literature is not for him to meddle with"

Jj

What is the difference between literature and journalism? Journalism is unreadable and literature is not read

Oscar Wilde

Jack Daniel's technically a Tennessee whiskey, not a bourbon

Jacuzzi trademark, named after its inventors, Roy and Candido Jacuzzi; call it a whirlpool bath unless it really is a Jacuzzi

al-Jazeera

jejune unsophisticated (not necessarily to do with being young)

jihad used by Muslims to describe three kinds of struggle: an individual's internal struggle to live out the Muslim faith as well as possible; the struggle to build a good Muslim society; and the struggle to defend Islam, with force if necessary (holy war)

Johns Hopkins University not John Hopkins

judgment call use this phrase only if you delete the word "call"

July 7 2005 the London bombings can appear as 7/7 in headlines

junior abbreviate to Jr not Jun or Jnr, eg Sammy Davis Jr

just deserts not just desserts, unless you only want pudding

Kk

The life of a journalist is poor, nasty, brutish and short.
So is his style

Stella Gibbons

Kaiser Chiefs band from Leeds (no "the"); **Kaizer Chiefs** football
club from Soweto; **Kaiser Wilhelm II** last German emperor and
king of Prussia

kebabs a doner kebab is made using meat from a rotating spit;
shish kebabs are made from skewered cubes of meat

key a useful headline word, but overused

Kings Road a road in Chelsea, west London; try not to call it "the
Kings Road"; no apostrophe, although until 1830 it was a private
royal road

Kirkcaldy not Kirkaldy; a town in Fife, not Fyfe

knots measure of nautical miles an hour, so do not say knots per
hour

koala not koala bear

koi not koi carp

krona plural **kronor** Sweden; **krona** plural **kronur** Iceland; **krone**
plural **kroner** Denmark; **krone** plural **kroner** Norway

Ll

"Away with him! Away with him! He speaks Latin."

William Shakespeare, Henry VI Part 2

laager South African encampment; **lager** beer

Lady Macbeth of Mtsensk Shostakovich opera, traditionally misspelt in the Guardian as Mtensk, with occasional variations such as Mtsenk

Lady Thatcher (and other ladies) not Baroness

larva (plural larvae) insects; **lava** volcanic magma; we often say the former when we mean the latter

laser word dating from 1960 formed from the phrase "light amplification by stimulated emission of radiation", and an example of why not all acronyms need to be capped up

later often redundant, as context will inform the reader: "They will meet this month" rather than "They will meet later this month"

Latin
Some people object to, say, the use of "decimate" to mean destroy on the grounds that in ancient Rome it meant to kill every 10th man; some of them are also likely to complain about so-called split infinitives, a prejudice that goes back to 19th-century Latin teachers who argued that as you can't split infinitives in Latin (they are one word) you shouldn't separate "to" from the verb in

English. Others might even get upset about our alleged misuse of grammatical "case" (including cases such as dative and genitive that no longer exist in English).

. As the Guardian is written in English, rather than Latin, do not worry about any of this even slightly

latitude like this: 21 deg 14 min S

launderette but Stephen Frears' 1985 film was My Beautiful Laundrette

lay off does not mean to sack or make redundant, but to send workers home on part pay because of a temporary lack of demand for their product

lay waste a hurricane can lay waste an island, or lay an island waste, but it does not lay it to waste or lay waste to it (the word comes from the same root as devastate)

led past tense of the verb "lead"; it is surprising how often such sentences as "he lead them to the scene of the crime" find their way into the paper

legal terms in England and Wales, in camera is now known as in secret and in chambers in private; a writ is a claim form and a plaintiff a claimant; leave to appeal is permission to appeal. Since the Children Act 1989, access has been known as contact and custody is known as residence; do not use the older terms

lent past tense of lend; we sometimes say "leant" as in "a gritty drama, leant added authenticity by Jean Tournier's monochrome photography ... "

less or fewer? less means smaller in quantity, eg less money; fewer means smaller in number, eg fewer coins

Lib Dems acceptable for Liberal Democrats after first mention and in headlines

licence noun; **license** verb; you might enjoy your drinks in a licensed premises or take them home from an off-licence

light year a measure of distance, not time

limpid means clear or transparent, not limp

linchpin not lynchpin

literally term used, particularly by sports commentators, to denote an event that is not literally true, as in "Manchester City literally came back from the dead"

Lord Lloyd-Webber but **Andrew Lloyd Webber**

loan noun; the verb is **lend**

loathe detest; **loth** unwilling, not loath

local an adjective, not a noun: talk about local people rather than "locals"

London assembly elected body of 25 members whose role is to hold the mayor of London to account. Together, assembly and mayor constitute the Greater London authority (GLA); note there is no such organisation as the "Greater London assembly"

London boroughs and counties
Parts of the traditional counties of Essex, Middlesex, Kent and Surrey that are close to London retain the county link in their postal addresses (eg Bromley, Kent), even when they are administratively part of a London borough (eg the London borough of Bromley), and represented in the London assembly.

This leads to inconsistencies, as when we refer to "Chingford, Essex" in one story and "Chingford, east London" in another. It is hard to be totally consistent – the preferences even of people who live in such places may vary (according to how long they have lived there, for example).

In general, use London rather than the traditional counties – Ilford, east London; Bexley, south-east London, etc – unless a group or organisation specifically includes a county designation in its title

London's do not say "London's Covent Garden" (or London's anything else); it is Covent Garden, London

longitude like this: 149 deg 18 min E

Lords, House of Lords but **the house**, not the House; **their lordships**

Lord's cricket ground

lowlife plural **lowlifes**, not lowlives (for an eloquent explanation, see Steven Pinker's Words and Rules)

lumpenproletariat

Lycra trademark; the briefly fashionable term "lycra louts" led to complaints from the Lycra lawyers

Mm

I see my name spelt with one word, I want to slap and choke people. If you do that, you got to be a moron ... It's on every poster, every album and every ticket as two words. If you spell it as one, you're an idiot. Bottom line

Meat Loaf

McDonald's hamburgers; the possessive is the same word, eg "McDonald's new vegan-friendly image"

machiavellian after Nicolo Machiavelli (1469-1527)

MB megabytes (storage capacity)

Mbps megabits per second (communication speed); take care to get such terms right: we referred to a "2mbps internet connection" which, at two millibits a second, is about the speed of smoke signals

McJob defined by the OED as "an unstimulating, low-paid job with few prospects, esp one created by the expansion of the service sector"

Mafikeng now spelt thus, though it was Mafeking when it was relieved in 1900

major a major case of overuse; avoid except in a military context: big, main and leading are among the alternatives

Mm

manoeuvre, manoeuvring

marshal (military rank) not marshall, a frequent error; a reader sent in this mnemonic: "Air Chief Marshal Marshall presided at the court martial of the martial arts instructor"

martial law

Mary Celeste not Marie Celeste

massacre the savage killing of large numbers of people, not Stockport County beating Macclesfield Town 5-0

massive massively overused

masterful imperious; **masterly** skilful

May Day May 1; **Mayday** distress signal (from the French *m'aidez!*)

meanwhile usually means "here's a slight change of subject"

Meat Loaf sings, **meatloaf** doesn't

Mecca holy city in Saudi Arabia

mecca as in "Ashton-under-Lyne is a mecca for tripe-eaters"

media plural of medium: the media are sex-obsessed, etc; but a convention of spiritualists would be attended by mediums

medieval not mediaeval

meet, met not meet with, met with someone

mega horrible; do not use

mental handicap, mentally handicapped, mentally retarded
Do not use: say person with learning difficulties

mental health

Take care using language about mental health issues. In addition to such clearly offensive and unacceptable words as loony, maniac, nutter, psycho and schizo, expressions to avoid – because they stereotype and stigmatise – include victim of, suffering from, and afflicted by; "a person with" is clear, accurate and preferable to "a person suffering from". Never use schizophrenic to mean "in two minds", or as a noun. And avoid writing "the mentally ill" – say mentally ill people, mental health patients or people with mental health problems

metric system

The Guardian uses the metric system for weights and measures; exceptions are the mile and the pint. Since understanding of the two systems is a matter of generations, conversions (in brackets) to imperial units should be provided wherever this seems useful, though usually one conversion – the first – will suffice. Imperial units in quoted matter should be retained, and converted to metric [in square brackets] if it doesn't ruin the flow of the quote.

It is not necessary to convert moderate distances between metres and yards, which are close enough for rough and ready purposes (though it is preferable to use metres), or small domestic quantities: two litres of wine, a kilogram of sugar, a couple of pounds of apples, a few inches of string. Small units should be converted when precision is required: 44mm (1.7in) of rain fell in two hours. But be sensible: don't convert a metric estimate into a precise imperial figure (round the conversion up or down). Tons and tonnes are close enough for most purposes to do without conversion; use tonnes (except in shipping tonnage).

Body weights and heights should always be converted in brackets: metres to feet and inches, kilograms to stones/pounds. Geographical heights and depths, of people, buildings, monuments, etc, should be converted, metres to feet. In square measurement, land is given in sq metres, hectares and sq km, with sq yards, acres or sq miles in brackets where there is space to provide a conversion. The floor areas of buildings are conventionally expressed in sq metres (or sq ft). Take great care in conversions of square and cubic measures

Middle-earth (Tolkien) not Middle Earth

Middle East never Mid, even in headlines

Middlesbrough, Teesside not Middlesborough, Teeside

militate or mitigate? to militate against something is to influence it (his record militated against his early release); to mitigate means to lessen an offence (in mitigation, her counsel argued that she came from a broken home)

million in copy use m for sums of money, units or inanimate objects: £10m, 45m tonnes of coal, 30m doses of vaccine; but million for people or animals: 1 million people, 23 million rabbits, etc; use m in headlines

Minnelli, Liza note that it's "Liza with a Zee, not Lisa with an Ess"

minority ethnic (adjective) rather than ethnic minority

Moby-Dick Herman Melville's classic is, believe it or not, hyphenated

mongooses (not mongeese) plural of mongoose

more than generally preferable to over: there were more than 20,000 people at the game, it will cost more than £100 to get it fixed; but she is over 18

mother of parliaments the great 19th-century Liberal politician and Manchester Guardian reader John Bright described England, the country (not Westminster, the institution), as the mother of parliaments

Mötley Crüe, Motörhead include "heavy metal umlauts"

Muhammad
Muslims consider Muhammad to be the last of God's prophets, who delivered God's final message. They recognise Moses and Jesus as prophets also. The above transliteration is our style for the

prophet's name and for most Muhammads living in Arab countries, though where someone's preferred spelling is known we respect it, eg Mohamed Al Fayed, Mohamed ElBaradei

mum or Mum? How is your mum? I don't know, I've not spoken to Mum for two years

Murphy's law "If there are two or more ways to do something, and one of those ways can result in a catastrophe, then someone will do it"; also known as sod's law

Muzak trademark; better to call it easy listening, loungecore, or a similar variant

myriad a large, unspecified number; use as an adjective (there are myriad people outside) or a noun (there is a myriad of people outside), but not "myriads of"

Nn

Trust your editor, and you'll sleep on straw

John Cheever

names

Prominent figures can just be named in stories, with their function at second mention: "Alistair Darling said last night ... " (first mention); "the chancellor added ... " (subsequent mentions). Where it is thought necessary to explain who someone is, write "Kevin Blackwell, the Sheffield United manager, said" or "the Sheffield United manager, Kevin Blackwell, said".

In such cases the commas around the name indicate there is only one person in the position, so write "the Tory leader, David Cameron, said" (only one person in the job), but "the former Tory prime minister John Major said" (there have been many).

Do not leave out the definite article in such constructions as "language guru David Marsh said ... " It should be "The language guru David Marsh" (if there are other language gurus) or "David Marsh, the language guru, ... " (if you feel only one person merits such a description)

nation

Do not use when you mean country or state; reserve nation to describe people united by language, culture and history so as to form a distinct group within a larger territory. And beware of attributing the actions of a government or a military force to a national population (eg, "The Israelis have killed 400 children during the intifada"). Official actions always have opponents within a population; if we don't acknowledge this, we oversimplify the situation and shortchange the opponents

Native Americans Geronimo was a Native American (not an American Indian or Red Indian); George Bush is a native American

naught nothing; **nought** the figure 0

neophilia
Even if you have always wanted to appear in Private Eye, resist the temptation to write such nonsense as "grey is the new black", "billiards is the new snooker", "Barnsley is the new Tuscany", etc

Netherlands, the not Holland, which is only part of the country; use Dutch as the adjective. Exception: the Dutch football team is generally known as Holland

new often redundant, as in "a new report said yesterday"

New Labour but old Labour

newspaper titles the Guardian, the New York Times, etc, do not write "the Sun newspaper" etc, patronising and unnecessary

no-brainer means something along the lines of "this is so obvious, you don't need a brain to know it" not "only someone with no brain would think this"

no doubt that, no question that are opposites: "There was no doubt that he was lying" means he was lying; "There was no question that he was lying" means he wasn't, although the two are routinely confused

no one not no-one

north north London, north Wales, north-west England, the north-west, etc

now useful for emphasis, but is now used far too often

numbers
Spell out from one to nine; numerals from 10 to 999,999; thereafter use m or bn for sums of money, quantities or inanimate

objects in copy, eg £10m, 5bn tonnes of coal, 30m doses of vaccine;
but million or billion for people or animals, eg 1 million people,
3 billion rabbits, etc; spell trillion in full at first mention, then tn;
in headlines use m, bn or tn

Nn

numeracy

Numbers have always contained power, and many a journalist will
tremble at the very sight of them. But most often the only maths
we need to make sense of them is simple arithmetic. Far more
important are our critical faculties, all too often switched off at
the first sniff of a figure.

It's easy to be hoodwinked by big numbers in particular. But are
they really so big? Compared with what? And what is being
assumed? A government announcement of an extra £X million a
year will look far less impressive if divided by 60 million (the
British population) and/or 52 (weeks in the year). That's quite
apart from the fact that it was probably trumpeted last week
already, as part of another, bigger number. We have to be
aggressive when interpreting the spin thrown at us.

The legal profession has, in the same way, been forced to put
DNA evidence in the dock. If the probability of the accused and
the culprit sharing the same genetic profile is one in 3million,
then there are 19 other people in Britain alone who share the
same DNA "match".

Never invent a big figure when a small one will do. Totting
jail sentences together ("the six men were jailed for a total of
87 years") is meaningless as well as irritating. Similarly, saying
that something has an area the size of 150 football pitches, or is
"eight times the size of Wales [or Belgium]", is cliched and may
not be helpful

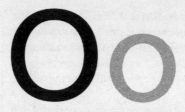

Oo

I try to leave out the parts that people skip

Elmore Leonard

OAPs, old age pensioners do not use: they are pensioners or old people; note also that we should take care using the word elderly – it should not be used to describe anyone younger than 70

obtuse "mentally slow or emotionally insensitive" (Collins); often confused with abstruse (hard to understand) or obscure

Occam's razor philosophical principle, attributed to the 14th-century English friar William of Ockham, that broadly means prefer the simplest explanation, adopting the one that makes the fewest assumptions and "shaving away" the rest

Oceania a preferable term to Australasia, it comprises Australia, New Zealand, Melanesia, Micronesia and Polynesia

Oh! not O!

OK is OK; okay is not

Olympic games or just Olympics or the games

ongoing prefer continuous or continual

on to not onto
Kingsley Amis, perhaps slightly overstating his case, argued: "I have found by experience that no one persistently using onto writes anything much worth reading"

Oo

or
Do not use "or" when explaining or amplifying – rather than "the NUT, or National Union of Teachers" say "The NUT (National Union of Teachers)" or, even better, "The National Union of Teachers" at first mention and then just "the NUT" or "the union"

outside not "outside of"

over not overly

overestimate, **overstate** take care that you don't mean underestimate or understate (we often get this wrong)

Oxford comma a comma before the final "and" in lists: straightforward ones (he had ham, eggs and chips) do not need one, but sometimes it can help the reader (he had cereal, kippers, bacon, eggs, toast and marmalade, and tea), and sometimes it is essential: compare
> I dedicate this book to my parents, Martin Amis, and JK Rowling
with
> I dedicate this book to my parents, Martin Amis and JK Rowling

oxymoron does not just vaguely mean self-contradictory; an oxymoron is a figure of speech in which apparently contradictory terms are used in conjunction, such as bittersweet, "darkness visible" (Paradise Lost), "the living dead" (The Waste Land); one of Margaret Atwood's characters thought "interesting Canadian" was an oxymoron

Pp

Journalism is the ability to meet the challenge of filling space

Rebecca West

pace Latin tag meaning "by the leave of", as a courteous nod to the views of a dissenting author, or "even acknowledging the existence of", not "such as"

palate roof of the mouth, sense of taste; **palette** used by an artist to mix paint; **pallet** hard bed, wooden frame moved by forklift truck

palindrome A man, a plan, a canal. Panama!

paparazzo plural **paparazzi**; named after a character in Fellini's 1960 film La Dolce Vita

Parkinson's law "Work expands so as to fill the time available for its completion"

parliament, parliamentary but cap up those parliaments referred to by their name in the relevant language, eg Knesset, Folketing, Duma, etc

Parthenon marbles official name, recognised by both Britain and Greece, for the Elgin marbles

patients are discharged from hospital, not released

pedaller cyclist; **peddler** drug dealer; **pedlar** hawker

per avoid; use English: "She earns £30,000 a year" is better than "per year". If you must use it, the Latin preposition is followed by another Latin word, eg per capita, not per head. Exception: miles per hour, which we write mph

per cent % in headlines and copy

percentage rises probably our most common lapse into "mythematics": an increase from 3% to 5% is a 2 percentage point increase or a 2-point increase, not a 2% increase; any sentence saying "such and such rose or fell by X%" should be considered and checked carefully

persons No! They are people (can you imagine Barbra Streisand singing "Persons who need persons"?)

photocall, photo-finish, photo opportunity

pi the ratio of the circumference of a circle to its diameter, as every schoolgirl knows

Pimm's the most popular version is Pimm's No 1 cup, which has gin as its base (the others are or were No 2, whisky; No 3, brandy; No 4, rum; No 5, rye; and No 6, vodka)

pin or **pin number** not Pin or PIN number

pixelated an image divided into pixels, the basic unit of representation on a TV or computer screen, or to display a person or object in pixels to disguise their identity; **pixilated** drunk

placename

planets cap up planets of our solar system: Mercury, Venus, Earth, Mars, Jupiter, Saturn, Uranus and Neptune; note that Pluto is now classified as a dwarf planet, along with Ceres and Eris; the sun and the Earth's moon are lc, but named moons are capped up: Europa, Io, etc

planning not "forward planning"

plea, pledge words used all the time by journalists (particularly when writing headlines), but only rarely by normal people

poetry
Separate the lines with spaces and a slash; italics are acceptable: I struck the board and cry'd, 'No more; / I will abroad.' / What, shall I ever sigh and pine? / My lines and life are free; free as the rode, / Loose as the winde, as large as store.

Polari
A form of language used mostly by gay men and lesbians, derived in part from slang used by sailors, actors and prostitutes and popularised in the 1960s BBC radio comedy Round the Horne by the characters Julian and Sandy. Example: "Vada the dolly eke on the bona omee ajax" (Look at the gorgeous face on that nice man over there); "naff" is an example of Polari that has passed into more general use, as are "butch", "camp" and "dizzy"

political correctness a term to be avoided on the grounds that it is, in Polly Toynbee's words, "an empty rightwing smear designed only to elevate its user"

political parties lc for word "party", eg Official Monster Raving Loony party

Portakabin, Portaloo trademark; say portable building, portable toilets

practising homosexual
Do not use this expression, or the equally grotesque "active homosexual"; where it is necessary to discuss someone's sex life, for example a story about gay clergy, it is possible to use other expressions, eg the Anglican church demands celibacy from gay clergy but permits the laity to have sexually active relationships
pre- redundant in such newly fashionable words as pre-booked, pre-reserved, pre-ordered, and even pre-rehearsed

presently means soon, not at present

press, the singular: the British press is a shining example to the rest of the world

pretext by its nature false, so while it may or may not be true that Tony Blair went to war on a pretext, it is tautologous to say he did so on a false one

prevaricate "to speak or act falsely with intent to deceive" (Collins); often confused with **procrastinate**, to put something off

primate another word for archbishop; Primate of All England: Archbishop of Canterbury; Primate of England: Archbishop of York; but "the primate" on second reference

primates higher members of the order *Primates*, essentially apes and humans

principal first in importance; principle standard of conduct

prison officer not warder, a term that the Prison Officers' Association regards as "degrading, insulting and historically inaccurate" (the Home Office changed it from warder in 1922)

proactive do not use this hideous jargon word with a hyphen. Or without one

probe a dental implement, not an inquiry or investigation

pro-choice but **anti-abortion** (not "pro-life")

prodigal wasteful or extravagant, not a returned wanderer; the confusion arises from the biblical parable of the prodigal son. A very common mistake

profile a noun, not a verb

Proms concerts; **proms** seafronts

prone face down; **supine** face up

proofreader, proofreading

prophecy noun; **prophesy** verb

protester not protestor

proved or proven? beware the creeping "proven", featuring (mispronounced) in every other TV ad; proven is not the normal past tense of prove, but a term in Scottish law ("not proven") and in certain English idioms, eg "proven record"

province avoid using this term to refer to Northern Ireland

public schools are actually private schools, so that is what we should call them

"There's nothing to it [subediting], really ... it's just a
matter of checking the facts and the spelling, crossing
out the first sentence, and removing any attempts at
jokes."

Michael Frayn, Towards the End of the Morning

al-Qaida Osama bin Laden's organisation; it means "the base"

quantum jump, quantum leap in any area other than physics,
a cliche best avoided (unless you are referring to the cult
70s band Quantum Jump or the cult 90s TV series Quantum Leap)

Queen, the if it is necessary to say so, she is Her Majesty or HM,
never HRH

Queen's Park Scotland's oldest football club, winners of the
Scottish Cup 10 times in the 19th century and twice runners-up in
the FA Cup

Queens Park Rangers (no apostrophe) English football club

queueing not queuing

quiz a suspect is questioned, not quizzed (however tempting for
headline purposes)

quotes

Take care with direct speech: our readers should be confident that words appearing in quotation marks accurately represent the actual words uttered by the speaker, though ums and ahems can be removed and bad grammar improved. If you aren't sure of the exact wording, use indirect speech.

Where a lot of material has been left out, start off a new quote with "He added: ... ", or signify this with an ellipsis. Take particular care when extracting from printed material, for example a minister's resignation letter.

Introduce the speaker from the beginning, or after the first sentence: it is confusing and frustrating to read several sentences or even paragraphs of a quote before finding out who is saying it.

Stories peppered with separately quoted words and short phrases are extremely irritating to the reader, and make it look as if we did not manage to catch the speaker's words properly. So when we reported that "the business community was accused of 'cynicism' in the fight against climate change yesterday" and "journalists said that the possible sale of the paper was 'dangerous' for their editorial independence" there is no need to quote the words cynicism and dangerous

Qur'an not Koran

Rr

'It will be proved to thy face that thou hast men about thee that usually talk of a noun and a verb, and such abominable words as no Christian ear can endure to hear.'

William Shakespeare, Henry VI Part 2

racial terminology
The words black and Asian should not be used as nouns, but as adjectives. Say African-Caribbean rather than Afro-Caribbean. Use the word "immigrant" with great care, not only because it is often incorrectly used to describe people who were born in Britain, but also because it has been used negatively for so many years.

Just as in the Balkans or anywhere else, internal African peoples should, where possible, be called ethnic groups or communities rather than "tribes"

rack and ruin; **rack** one's brains; **racked** by guilt or pain, not wracked

radiographer takes x-rays; **radiologist** reads them

raft something you float on; do not say "a raft of measures", which has very rapidly become a cliche (particularly in political reporting)

Rangers not Glasgow Rangers

re or re-?
Use re- (with hyphen) when followed by the vowels e or u (not pronounced as "yu"): eg re-entry, re-examine, re-urge.

Use re (no hyphen) when followed by the vowels a, i, o or u (pronounced as "yu"), or any consonant: eg rearm, rearrange, reassemble, reiterate, reorder, reread, reuse, rebuild, reconsider.

Exceptions (where confusion with another word would arise): re-cover/recover, re-form (to form again)/reform (to change for the better), re-creation/recreation, re-sign/resign

recent avoid: if the date is relevant, use it

refute use this much abused word only when an argument is disproved; otherwise contest, deny, rebut

regalia plural, of royalty; "royal regalia" is tautologous

register office not registry office

repellant noun; **repellent** adjective: you fight repellent insects with an insect repellant

residents has a rather old-fashioned feel to it, especially in the deadly form "local residents"; on the whole, better to call them people

reticent unwilling to speak; do not confuse with reluctant, as in this example from the paper: "Like most graduates of limited financial means, Louise Clark was reticent about handing over a huge wad of dosh"

the Rev at first mention, thereafter surname only: eg the Rev Joan Smith, subsequently Smith; never say "Reverend Smith", "the Reverend Smith" or "Rev Smith"

Revelation last book in the New Testament: not Revelations, a very common error; its full name is The Revelation of St John the Divine (anyone calling it "Revelations" will burn in hell for eternity)

Richter scale expresses the magnitude of an earthquake, but now largely superseded by the moment magnitude scale

riffle to flick through a book, newspaper or magazine; often confused with **rifle**, to search or ransack and steal from, eg rifle goods from a shop

rock'n'roll one word

routeing or routing? They are routeing buses through the city centre after the routing of the protesters

Rovers Return, the (no apostrophe) Coronation Street's pub

royal family

Rule, Britannia!

Ss

The practice of hinting by single letters those expletives with which profane and violent people are wont to garnish their discourse, strikes me as a proceeding which, however well meant, is weak and futile. I cannot tell what good it does – what feeling it spares – what horror it conceals

Charlotte Brontë

saccharin noun; **saccharine** adjective

sacrilegious not sacreligious

Sad seasonal affective disorder

said normally preferable to added, commented, declared, pointed out, ejaculated, etc; you can avoid too many "saids", whether quoting someone or in reported speech, quite easily

Saint in running text should be spelt in full: Saint John, Saint Paul. For names of towns, churches, etc, abbreviate St (no point) eg St Mirren, St Stephen's church

St James Park home of Exeter City; **St James' Park** home of Newcastle United; **St James's Park** royal park in London

St John Ambulance not St John's and no longer "Brigade"

Samaritans the organisation has dropped "the" from its name

Ss

San Serriffe island nation profiled in the Guardian on April 1 1977; **sans serif** typeface

Satan but **satanist, satanism**

satnav

Sats standard assessment tasks

SATs scholastic aptitude tests (in the US, where they are pronounced as individual letters)

schizophrenia, schizophrenic use only in a medical context, never to mean "in two minds", contradictory, or erratic, which is wrong, as well as offensive to people diagnosed with this illness; schizophrenic should never be used as a noun

Schwarzenegger, Arnold Arnie is acceptable in headlines

scientific names in italics, with the first name (denoting the genus) capped, the second (denoting the species) lc; *Escherichia coli, Quercus robur.* The name can be shortened by using the first initial: *E coli, Q robur* (but we do not use a full point after the initial)

scientific terms some silly cliches you may wish to avoid: you would find it difficult to hesitate for a nanosecond (the shortest measurable human hesitation is probably about 250 million nanoseconds, or a quarter of a second); "astronomical sums" when talking about large sums of money is rather dated (the national debt surpassed the standard astronomical unit of 93 million [miles] 100 years ago)

Scotland
The following was written by a Scot who works for the Guardian and lives in London. Letters expressing similar sentiments come from across Britain (and, indeed, from around the world):
We don't carry much coverage of events in Scotland and to be honest, even as an expat, that suits me fine. But I do care very much that we acknowledge that Scotland is a separate nation and

Ss

in many ways a separate country. It has different laws, education system (primary, higher and further), local government, national government, sport, school terms, weather, property market and selling system, bank holidays, right to roam, banks and money, churches etc.

If we really want to be a national newspaper then we need to consider whether our stories apply only to England (and Wales) or Britain, or Scotland only. When we write about teachers' pay deals, we should point out that we mean teachers in England and Wales; Scottish teachers have separate pay and management structures and union. When we write about it being half term, we should remember that there's no such thing in Scotland. When we write about bank holiday sunshine/rain, we should remember that in Scotland the weather was probably different and it possibly wasn't even a bank holiday. When we write a back-page special on why the English cricket team is crap, we should be careful not to refer to it as "we" and "us". When the Scottish Cup final is played, we should perhaps consider devoting more than a few paragraphs at the foot of a page to Rangers winning their 100th major trophy (if it had been Manchester United we'd have had pages and pages with Bobby Charlton's all-time fantasy first XI and a dissertation on why English clubs are the best in Europe).

These daily oversights come across to a Scot as arrogance. They also undermine confidence in what the paper is telling the reader

---

Scott, Charles Prestwich (1846-1932) editor of the Manchester Guardian for 57 years and its owner from 1907 until his death (his uncle, John Edward Taylor, had founded the paper in 1821). Scott, who was editor when the first "Style-book of the Manchester Guardian" – forerunner of this publication – appeared in 1928, is most famous for his "comment is free, but facts are sacred"

Scouts not "Boy Scouts" (in the UK, at least); the organisation is the Scout Association

Scoville scale system that measures the heat level of chillies

seal pups not "baby seals" for the same reason we don't call lambs "baby sheep"

seas, **oceans** uc, eg Black Sea, Caspian Sea, Pacific Ocean

Ss

seasons spring, summer, autumn, winter, all lc

seize not sieze

senior abbreviate to Sr not Sen or Snr, eg George Bush Sr

September 11 9/11 is acceptable

set to
It is very tempting to use this, especially in headlines, when we think something is going to happen, but aren't all that sure; try to resist this temptation. It is even less excusable when we do know that something is going to happen: one of our readers counted no fewer than 16 uses of the phrase in the paper in two days; in almost every case, the words could have been replaced with "will", or by simply leaving out the "set", eg "the packs are set to come into force as part of the house-selling process"

Sgt Pepper's Lonely Hearts Club Band 1967 album by a popular beat combo of the day; not Sergeant Pepper's Lonely Hearts Club Band

Shetland or **the Shetland Isles** but never "the Shetlands"

shiatsu massage; **shih-tzu** dog

ships not feminine: it ran aground, not she ran aground

shoo-in not shoe-in

shrank not shrunk, except in the film title Honey, I Shrunk the Kids (and perhaps the occasional piece of wordplay based on it)

siege not seige

silicon computer chips; **silicone** breast implants – we have been known to confuse the two, as in "Silicone Valley"

Ss

Sinn Féin

slavery was not abolished in 1807, as we sometimes say: slavery in Britain became illegal in 1772, the slave trade in the British empire was abolished in 1807, but slavery remained in the colonies until the Slavery Abolition Act 1833

so-called overused: as a reader pointed out when we used the term "so-called friendly fire", the expression is "obviously ironic and really doesn't need such ham-fisted pointing out"

soi-disant means self-styled, not so-called; both phrases should be used sparingly

some do not use before a figure: if you are not sure, about or approximately are better, and if you are, it sounds daft: "some 12 people have died from wasp stings this year alone" was a particularly silly example that found its way into the paper

spacehopper

spark overused in headlines of the "rates rise sparks fury" variety

spellchecker
If you use one, read through your work afterwards: a graphic on our front page was rendered nonsensical when a spellcheck turned the species *Aquila adalberti* into "alleyway adalberti", while *Prunella modularis* became "pronely modularise"; also note that most use American English spellings

spelled or spelt? she spelled it out for him: "the word is spelt like this"

spinster avoid this old-fashioned term, which has acquired a pejorative tone; say, if relevant, that someone is an unmarried woman

spiral, spiralling prices (and other things) can spiral down as well as up; try a less cliched word that doesn't suggest a circular movement

Ss

staff are plural

stalemate in chess, a stalemate is the end of the game, and cannot be broken or resolved; deadlock or impasse are more suitable for metaphorical use

stationary not moving; **stationery** writing materials

stepchange avoid, unless you are quoting someone; change is perfectly adequate

still life plural **still lifes**

stone age
As recently as 2006, we used the phrase "stone age tribe" in a headline to describe the inhabitants of the Andaman Islands. The charity Survival says: " 'Stone age' and 'primitive' have been used to describe tribal people since the colonial era, reinforcing the idea that they have not changed over time and that they are backward. This idea is both incorrect and very dangerous: incorrect because all societies adapt and change, and dangerous because it is often used to justify the persecution or forced 'development' of tribal people"

stylebook but **style guide**

Subbuteo table football game where players "flick to kick", named after the bird of prey *Falco subbuteo* (the hobby)

sudoku

suffer little children nothing to do with suffering, this frequently misquoted or misunderstood phrase was used by Christ (Luke 18:16) to mean "allow the little children to come to me"; it is also the title of a song about the Moors murders on the first Smiths album

suicide
Say that someone killed him or herself rather than "committed suicide"; suicide has not been a crime in the UK for many years

Ss

and this old-fashioned term can cause unnecessary further distress to families who have been bereaved in this way.

Journalists should exercise particular care in reporting suicide or issues involving suicide, bearing in mind the risk of encouraging others. This applies to presentation, including the use of pictures, and to describing the method of suicide. Any substances should be referred to in general rather than specific terms.

When appropriate, a helpline number (eg Samaritans) should be given. The feelings of relatives should also be carefully considered

supermarkets Marks & Spencer or M&S, Morrisons, Safeway, Sainsbury's, Tesco (no wonder people get confused about apostrophes)

supermodel every new face who makes a name for herself these days is labelled a supermodel; model is normally sufficient

surge prefer rise or increase, if that is the meaning; but surge is preferable to "upsurge"

supersede not supercede

svengali (lc) although named after the sinister Svengali in George du Maurier's 1894 novel Trilby

swap not swop

swath, **swaths** broad strip, eg cut a wide swath; **swathe**, **swathes** baby clothes, bandage, wrappings

swearwords
The Guardian editor's guidelines are as follows:

First, remember the reader, and respect demands that we should not casually use words that are likely to offend.

Second, use such words only when absolutely necessary to the facts of a piece, or to portray a character in an article; there is almost never a case in which we need to use a swearword outside direct quotes.

Third, the stronger the swearword, the harder we ought to think about using it.

Finally, never use asterisks, which are just a cop-out (as elegantly put by Charlotte Brontë in the quotation at the beginning of this section)

Ss

Tt

I will have none of your damned cutting and slashing ...
You shan't make canticles out of my canto [Don Juan] ...
I will not give way to all the cant of Christendom

Lord Byron

T (not tee) as in it suited her to a T, he had it down to a T

Taliban plural (it means "students")

Tamiflu not a vaccine for bird flu, as often described: it's an antibiotic used to treat it

Tate the original London gallery in Millbank, now known as Tate Britain, houses British art from the 16th century; Tate Modern, at Southwark, south London, Tate Liverpool and Tate St Ives, in Cornwall, all house modern art

tax avoidance is legal; **tax evasion** is illegal

teams
Sports teams take plural verbs: Australia have won by an innings, Wednesday were relegated again, etc; but note that in a business context they are singular like other companies, eg Leeds United reported its biggest loss to date

Teletubbies they are: Tinky Winky (purple); Laa-Laa (yellow); Dipsy (green); and Po (red)

temperatures thus: 30C (85F) – ie celsius, with fahrenheit in brackets on first mention

Ten Commandments

terrorism
A terrorist act is directed against victims chosen either randomly or as symbols of what is being opposed (eg workers in the World Trade Centre, tourists in Bali, Spanish commuters). It is designed to create a state of terror in the minds of a particular group of people or the public as a whole for political or social ends. Although most terrorist acts are violent, you can be a terrorist without being overtly violent (eg poisoning a water supply or gassing people on the underground).

Does having a good cause make a difference? The UN says no: "Criminal acts calculated to provoke a state of terror in the general public are in any circumstances unjustifiable, whatever the considerations of a political, philosophical, ideological, racial, ethnic, religious or other nature that may be invoked to justify them."

Whatever one's political sympathies, suicide bombers, the 9/11 attackers and most paramilitary groups can all reasonably be regarded as terrorists (or at least groups some of whose members perpetrate terrorist acts). Nonetheless we need to be very careful about using the term: it is still a subjective judgment – one person's terrorist may be another person's freedom fighter, and there are former "terrorists" holding elected office in many parts of the world. Some critics suggest that, for the Guardian, all terrorists are militants – unless their victims are British. Others may point to what they regard as "state terrorism".

Often, alternatives such as militants, radicals, separatists, etc, may be more appropriate and less controversial, but this is a difficult area: references to the "resistance", for example, imply more sympathy to a cause than calling such fighters "insurgents". The most important thing is that, in news reporting, we are not seen – because of the language we use – to be taking sides.

Note that the phrase "war on terror" should always appear in quotes, whether used by us or (more likely) quoting someone else

Tt

Tt

the
Leaving "the" out often reads like jargon: say the conference
agreed to do something, not "conference agreed"; the government
has to do, not "government has to"; the Super League (rugby), not
"Super League".

Avoid the "prime minister Gordon Brown" syndrome: do not
use constructions such as "prime minister Gordon Brown said".
Prominent figures can just be named, with their function at
second mention: "Gordon Brown said last night" (first mention);
"the prime minister said" (subsequent mentions).

lc for newspapers (the Guardian), magazines (the New
Statesman), pubs (the Coach and Horses), bands (the Beatles, the
Black Eyed Peas, the The), nicknames (the Hulk, the Red Baron),
and sports grounds (the Oval).

uc for books (The Lord of the Rings), films (The Matrix), poems
(The Waste Land), television shows (The West Wing), and
placenames (The Hague)

theirs no apostrophe

thinktank one word

third world meaning not the west (first) or the Soviet Union
(second), so today an outdated (as well as objectionable) term; use
developing countries or developing nations

tidal wave just what it says it is; tsunami huge wave caused by an
underwater earthquake

times noon, midnight, 1am, 6.30pm, etc; 10 o'clock last night but
10pm yesterday; half past two, a quarter to three, 10 to 11, etc; for
24-hour clock, 00.47, 23.59

Tipp-Ex trademark; use correction fluid (not that many people do
any more)

told the Guardian we use this phrase too often: it should
normally be replaced by "said" and reserved for occasions when it
genuinely adds interest or authority to a story (if someone got an
exclusive interview with, say, Osama bin Laden)

Tolkien, JRR (1892-1973) British author and philologist, notable for writing The Lord of the Rings and not spelling his name "Tolkein".

Tt

tomato plural tomatoes

tortuous a tortuous road is one that winds or twists

torturous a torturous experience is one that involves pain or suffering

Townshend, Pete one of the two members of the Who who didn't die before he got old (the other is Roger Daltrey)

trademarks
Take care: use a generic alternative unless there is a very good reason not to, eg ballpoint pen, not biro (unless it really is a Biro, in which case it takes a cap B); say photocopy rather than Xerox, etc; you will save our lawyers, and those of Portakabin and various other companies, a lot of time and trouble

Travellers capped: they are recognised as an ethnic group under the Race Relations Act; but note **new age travellers**

Trekkers how to refer to Star Trek fans unless you want to make fun of them, in which case they are **Trekkies**

trillion a thousand billion (1 followed by 12 noughts), abbreviate like this: $25tn

try to never "try and", eg "I will try to do something about this misuse of language"

turgid does not mean apathetic or sluggish – that's torpid – but swollen, congested, or (when used of language) pompous or bombastic

Uu

I believe more in the scissors than I do in the pencil

Truman Capote

uber no accent if you are saying something like uber-hip, but use the umlaut if you are quoting German

UK or **Britain** in copy and headlines for the United Kingdom of Great Britain and Northern Ireland (but note Great Britain comprises just England, Scotland and Wales)

Ukraine no "the"; adjective Ukrainian

Ulster avoid if possible but acceptable in headlines to mean Northern Ireland, which in fact comprises six of the nine counties of the province of Ulster

Uluru formerly known as Ayers Rock

uncharted not unchartered

under way not underway

uneducated "with no formal education" may be more appropriate

unique one of a kind, so cannot be qualified as "absolutely unique", "very unique" etc

until not "up until"

unveiled pictures are, as are cars sometimes, but these days almost everything seems to be – so the government "unveiled a raft of new policies" (two cliches and a redundant "new" in six words) or a company "unveiled record profits". There is nothing wrong with announcing, reporting, presenting or publishing

upcoming the coining and, even worse, use of such jargon words is likely to make many otherwise liberal, enlightened Guardian readers (and stylebook editors) wonder if there is not after all a case to bring back capital, or at least corporal, punishment for crimes against the English language; an editor once told his staff: "If I read upcoming in the Wall Street Journal again, I shall be downcoming and somebody will be outgoing"

US for United States, not USA; no need to spell out, even at first mention; America is also acceptable

U-turn

Uu

Vv

Substitute 'damn' every time you're inclined to write 'very'. Your editor will delete it and the writing will be just as it should be

Mark Twain

v (roman) for versus, not vs: England v Australia, Rushden & Diamonds v Sheffield Wednesday, etc

Valium trademark; a brand of diazepam

venal open to bribery; **venial** easily forgiven

very usually very redundant

vicar a cleric of the Anglican church (which also has rectors and curates, etc), not of any other denomination. A priest writes: "A vicar is a person who is the incumbent of a parish, and the term is a job description in the same way that editor is a job description. All editors are journalists but not all journalists are editors. In the same way, all vicars are priests, but not all priests are vicars. Some priests are chaplains; some (like me) are forensic social workers; some are retired; some are shopworkers; some are police officers"

virus not the same as a bacterium, but we often confuse the two. MRSA, TB and legionnaires' disease are examples of bacteria; HIV, measles and influenza are viruses

vortex plural **vortices**

Some editors are failed writers, but so are most writers

TS Eliot

Wags wives and girlfriends (generally of footballers: the term was popularised during the 2006 World Cup); the singular is Wag. Now in danger of overuse, and arguably sexist – although variations include Habs (husbands and boyfriends)

Wahhabism branch of Islam practised by followers of the teachings of Muhammad ibn Abd-al-Wahhab (1703-92)

wake "in the wake of" is overused; nothing wrong with "as a result of" or simply "after"

Wales avoid the word "principality"; not a unit of measurement ("50 times the size of Wales")

"war on terror" always in quotes

wars
first world war, second world war (do not say "before the war" or "after the war" when you mean the second world war)

Waste Land, The poem by TS Eliot (not Wasteland)

Waterstone's bookshop

Watford Gap a service area on the M1 in Northamptonshire, named after a nearby village 80 miles north of London; nothing to

do with the Hertfordshire town of Watford, with which it is sometimes confused by lazy writers who think such phrases as "anyone north of the Watford Gap" a witty way to depict the unwashed northern hordes

wayzgoose traditional term for a printers' works outing

web, **webpage**, **website**, **world wide web**

welch (not welsh) to fail to honour an obligation

well-known as with famous, if someone or something is well-known, it should not be necessary to say so

West Bank barrier should always be called a barrier when referred to in its totality, as it is in places a steel and barbed-wire fence and in others an 8 metre-high concrete wall

what is a phrase that, while occasionally helpful to add emphasis, has become overused to the point of tedium; examples from the paper include:

"Beckham repaid the committed public support with what was a man-of-the-match performance ... "

"Principal among Schofield's 19 recommendations in what is a wide-ranging report ... "

What is clear is that these sentences would be improved by what would be the simple step of removing the offending phrase

wheelchair say (if relevant) that someone uses a wheelchair, not that they are "in a wheelchair" or "wheelchair-bound" – stigmatising and offensive, as well as inaccurate

whence means where from, so don't write "from whence"

whereabouts singular: her whereabouts is not known

while not whilst

whisky plural **whiskies**; but Irish and US **whiskey**

Wi-Fi trademark; the generic term is wireless computer network

Windermere not Lake Windermere; note that Windermere is also the name of the town

Worcestershire sauce not Worcester

World Trade Centre but **twin towers**

worldwide but **world wide web**

wrinklies patronising, unfunny way to refer to elderly people; do not use

WWE World Wrestling Entertainment, formerly the World Wrestling Federation

WWF formerly the World Wide Fund for Nature (or, in the US, World Wildlife Fund)

Ww

XxYyZz

Editors are craftsmen, ghosts, psychiatrists, bullies, sparring partners, experts, enablers, ignoramuses, translators, writers, goalies, friends, firemen, wimps, ditch diggers, mind readers, coaches, bomb throwers, muses and spittoon – sometimes all while working on the same piece

Gary Kamiya, Salon.com

Xbox

xenophobe, xenophobia, xenophobic

Xerox trademark; say photocopy

Xhosa South African ethnic group and language

Xi'an city in China where the Terracotta Warriors are located

Xmas avoid; use Christmas unless writing a headline, up against a deadline, and desperate

x-ray

years 2007-10; but between 2007 and 2010, not "between 2007-10"

yes campaign, no campaign not Yes or "yes" campaign

yesterday
Take care where you place the time element in a story: do not automatically place it at the start ("Gordon Brown last night insisted ... "). Constructions such as "the two sides were today to consider", as we have been known to say, sound ugly and artificial.

As with headlines, try reading out loud to find the most natural arrangement

Yorkshire North Yorkshire, South Yorkshire, West Yorkshire but east Yorkshire

yorkshire pudding, yorkshire terrier

young turks

yours no apostrophe

yuan Chinese currency; we don't call it renminbi

-ze endings: use -se, even if this upsets your (American) spellchecker, eg emphasise, realise; but capsize

zeitgeist

zero plural zeros

Zeta-Jones, Catherine

zeugma eg "The queen takes counsel and tea"
(Alexander Pope)

zhoosh an example of gay slang (see Polari), used in the fashion industry and on US television shows such as Will and Grace and Queer Eye for the Straight Guy, it has various shades of meaning: (noun) clothing, ornamentation; (verb) zhoosh your hair, zhoosh yourself up; zhooshy (adjective) showy

Zimmer trademark; if it's not a Zimmer frame, call it a walking frame

Zionist refers to someone who believes in the right for a Jewish national home to exist within historic Palestine; someone who wants the borders of that entity to be expanded is not an "ultra-Zionist" but might be described as a hardliner, hawk or rightwinger

I am about to – or I am going to – die; either expression is used
Last words of 17th-century French Jesuit grammarian Dominique Bouhours

Writers' directory

Approaching publishers and agents

On the following pages you'll find a comprehensive list of publishers, agents and associations, with details. Linda Newbery offers advice on how to make that all-important first contact.

It's a bit of a catch-22, whether to approach an agent first or go directly to publishers. It's hard to get a book published without an agent; it's hard to attract an agent if you're not published yet. However, both publishers and agents are always on the lookout for new talent. Whichever you go for, your work needs to stand out, and catch someone's eye. To editors, unsolicited typescripts – that is, work not submitted through an agent, or already commissioned from the author – constitute what's known as the 'slush pile', which doesn't sound at all encouraging, but does give an indication of the quality of much of the work waiting there. Most submissions on this pile will be rejected, often with a standard letter or card.

So: what are the biggest turn-offs for an editor? David Fickling, who has his own imprint under the Random House umbrella, is repelled by "bad writing, boring writing, uncorrected writing, poor structure, no structure, no coherence, blatant plagiarism, trend following or commercial copy-catting for the wrong reasons, and above all the absence of heart and feeling and connection." Jon Appleton, of Orion Children's Books, stresses the importance of presentation: "Submissions should be written to impress. Single-spaced typing, ribbons, elaborate clips, foolscap paper, picture book texts supplied with amateurish illustrations by the writer's friend – all these are a deterrent." Don't risk putting off an editor before he or she has even started reading.

An alternative preliminary stage is to send your work to a consultancy, such as *Cornerstones* or *The Literary Consultancy*. For a fee, a tutor, usually a published author or someone with experience in publishing or agenting, will assess your work and advise you on improving and then submitting it.

Writing groups and courses

Whether or not writing can be taught is open to debate. Some people seem to be naturally gifted; for others, hard work and persistence bring rewards. Determination is probably the most important quality; even the most talented writer won't succeed without it.

Writing can be a lonely business. There's probably a writers' group of some kind near you; these vary tremendously in scope and ambition, but do give you an audience for your work, and maybe local publication. Or, for an intensive few days working with professional authors, try The Arvon Foundation, which offers residential courses such as Fiction, Novel Writing, Starting to Write and, for those interested in writing for young people, Writing for Children, Writing for Teens and Young Adults, and Poetry for Children. The Society of Authors is for published writers only, but The Society of Children's Book Writers and Illustrators (SCBWI) is an international organisation with both published and aspiring authors among its members.

Many universities now offer Creative Writing first degree and MA courses, with some offering prizes such as representation by leading literary agencies. There are also various competitions for unpublished novels, with publication as the prize.

Make it happen

If you're serious, write today. Write tomorrow. Write the next day. Make it part of your life.

Publishers

A&C Black
(see Bloomsbury Publishing)

AA Publishing
The Automobile Association,
14th Floor, Fanum House,
Basingstoke, Hampshire RG21 4EA
01256 491519
ian.harvey@theaa.com
www.theaa.co.uk
Maps, atlases and guidebooks

Abacus
(see Little, Brown Book Group)

ABC-Clio
PO Box 1437, Oxford, OX4 9AZ
01865 481403
salesuk@abc-clio.com
www.abc-clio.com
Academic and general reference

Absolute Press
Scarborough House,
29 James Street West,
Bath BA1 2BT
01225 316013
office@absolutepress.co.uk
www.absolutepress.co.uk
Non-fiction

Abson Books London
5 Sidney Square, London E1 2EY
020 7790 4737
absonbooks@aol.com
www.absonbooks.co.uk
Language glossaries

Acair
7 James Street, Stornoway,
Isle of Lewis HS1 2QN
01851 703020
info@acairbooks.com
www.acairbooks.com
Scottish history and culture, Gaelic

Acumen Publishing
Stocksfield Hall,
Stocksfield NE43 7TN
01661 844865
enquiries@acumenpublishing.co.uk
www.acumenpublishing.co.uk
*Philosophy, history, classics and
politics*

Addison-Wesley
(see Pearson Education)

Age Concern Books
Astral House, 1268 London Road,
London SW16 4ER
020 8765 7397
books@ace.org.uk
www.ageconcern.org.uk

Aidan Ellis Publishing
Cobb House,
Nuffield, Henley on Thames,
Oxfordshire RG9 5RT
01491 641496
mail@aidanellispublishing.co.uk
www.aepub.demon.co.uk
General publishing and non-fiction

Allen & Unwin
(see Orion Publishing Group)

Allen Lane
(see Penguin Books)

Alligator Books
Gadd House, Arcadia Avenue,
London N3 2JU
020 8371 6622
sales@pinwheel.co.uk
www.pinwheel.co.uk
*Pinwheel is a division. Imprints:
Gullane (children's picture); Pinwheel
(novelty); Andromeda (education)*

Allison & Busby
13 Charlotte Mews,
London W1T 4EJ
020 7580 1080
susie@allisonandbusby.com
www.allisonandbusby.com
Crime; literary fiction and non-fiction

Allyn & Bacon
(see Pearson Education)

Alma Books
London House,
243 -253 Lower Mortlake Road
Richmond, Surrey TW9 2LL
020 8948 9550
info@almabooks.com
www.almabooks.co.uk
*Contemporary literary fiction and
some non-fiction*

Amber Lane Press
Cheorl House, Church Street,
Charlbury, Oxfordshire OX7 3PR
01608 810024
sales@amberlanepress.co.uk
www.amberlanepress.co.uk
Plays and theatre

Andersen Press
20 Vauxhall Bridge Road,
London SW1V 2SA
020 7840 8701
anderseneditorial@randomhouse.
co.uk
www.andersenpress.co.uk
Children's books and fiction

Anness Publishing
Hermes House,
88–89 Blackfriars Road,
London SE1 8HA
020 7401 2077
info@anness.com
www.annesspublishing.com
General non-fiction

Imprints: Aquamarine (lifestyle, cookery, craft); Hermes House (illustrated practical books); Lorenz Books (lifestyle, mind, body and spirit); Southwater (lifestyle, mind, body and spirit)

Anova Books
The Old Magistrates Court,
Soughcombe Street,
London W14 0RA
reception@anovabooks.com
www.anovabooks.com
- Batsford – *Specialist and technical illustrated non-fiction: embroidery, lace, chess, bridge, practical art, film and furniture*
- Collins & Brown – *Illustrated non-fiction: photography, crafts and practical arts; national magazine branded books; health, mind, body and spirit (formerly Vega)*
- Conway – *Maritime history, ship modelling and naval*
- National Trust – *Non-fiction: English culture, environment, gardening, cookery*
- Paper Tiger – *Science fiction and fantasy art*
- Pavilion – *High-end coffee table books: celebrity, lifestyle, interiors, cookery, garden, art and photography*
- Portico – *Non fiction: humour, general interest, popular culture*
- Robson – *Sports, humour and biography, especially celebrity; some fiction*
- Salamander – *Packager of made-to-order books*

Anthem Press
(see Wimbledon Publishing Press)

Antique Collectors' Club
Sandy Lane, Old Martlesham,
Woodbridge, Suffolk IP12 4SD
01394 389950
sales@antique-acc.com
www.antiquecollectorsclub.com

Anvil Press Poetry
Neptune House, 70 Royal Hill,
London SE10 8RF
020 8469 3033
info@anvilpresspoetry.com
www.anvilpresspoetry.com
Poetry

Appletree Press
The Old Potato Station,
14 Howard Street South,
Belfast BT7 1AP
028 9024 3074
reception@appletree.ie
www.appletree.ie
Cookery, Celtic interest, general non-fiction, bespoke publications

Arc Publications
Nanholme Mill, Shaw Wood Road,
Todmorden, Lancashire OL14 6DA
01706 812338
arc.publications@btconnect.com
www.arcpublications.co.uk
Contemporary poetry

Arcadia Books
15–16 Nassau Street,
London W1W 7AB
020 7436 9898
info@arcadiabooks.co.uk
www.arcadiabooks.co.uk
Literary fiction, crime, biography, gender studies and travel. Imprints: Arcadia Books (literary fiction, biography, gender studies, travel literature); Black Amber (Black and Asian writing); Bliss Books (popular fiction and non-fiction); Euro Crime (European Crime writing)

Architectural Association Publications
36 Bedford Square,
London WC1B 3ES
020 7887 4021
publications@aaschool.ac.uk
www.aaschool.ac.uk/publications
Publishing arm of Architectural Association School of Architecture

Arcturus Publishing
26/27 Bickels Yard,
151–153 Bermondsey Street,
London SE1 3HA
020 7407 9400
info@arcturuspublishing.com
www.arcturuspublishing.com
Non-fiction

Arrow
(see Random House Group)

Ashgrove Publishing
3 Town Barton, Norton St Philip,
Bath BA2 7LN
01373 834 900
sales@ashgrovepublish.demon.co.uk
www.gmo73.dial.pipex.com/ashgrove
Owned by Hollydata Publishers. Mind, body and spirit

Ashley Drake Publishing
PO Box 733, Cardiff CF14 7ZY
029 2056 0343
post@ashleydrake.com
www.ashleydrake.com
Imprints: Welsh Academic Press (academic titles in English); St David's Press (general trade); Y Ddraig Fach (children's books in Welsh); Gwasg Addysgol Cymru (educational in Welsh)

Ashmolean Museum Publications
(see Oxford University)

Atlantic Books
Ormond House,
26–27 Boswell Street,
London WC1N 3JZ
020 7269 1610
enquiries@groveatlantic.co.uk
www.atlantic-books.co.uk
Literary fiction, non-fiction and reference

Atom
(see Little, Brown Book Group)

Aurum Press
7 Greenland Street, London
NW1 0ND
020 7284 7160
www.aurumpress.co.uk
Non-fiction

Australian Consolidated Press UK
Moulton Park Business Centre,
10 Scirocco Close,
Moulton Park Office Village,
Northampton NN3 6AP
01604 642200
books@acpuk.com
www.acpuk.com
Home interest

Authentic Media
9 Holdom Avenue, Bletchley,
Milton Keynes MK1 1QR
01908 364200
info@authenticmedia.co.uk
www.authenticmedia.co.uk

Imprints: Authentic (Christian life); Paternoster (academic and theological titles and theses); Authentic Music

Autumn Publishing
Appledram Barns,
Birdham Road, near Chichester,
West Sussex PO20 7EQ
01243 531660
autumn@autumnpublishing.co.uk
www.autumnchildrensbooks.co.uk
Early learning. Imprint: Byeway Books

Award Publications
The Old Riding School,
Welbeck Estate, Worksop,
Nottinghamshire S80 3LR
01909 478170
info@awardpublications.co.uk
www.awardpublications.co.uk
*Children's fiction and reference.
Imprint: Horus Editions*

Axis Publishing
8C Accommodation Road,
London NW11 8ED
020 8731 8080
admin@axispublishing.co.uk
www.axispublishing.co.uk
Illustrated full colour books

Bantam/Bantam Press
(see Random House Group)

Barefoot Books
124 Walcot Street, Bath BA1 5BG
01225 322400
info@barefootbooks.co.uk
www.barefoot-books.com
Highly illustrated children's picture books

Barny Books
The Cottage,
Hough on the Hill, near Grantham,
Lincolnshire NG32 2HL
01400 250246
info@barnybooks.biz
www.barnybooks.biz
Children's books, adult fiction and non-fiction

Barrington Stoke
18 Walker Street, Edinburgh EH3 7LP
0131 225 4113
barrington@barringtonstoke.co.uk
www.barringtonstoke.co.uk
Remedial children's reading for dyslexic, struggling and reluctant readers.

Batsford
(see Anova Books)

BBC Books
(See Random House Group)

Beautiful Books
36-38 Glasshouse Street,
London W1B 3DL
020 7734 4448
office@beautiful-books.co.uk
www.beautiful-books.co.uk
Adult fiction and non-fiction

Benjamin Cummings
(see Pearson Education)

Berg Publishers
1st Floor Angel Court,
81 St Clements Street,
Oxford OX4 1AW
01865 245104
enquiry@bergpublishers.com
www.bergpublishers.com
Various academic

Berghahn Books
3 Newtec Place, Magdalen Road,
Oxford OX4 1RE
01865 250011
salesuk@berghahnbooks.com
www.berghahnbooks.com
Academic books and journals

Berlitz Publishing
(See Insight Guides/Berlitz Publishing)

BFI Publishing
(See Macmillan Publishers)

BFP Books
Focus House, 497 Green Lanes,
London N13 4BP
020 8882 3315
info@thebfp.com
www.thebfp.com
Publishing arm of the Bureau of Freelance Photographers

BIOS Scientific Publishers
(see T&F Informa)

Birlinn
West Newington House,
10 Newington Road,
Edinburgh EH9 1QS
0131 668 4371
info@birlinn.co.uk

www.birlinn.co.uk
History, folklore, Scottish interest and fiction. Imprints: Birlinn; Canongate Classics; House of Lochar; John Donald; Mercat; Polygon; Tuckwell; Maclean Dubois

Black & White Publishing
29 Ocean Drive,
Edinburgh EH6 6JL
0131 625 4500
mail@blackandwhitepublishing.com
www.blackandwhitepublishing.com
General fiction and non-fiction

Black Ace Books
PO Box 7547, Perth PH2 1AU
01821 642 822
www.blackacebooks.com
Adult fiction and non-fiction

Black Lace
(See Virgin Books)

Black Spring Press
Curtain House,
134–146 Curtain Road,
London EC2A 3AR
020 7613 3066
enquiries@blackspringpress.co.uk
www.blackspringpress.co.uk
Fiction and non-fiction

Black Swan
(see Random House Group)

Blackstaff Press
4c Heron Wharf,
Sydenham Business Park,
Belfast BT3 9LE
028 9045 5006
info@blackstaffpress.com
www.blackstaffpress.com
Fiction, non-fiction and poetry

Bloodaxe Books
Highgreen, Tarset,
Northumberland NE48 1RP
01434 240500
publicity@bloodaxebooks.com
www.bloodaxebooks.com
Poetry

Bloomsbury Publishing
36 Soho Square, London W1D 3QY
020 7494 2111
customerservices@bloomsbury.com
www.bloomsbury.com

Adult and children's fiction and non-fiction (including Harry Potter)

A&C Black (Publishers)
36 Soho Square, London W1D 3QY
020 7758 0200
publicity@acblack.com
www.acblack.com
Reference and non-fiction; Writers' and Artists' Yearbook

The Bodley Head
(see Random House Group)

Book Guild
Pavilion View, 19 New Road,
Brighton BN1 1UF
01273 720900
info@bookguild.co.uk
www.bookguild.co.uk
Fiction, non-fiction and children's

Boulevard Books & The Babel Guides
71 Lytton Road, Oxford OX4 3NY
01865 712931
info@babelguides.com
www.babelguides.com
Contemporary world fiction and guides

Bowker (UK)
1st Floor, Medway House,
Cantelupe Road, East Grinstead,
West Sussex RH19 3BJ
01342 310450
sales@bowker.co.uk
www.bowker.co.uk
Part of the Cambridge Information Group (CIG). Reference and biography

Boydell & Brewer
Whitwell House,
St Audry's Park Road, Melton,
Woodbridge,
Suffolk, 1P12 1SY
01394 610600
trading@boydell.co.uk
www.boydell.co.uk
Non-fiction, principally medieval studies

Boxtree
(see Macmillan Publishers)

Bradt Travel Guides
23 High Street, Chalfont St Peter,
Buckinghamshire SL9 9QE
01753 893444
info@bradtguides.com
www.bradt-travelguides.com
Travel guides

Breedon Books Publishing Co
3 The Parker Centre,
Mansfield Road,
Derby DE21 4SZ
01332 384235
sales@breedonpublishing.co.uk
www.breedonbooks.co.uk
Local history and heritage, sport

British Academy
10 Carlton House Terrace,
London SW1Y 5AH
020 7969 5200
secretary@britac.ac.uk
www.britac.ac.uk

British Library
96 Euston Road, London NW1 2DB
020 7412 7469
blpublications@bl.uk
www.bl.uk

British Museum Press
38 Russell Square,
London WC1B 3QQ
020 7323 1234
sales@britishmuseum.co.uk
www.britishmuseum.co.uk

Brooklands Books
PO Box 146, Cobham,
Surrey KT11 1LG
01932 865051
sales@brooklands-books.com
www.brooklands-books.com
Motoring titles and technical catalogues

Brown Watson
The Old Mill, 76 Fleckney Road,
Kibworth Beauchamp,
Leicestershire LE8 0HG
0116 279 6333
books@brownwatson.co.uk
www.brownwatson.co.uk
General children's interest

Brown, Son & Ferguson
4–10 Darnley Street,
Glasgow G41 2SD
0141 429 1234
info@skipper.co.uk
www.skipper.co.uk
Nautical textbooks. Sister company is Scottish Plays

Browntrout Publishers
PO Box 201, Bristol BS99 5ZE
0117 973 9191
sales@browntroutuk.com
www.browntroutuk.com
Fine art and photography calendars

Brunner-Routledge
(see T&F Informa)

Bryntirion Press
Bryntirion, Bridgend,
Mid-Glamorgan CF31 4DX
01656 655886
office@emw.org.uk
www.emw.org.uk
Owned by the Evangelical Movement of Wales. Christian books in English and Welsh

Business Education Publishers
Cygnet Way,
Rainton Bridge Business Centre,
Houghton-le-Spring,
Tyne and Wear DH4 5QY
0191 305 5165
info@bepl.com
www.bepl.com

Butterworths/ Butterworth-Heinemann
(see Reed Elsevier)

Cadogan Guides
(See New Holland Publishers)

Calder Publications
(See Oneworld Classics)

Cambridge University Press
The Edinburgh Building,
Shaftesbury Road,
Cambridge CB2 2RU
01223 312393
information@cambridge.org
www.cambridge.org

Campbell Books
(see Macmillan Publishers)

Canongate Books
14 High Street, Edinburgh EH1 1TE
0131 557 5111
info@canongate.co.uk
www.canongate.net
Literary fiction and non-fiction, music

Capall Bann Publishing
Auton Farm, Milverton,
Somerset TA4 1NE
01823 401528
enquiries@capallbann.co.uk
www.capallbann.co.uk
British traditional works and folklore

Capstone Publishing
(see Wiley Europe)

Carcanet Press
4th Floor, Alliance House,
30 Cross Street,
Manchester M2 7AQ
0161 834 8730
info@carcanet.co.uk
www.carcanet.co.uk
*Poetry, academic works, literary
biography, fiction in translation*

Cardiff Academic Press
St Fagans Road, Fairwater,
Cardiff CF5 3AE
029 2056 0333
cap@drakeed.com
www.drakeed.com/cap

Carfax
(see T&F Informa)

Carlton Publishing Group
20 Mortimer Street,
London W1T 3JW
020 7612 0400
enquiries@carltonbooks.co.uk
www.carltonbooks.co.uk
*Illustrated entertainment and leisure
titles. Imprints: Carlton Books, Andre
Deutsche and Prion Books*

Carroll & Brown Publishers
20 Lonsdale Road,
London NW6 6RD
020 7372 0900
mail@carrollandbrown.co.uk
www.carrollandbrown.co.uk
Lifestyle

Cassell Illustrated
(See Octopus Publishing Group)

Cassell Reference
(see Orion Publishing Group)

Catholic Truth Society (CTS)
40–46 Harleyford Road,
London SE11 5AY
020 7640 0042
editorial@cts-online.org.uk
www.cts-online.org.uk
*Roman Catholic books, including
Vatican documents*

Cavendish Publishing
(See T&F Informa)

**CBA (Publishing
Department)**
St Mary's House, 66 Bootham,
York YO30 7BZ
01904 671417
info@britarch.ac.uk
www.britarch.ac.uk
*Publishing arm of the Council for
British Archaeology. Archaeology,
practical handbooks*

CBD Research
Chancery House, 15 Wickham
Road, Beckenham, Kent BR3 5JS
0871 222 8440
cbd@cbdresearch.com
www.cbdresearch.com
Directories

Century
(see Random House Group)

**Chambers Harrap
Publishers**
7 Hopetoun Crescent,
Edinburgh EH7 4AY
0131 556 5929
admin@chambersharrap.co.uk
www.chambersharrap.com
Dictionaries and reference

Channel 4 Books
(see Random House Group)

Chapman Publishing
4 Broughton Place,
Edinburgh EH1 3RX
0131 557 2207
chapman-pub@blueyonder.co.uk
www.chapman-pub.co.uk
*Scottish writers including poetry,
drama, short stories*

**Chartered Institute
of Personnel and
Development**
151 The Broadway,
London SW19 1JQ
020 8612 6200
publish@cipd.co.uk
(books);editorial@
peoplemanagement.co.uk
www.cipd.co.uk
Part of CIPD Enterprises (magazine)

Chatto & Windus
(see Random House Group)

Chicken House Publishing
2 Palmer Street, Frome,
Somerset BA11 1DS
01373 454 488
chickenhouse@doublecluck.com
www.doublecluck.com
Children's fiction

Child's Play (International)
Ashworth Road, Bridgemead,
Swindon, Wiltshire SN5 7YD
01793 616286
office@childs-play.com
www.childs-play.com

Chipmunka Publishing
Quay House, 2 Admirals Way,
Marsh Wall, London E14 9XG
020 7868 1530
info@chipmunkapublishing
www.chipmunkapublishing.co.uk
Mental health issues

Chris Andrews Publications
15 Curtis Yard, North Hinksey Lane,
Oxford OX2 0LX
01865 723404
enquiries@cap-ox.com
www.oxfordpicturelibrary.co.uk
*Owns the Oxford Picture Library. Coffee
table books, calendars and diaries*

Christian Focus Publications
Geanies House, Fearn, Tain,
Rosshire IV20 1TW
01862 871011
info@christianfocus.com
www.christianfocus.com
*Christian books for adults and
children*

Chrysalis Books
(incorporated into Anova Books)

Cicerone Press
2 Police Square, Milnthorpe,
Cumbria LA7 7PY
01539 562069
info@cicerone.co.uk
www.cicerone.co.uk
Guidebooks for outdoor enthusiasts

Cico Books
20-21 Jockey's Fields,
London WC1R 4BW
020 7025 2280
mail@cicobooks.co.uk
*Lifestyle and interiors, crafts, mind,
body and spirit*

Cisco Press
(see Pearson Education)

Co & Bear Productions (UK)
63 Edith Grove, London SW10 0LB
020 7351 5545
info@cobear.co.uk
www.scriptumeditions.co.uk
*High quality illustrated books.
Imprint: Scriptum Editions*

Colin Smythe
PO Box 6, Gerrards Cross,
Buckinghamshire SL9 8XA
01753 886000
cpsmythe@aol.com
www.colinsmythe.co.uk
Anglo-Irish literature and criticism

Collins
(see HarperCollins Publishers)

Collins & Brown
(see Anova Books)

Colourpoint Books
Colourpoint House,
Jubilee Business Park,
21 Jubilee Road, Newtownards,
Co Down BT23 4YH
028 9182 0505
info@colourpoint.co.uk
www.colourpoint.co.uk
*School textbooks, transport, Irish
interest*

Compendium Publishing
1st Floor, 43 Frith Street,
London W1D 4SA
020 7287 4570
info@compendiumpublishing.com
Historical

Constable & Robinson
3, The Lanchesters,
162 Fulham Palace Road,
London W6 9ER
020 8741 3663
enquiries@constablerobinson.com
www.constablerobinson.com
*Fiction and non-fiction: lifestyle,
reference, current affairs
and politics*

**Continuum International
Publishing Group**
The Tower Building, 11 York Road,
London SE1 7NX
020 7922 0880
info@continuumbooks.com
www.continuumbooks.com
Imprints:
• Constable – *Non-fiction and
  hardback crime fiction*
• Robinson – *Crime fiction
  paperbacks*
• Right Way – *Practical books,
  puzzles, lifestyle*
• Magpie – *Promotional books*

Conway
(see Anova Books)

Corgi
(see Random House Group)

Country Publications
The Watermill, Broughton Hall,
Skipton, North Yorkshire BD23 3AG
01756 701033
editorial@thecountryman.co.uk
www.dalesman.co.uk
*Magazines and regional books
(Countryman, Cumbria, Dalesman
and the Yorkshire nostalgia magazine
Down Your Way)*

Countryside Books
Highfield House, 2 Highfield
Avenue, Newbury,
Berkshire RG14 5DS
01635 43816
info@countrysidebooks.co.uk
www.countrysidebooks.co.uk
Local interest and walking books

CRC Press
(see T&F Informa)

Cressrelles Publishing Co
10 Station Road Industrial Estate,
Colwall, Malvern,
Worcestershire WR13 6RN
01684 540154
simon@cressrelles.co.uk
*Plays and theatre texts. Imprints:
Actinic Press; J. Garnet Miller; Kenyon
Deane; New Playwrights Network*

Crowood Press
The Stable Block, Crowood Lane,
Ramsbury, Marlborough,
Wiltshire SN8 2HR
01672 520320
enquiries@crowood.com
www.crowoodpress.co.uk
*Aviation, military history, country,
sports, hobby and leisure pursuits.
Imprint: Airlife publishing*

Curzon Press
(see T&F Informa)

CW Daniel Company
(see Random House Group)

Darton, Longman & Todd
1 Spencer Court,
140–142 Wandsworth High Street,
London SW18 4JJ
020 8875 0155
mail@darton-longman-todd.co.uk
www.darton-longman-todd.co.uk
Spirituality, theology and Christianity

David & Charles Publishers
Brunel House, Forde Close,
Newton Abbot, Devon TQ12 4PU
01626 323200
postmaster@davidandcharles.co.uk
www.davidandcharles.co.uk
*Subsidiary of F&W, USA. Illustrated
non-fiction*

David Fickling Books
(see Random House Group)

David Fulton (Publishers)
(see T&F Informa)

Debrett's
18–20 Hill Rise, Richmond,
Surrey TW10 6UA
020 8939 2250
enquiries@debretts.co.uk
www.debretts.co.uk
Specialist reference works

Dedalus
Langford Lodge, St Judith's Lane,
Sawtry, Cambridgeshire PE28 5XE
01487 832382
info@dedalusbooks.com
www.dedalusbooks.com
*English contemporary fiction and
European fiction in translation,
concept books such as The Decadent
Handbook and The Dedalus Book of
Absinthe*

Dewi Lewis Publishing
8 Broomfield Road, Heaton Moor,
Stockport SK4 4ND
0161 442 9450
mail@dewilewispublishing.com
www.dewilewispublishing.com
Fiction, photography and visual arts

Dorling Kindersley
(see Penguin Books)

**Doubleday/Doubleday
Children's Books**
(see Random House Group)

**Drake Educational
Associates**
St Fagans Road, Fairwater,
Cardiff CF5 3AE
029 2056 0333
enquiries@drakeed.com
www.drakeed.com
Audio-visual, educational

Dref Wen
28 Church Road, Whitchurch,
Cardiff CF14 2EA
029 2061 7860
sales@drefwen.com
Welsh language

Duncan Baird Publishers
29 Jewry Stree,t, Winchester,
Hampshire, SO23 8RY
01962 841 411
enquiries@dbp.co.uk
www.dbp.co.uk
General non-fiction

**Duncan Petersen
Publishing**
C7, Old Imperial Laundry,
Warriner Gardens, London SW11 4XW
020 7371 2356
charmingsmall.hotels@zen.co.uk
www.charmingsmallhotels.co.uk
Non-fiction

**Ebury Publishing/ Ebury
Press**
(see Random House Group)

Eden Books
(see Random House Group)

Edinburgh University Press
22 George Square, Edinburgh
EH8 9LF
0131 650 4218
editorial@eup.ed.ac.uk
www.euppublishing.com

Edward Elgar Publishing
The Lypiatts, 15 Lansdown Road,
Cheltenham, Gloucestershire,
GL50 2JA
01242 226934
info@e-elgar.co.uk
www.e-elgar.com
Economics, business and environment

Egmont Books
239 Kensington High Street,
London W8 6SA
020 7761 3500
info@egmont.com
www.egmont.co.uk
*Children's entertainment. Imprints:
Heinemann Young Books; Methuen
Children's Books; Hamlyn Children's
Books; Mammoth; Dean*

Eland Publishing
Third Floor, 61 Exmouth Market,
Clerkenwell, London EC1R 4QL
020 7833 0762
info@travelbooks.co.uk
www.travelbooks.co.uk
*Classic travel literature, Spirit of
Place novels, poetry and history of the
Islamic world*

Element
(See HarperCollins)

Elliot Right Way Books
(See Constable & Robinson)

Elliott & Thompson
27 John Street, London WC1N 2BX
020 7831 5013
mark@eandtbooks.com
www.elliottthompson.com
History, biography, literary and fiction

**ELM Publications and
Training**
Seaton House,
Kings Ripton, Huntingdon,
Cambridgeshire PE28 2NJ
01487 773254
elm@elm-training.co.uk
www.elm-training.co.uk
Educational aids

Elsevier
(see Reed Elsevier)

Emissary Publishing
PO Box 33, Bicester,
Oxfordshire OX26 4ZZ
01869 323447
enquiries@peterpook.com
www.peterpook.com
Humorous paperbacks

Emma Treehouse
The Studio, Church Street, Nunney,
Frome, Somerset BN1 4LW
01373 836233
info@emmatreehouse.com
www.emmatreehouse.com
Children's pre-school

**Encyclopaedia Britannica
(UK)**
2nd Floor, Unity Wharf, Mill Street,
London SE1 2BH
020 7500 7800
enquiries@britannica.co.uk
www.britannica.co.uk

**English Heritage
(Publishing)**
Kemble Drive, Swindon SN2 2GZ
01793 414619
customers@english-heritage.org.uk
www.english-heritage.org.uk
General and specialist history

Enitharmon Press
26B Caversham Road,
London NW5 2DU
020 7482 5967
info@enitharmon.co.uk
www.enitharmon.co.uk
*Poetry, literary criticism, fiction,
art and photography, memoirs and
translations*

Euromonitor
60–61 Britton Street,
London EC1M 5UX
020 7251 8024

info@euromonitor.com
www.euromonitor.com
Business reference, market analysis and information directories

Europa Publications
(see T&F Informa)

Evans Publishing Group
2a Portnam Mansions, Chiltern Street, London EC1V 0AT
020 7487 0926
sales@evansbooks.co.uk
www.evansbooks.co.uk

Everyman
(see Orion Publishing Group)

Everyman's Library
Northburgh House,
10 Northburgh Street,
London EC1V 0AT
020 7566 6350
books@everyman.uk.com
Imprint of Alfred A Knopf (subsidiary of Random House, USA). Literature, poetry, children's and travel

Exley Publications
16 Chalk Hill, Watford,
Hertfordshire WD19 4BG
01923 250505
enquiries@exleypublications.co.uk
www.helenexleygiftbooks.com
Giftbooks, quotation anthologies and humour

Expert Books
(see Random House Group)

Faber & Faber
Bloomsbury House,
74-77 Great Russell Street,
London WC1B 3DA
020 7927 3800
gasales@faber.co.uk
www.faber.co.uk
Fiction, non-fiction and poetry

Facet Publishing
7 Ridgmount Street,
London WC1E 7AE
020 7255 0590/0505 (text phone)
info@facetpublishing.co.uk
www.facetpublishing.co.uk
Publishing arm of CILIP (Chartered Institute of Library and Information Professionals). Library and information science

Fig Tree
(See Penguin Group)

Findhorn Press
305a The Park, Findhorn, Forres,
Morayshire IV36 3TE
01309 690582
info@findhornpress.com
www.findhornpress.com
New Age, personal development and alternative health

First & Best in Education
Hamilton House Mailings Plc,
Earlstrees Court, Earlstrees Road,
Corby, Northants, NN17 4HH
01536 399005
info@firstandbest.co.uk
www.firstandbest.co.uk
Educational books for schools.
Imprints: School Improvement Reports

Floris Books
15 Harrison Gardens,
Edinburgh EH11 1SH
0131 337 2372
floris@florisbooks.co.uk
www.florisbooks.co.uk
Scientific, religion, holistic health, children's, bio dynamics and organics

Folens Publishers
Waterslade House, Thame Road,
Haddenham, Buckinghamshire
HP17 8NT
08445 768115
folens@folens.com
www.folens.com
Educational books. Imprint: Belair

Footprint Handbooks
6 Riverside Court,
Lower Bristol Road, Bath BA2 3DZ
01225 469141
wwwinfo@footprintbooks.com
www.footprintbooks.com
Travel. Activity guides to hundreds of cities and countries

For Dummies
(see Wiley Europe)

Fourth Estate
(see HarperCollins Publishers)

Frances Lincoln Publishers
4 Torriano Mews, Torriano Avenue,
London NW5 2RZ
020 7284 4009
reception@frances-lincoln.com
www.franceslincoln.com
Highly illustrated non-fiction

Frank Cass
(see T&F Informa)

Free Association Books
PO Box 37664, London NW7 2XU
020 8906 0396
info@fabooks.com
www.fabooks.com
Psychoanalysis and psychotherapy, social science, psychology

Frommer's
(see Wiley Europe)

FT Prentice Hall
(see Pearson Education)

Gaia Books
(See Octopus Publishing Group)

Garland Science
(see T&F Informa)

Garnet Publishing
8 Southern Court, South Street,
Reading, Berkshire RG1 4QS
0118 959 7847
enquiries@garnetpublishing.co.uk
www.garnetpublishing.co.uk
Imprints: Garnet (Middle East); Ithaca Press (business books)

Geddes & Grosset
David Dale House,
New Lanark ML11 9DJ
01555 665000
info@geddesandgrosset.co.uk
www.geddesandgrosset.co.uk
Children's and reference books.
Imprints:Waverley Books (Scottish interest, graphic novel adaptations); Beanobooks (children's)

Geological Society Publishing House
Unit 7, Brassmill Enterprise Centre,
Brassmill Lane, Bath BA1 3JN
01225 445046
sales@geolsoc.org.uk
www.geolsoc.org.uk/bookshop
Publishing arm of the Geological

Society. Undergraduate and postgraduate texts in the earth sciences

Gibson Square
47 Lonsdale Square,
London N1 1EW
020 7096 1100
media@gibsonsquare.com
www.gibsonsquare.com/
Biography and current issues.
Imprints: Gibson Square, New Editions

Giles de la Mare Publishers
PO Box 25351, London NW5 1ZT
020 7485 2533
gilesdelamare@dial.pipex.com
www.gilesdelamare.co.uk
Art and architecture, biography, history, music

Gollancz
(see Orion Publishing Group)

Gomer Press
Llandysul, Ceredigion SA44 4JL
01559 362371
gwasg@gomer.co.uk
www.gomer.co.uk
Adult fiction and non-fiction.
Imprint: Pont Books

Granada Learning Group
The Chiswick Centre,
414 Chiswick High Road,
London W4 5TF
020 8996 3333
info@granada-learning.com
www.granada-learning.com
Tests, assessments and assessment services

Granta Publications
12 Addison Avenue, Holland Park,
London W11 4QR
020 7605 1360
info@granta.com
www.granta.com
Literary fiction and general non-fiction. Imprint: Granta Books

Green Books
Foxhole, Dartington, Totnes,
Devon TQ9 6EB
01803 863260
edit@greenbooks.co.uk
www.greenbooks.co.uk
Green issues

Gresham Books
46 Victoria Road, Summertown,
Oxford OX2 7QD
01865 513582
info@gresham-books.co.uk
www.gresham-books.co.uk
Hymn and service books for children.

Griffith Institute
(see Oxford University)

Grub Street Publishing
4 Rainham Close,
London SW11 6SS
020 7924 3966/7738 1008
post@grubstreet.co.uk
www.grubstreet.co.uk
Lifestyle and aviation history

Guardian Books
Guardian News and Media
Kings Place
90 York Way
London N1 9AG
020 3353 4338
www.guardianbooks.co.uk
General non-fiction and reference

Guild of Master Craftsman Publications
166 High Street, Lewes,
East Sussex BN7 1XU
01273 477374
www.gmcbooks.com
Craft and woodworking

Guinness World Records
184-192 Drummond Street,
3rd Floor, London NW1 3HP
020 7891 4567
press@guinnessworldrecords.com
www.guinnessworldrecords.com

Gullane Children's Books
(see Alligator Books)

Gwasg Carreg Gwalch
12 Iard yr Orsaf, Llanrwst,
Conwy LL26 0EH
01492 642031
llanrwst@carreg-gwalch.co.uk
www.carreg-gwalch.com
Welsh fiction and non-fiction; books on Wales

Hachette Children's Books
338 Euston Road, London NW1 3BH
020 7873 6000
www.hodderchildrens.co.uk
www.hachettelivre.co.uk
Children's fiction and non-fiction
Imprints:
- Hodder Children's Books – *fiction and non-fiction, picture books*
- Orchard Books – *fiction, picture and novelty*
- Franklin Watts – *non-fiction*
- Wayland – *non-fiction*

Hachette Livre
338 Euston Road,
London NW1 3BH
020 7873 6000
www.hachettelivre.co.uk
Comprises of the following group companies based in the UK: Hachette Books Scotland; Hachette Children's Books; Headline Publishing Group; Hodder Education Group; Hodder & Stoughton; Hodder & Stoughton Faith Books; John Murray; Little, Brown Book Group; Octopus Publishing Group; Orion Publishing Group.

Halban Publishers
22 Golden Square,
London W1F 9JW
020 7437 9300
books@halbanpublishers.com
www.halbanpublishers.com
Fiction, memoirs, history, biography, books on the Middle East and of Jewish interest

Halsgrove Publishing
Ryelands Industrial Estate,
Bagley Road, Wellington,
Somerset TA21 9PZ
01823 653777
sales@halsgrove.com
www.halsgrove.com
South-west regional books, cookery, biography and art

Hambledon and London
PO Box 55661, London W9 3SW
0845 070 5444
office@hambledon.co.uk
www.hambledon.co.uk
History and biography

Hamish Hamilton
(see Penguin Books)

Harlequin Mills & Boon
Eton House, 18–24 Paradise Road,
Richmond, Surrey TW9 1SR
020 8288 2800
www.millsandboon.co.uk
Subsidiary of Harlequin, Canada.
Popular fiction. Imprints: Mills &
Boon Romance; Mira Books; Modern
Extra; Modern Romance; Red Dress
Ink; Silhouette

HarperCollins Publishers
77–85 Fulham Palace Road,
London W6 8JB
020 8741 7070
enquiries@harpercollins.co.uk
www.harpercollins.co.uk
Collins – www.collins.co.uk
Reference books, cartography,
education, dictionaries.
Imprints: Collins; Collins Geo; Collins
Language; Collins Educational
HarperCollins Children's
Books
HarperCollins Children's Books. Picture
books, fiction and properties (Dr Seuss,
Paddington Bear, Noddy etc.)
HarperFiction
Imprints: HarperFiction (popular
fiction); Voyager (fantasy and science
fiction); Angry Robot (science fiction
and fantasy in physical and digital
form); Avon (commercial women's
fiction); Blue Door (commercial fiction)
Press Books
Imprints: Fourth Estate (innovative
fiction and non-fiction); HarperPress
(wide range of fiction and non-fiction);
Harper Perennial (literary paperback
imprint for HarperPress and Fourth
Estate); The Friday Project (talent
found on the web);
Harper NonFiction
Imprints: HarperThorsons/Element
(health, personal development and
spirituality titles); HarperNonFiction
(non-fiction, celebrity writers);
HarperTrue (inspirational memoirs);
HarperSport (sporting biographies,
guides and histories)

Harvard University Press/
MIT Press
Fitzroy House, 11 Chenies Street,
London WC1E 7EY
020 7306 0603
info@HUP-MITpress.co.uk
ww.hup.harvard.edu
European office of US company

Harvill Secker
(see Random House Group)

Haynes Publishing
Sparkford, Near Yeovil,
Somerset BA22 7JJ
01963 440635
www.haynes.co.uk
Car and motorcycle service and repair
manuals.

Headline Publishing Group
338 Euston Road,
London NW1 3BH
020 7873 6000
www.headline.co.uk
www.hachettelivre.co.uk
Commercial and literary fiction
and popular non-fiction. Imprints:
Headline, Headline Review; Little
Black Dress; Headline Springboard;
Business Plus

Heinemann
(see Pearson Education)

Helicon Publishing
RM, New Mill House,
183 Milton Park, Abingdon,
Oxfordshire OX14 4SE
08450 700 300
helicon@rm.com
www.helicon.co.uk
CD-Roms and online reference and
cartography

Helm Information
Crowham Manor, Main Road,
Westfield, Hastings,
East Sussex TN35 4SR
01424 882422
amandahelm@helm-information.
co.uk
www.helm-information.co.uk
Academic

Helter Skelter Publishing
18a Radbourne Road, Balham,
London SW12 0DZ
020 8673 6320

sales@helterskelterpublishing.com
www.helterskelterbooks.com
Obscure music. Firefly Publishing
(mainstream rock and pop)

Hesperus Press
4 Rickett Street, London SW6 1RU
020 7610 3331
info@hesperuspress.com
www.hesperuspress.com
Classic fiction in paperback

History Press
The Mill, Briscombe Port, Stroud,
Gloucester GL5 2QG
01453 883 300
www.thehistorypress.co.uk
Specialist history publisher. Imprints:
Jarrold; Nonsuch; Phillmore; Pitkin;
Spellmount; Sutton; Tempus

Hobsons Publishing
Challenger House, 42 Adler Street,
London E1 1EE
020 7958 5000
info@hobsons.co.uk
www.hobsons.co.uk
Part of the Daily Mail & General Trust.
Course and career guides

Hodder Headline Group
338 Euston Road,
London NW1 3BH
020 7873 6000
www.hodderheadline.co.uk
www.hachettelivre.co.uk
General
• Hodder & Stoughton *Commercial*
  and literary fiction. Imprints:
  Sceptre (literary); NEL (crime);
  Coronet (commercial fiction); Mobius
  (mind, body & spirit);
• Headline *Commercial and literary*
  fiction
• John Murray – *Fiction, history,*
  travel, literature and memoir
Education
www.hoddereducation.co.uk
• Hodder Arnold – *Imprints: Teach*
  Yourself (home reference); Hodder &
  Stoughton (reference including FA
  Guides and Michel Thomas)
• Hodder Education
• Hodder Gibson – *Textbooks and*
  revision support for the Scottish
  market
• Hodder Murray – *Curriculum*
  materials

- Philip Allan - *Textbooks, revision guides and other resources*
- Chambers Harrop – *Dictionaries etc.*

Religious
www.hodderreligious.co.uk
- Hodder Faith

Children's
- Hodder Children's Books – (See Hachette Children's Books)

Hodder Headline Ireland
8 Castlecourt Centre, Castleknock, Dublin 15
00 353 1 824 6288
Adult fiction and non-fiction.
Imprint: HHI Lir (fiction)
info@hhireland.ie

Honeyglen Publishing
56 Durrels House, Warwick Gardens, London W14 8QB
020 7602 2876
History and fiction

Honno Welsh Women's Press
Unit 14, Creative Units, Aberystwyth Arts Centre, Penglais Campus, Aberystwyth, Ceredigion, SY23 3GL
post@honno.co.uk
www.honno.co.uk
Reprints of classics, children's, fiction, poetry, short stories and Welsh women writers

House of Lochar
Isle of Colonsay, Argyll PA61 7YR
01951 200232
lochar@colonsay.org.uk
www.houseoflochar.com
Mostly Scottish titles. Imprint: Colonsay Books

How To Books
Spring Hill House, Spring Hill Road, Begbroke, Oxford OX5 1RX
01865 375794
info@howtobooks.co.uk
www.howtobooks.co.uk
Reference and self-help books

Hurst Publishers
41 Great Russell Street, London WC1B 3PL
020 7255 2201
hurst@atlas.co.uk
www.hurstpub.co.uk

Current affairs, politics, contemporary history

Hutchinson
(see Random House Group)

Ian Allan Publishing
Riverdene Business Park, Molesey Road, Hersham, Surrey KT12 4RG
01932 266600
info@ianallanpublishing.co.uk
www.ianallan.com
Maritime, road, rail, aviation, militaria and military history.
Imprints: Midland Publishing, OPC Railway, Classic Publications, Lewis Masonic

Ian Henry Publications
20 Park Drive, Romford, Essex RM1 4LH
01708 749119
info@ian-henry.com
www.ian-henry.com
History and Sherlock Holmes

IB Tauris
6 Salem Road, London W2 4BU
0207 243 1225
www.ibtauris.com
General non-fiction, humanities, social sciences

Icon Books
Omnibus Business Centre, 39-41 North Road, London N7 9DP
info@iconbooks.co.uk
www.iconbooks.co.uk
History, game books, children's non-fiction, adult non-fiction

Independent Music Press
PO Box 69, Church Stretton, Shropshire SY6 6WZ
0169 472 0049
info@impbooks.com
www.impbooks.com
Music biography and youth culture

Infinite Ideas
36 St Giles, Oxford OX1 3LD
01865 514 888
info@infideas.com
www.infideas.com
Inspirational, mind, body and spirit

Insight Guides/Berlitz Publishing
58 Borough High Street, London SE1 1XF
www.insightguides.com
www.berlitzpublishing.com
Travel guides

Interpet
Interpet House, Vincent Lane, Dorking, Surrey RH4 3YX
01306 873840
publishing@interpet.co.uk
Pet, aquatic and water gardening books

Inter-Varsity Press
Norton Street, Nottingham NG7 3HR
0115 978 1054
ivp@ivpbooks.com
www.ivpbooks.com
Christian belief and lifestyle.
Imprints: IVP, Apollos, Crossway

Ithaca Press
(see Garnet Publishing)

James Clarke & Co Lutterworth Press
PO Box 60, Cambridge CB1 2NT
01223 350865
publishing@jamesclarke.co.uk
www.lutterworth.com
Parent company of The Lutterworth Press. Theological, directory and reference

James Currey Publishers
Box 242, 266 Banbury Road, Oxford OX2 7DL
01865 559 200
editorial@jamescurrey.co.uk
www.jamescurrey.co.uk
Academic books on Africa and third world

Jane's Information Group
163 Brighton Road, Coulsdon, Surrey CR5 2YH
020 8700 3700
info@janes.com
www.janes.com
Defence, aerospace and transport

Janus Publishing Company
105–107 Gloucester Place,
London W1U 6BY
020 7486 6633
publisher@januspublishing.co.uk
www.januspublishing.co.uk
Fiction and non-fiction. Imprint:
Empiricus Books

Jarrold Publishing
Whitefriars, Norwich,
Norfolk NR3 1JR
01603 763300
publishing@jarrold.com
www.jarrold-publishing.co.uk
Heritage and leisure, walking guides.
Imprints: Pitkin, Unichrome

Jessica Kingsley Publishers
116 Pentonville Road,
London N1 9JB
020 7833 2307
post@jkp.com
www.jkp.com
Social and behavioural sciences

John Blake Publishing
3 Bramber Court, 2 Bramber Road,
London W14 9PB
020 7381 0666
words@blake.co.uk
www.johnblakepublishing.co.uk
General non-fiction, esp true crime,
popular culture, general biography.
Includes Richard Cohen, Smith
Gryphon and Blake Publishing.
Imprints: Metro Books (health, fitness,
cookery and lifestyle), Smith Gryphon

John Hunt/ O-Books
Publishing
The Bothy, Deershot Lodge,
Park Lane, Ropley,
Hampshire SO24 0BE
01962 773768
office1@o-books.com
www.johnhunt-publishing.com
www.o-books.com
World religions. Imprint: O Books
(mind, body and spirit)

John Murray
(see Hodder Headline Group)

Jonathan Cape
(see Random House Group)

Kahn & Averill
9 Harrington Road,
London SW7 3ES
020 8743 3278
kahn@averill23.freeserve.co.uk
Books on music

Kenilworth Press
Wykey House, Wykey, Shrewsbury,
Shropshire SY4 1JA
01939 261616
admin@quillerbooks.com
www.kenilworthpress.co.uk
Equestrian

Kenneth Mason
Publications
The Book Barn, Westbourne,
Emsworth, Hampshire PO10 8RS
01243 377977
info@researchdisclosure.com
www.researchdisclosure.com
Lifestyle, nutrition and nautical.
Imprint: Research Disclosure

Kevin Mayhew Publishers
Buxhall, Stowmarket,
Suffolk IP14 3BW
01449 737978
info@kevinmayhewltd.com
www.kevinmayhew.com
Christian music resources

Kingfisher Publications
(See Macmillan Publishers)

Kogan Page
120 Pentonville Road,
London N1 9JN
020 7278 0433
kpinfo@kogan-page.co.uk
www.kogan-page.co.uk
Business and management

Kyle Cathie
122 Arlington Road,
London NW1 7HP
020 7692 7215
general.enquiries@kyle-cathie.com
www.KyleCathie.com
Lifestyle

Ladybird
(see Penguin Books)

Landmark Publishing
The Oaks, Moor Farm Road West,
Ashbourne, DE6 1HD
01335 347349
landmark@clara.net
www.landmarkpublishing.co.uk
Travel guides, and industrial and
local history

Laurence King Publishing
361-373 City Road,
London EC1V 1LR
020 7841 6900
enquiries@laurenceking.co.uk
www.laurenceking.com
Illustrated arts

Lawrence & Wishart
99A Wallis Road, London E9 5LN
020 8533 2506
info@lwbooks.co.uk
www.lwbooks.co.uk
Current and world affairs

Leckie and Leckie
(see Granada Learning Group)

Lennard Associates
Windmill Cottage, Mackerye End,
Harpenden, Hertfordshire AL5 5DR
01582 715866
stephenson@lennardqap.co.uk
Sporting yearbooks. Imprints and
divisions include: Lennard Publishing,
Queen Anne Press

Letts Educational
4 Grosvenor Place,
London SW1X 7DL
020 7096 2900
mail@letts-educational.com
www.letts-educational.com
Study and revision guides

LexisNexis
(see Reed Elsevier)

Lion Hudson
Wilkinson House, Jordan Hill Road,
Oxford, OX2 8DR
01865 302750
info@lionhudson.com
www.lionhudson.com
Formed through merger of Lion
Publishing and Angus Hudson.
Christian books. Imprints: Lion, Lion
Children's, Candle, Monarch

Little, Brown Book Group
100 Victoria Embankment,
London EC4Y 0DY
020 7911 8000
uk@littlebrown.co.uk
www.littlebrown.co.uk
Hardback and paperback fiction and
non-fiction
Divisions and imprints:
• Abacus – fiction and non-fiction
• Atom – fantasy teen fiction
• Hachette Digital – (formerly
  Hachette Audio)
• Little, Brown – politics,
  biography, fiction
• Orbit – science fiction and
  fantasy
• Piatkus – fiction and non-fiction
• Sphere – commercial fiction
  and non-fiction, hardbacks and
  paperbacks
• Virago – fiction and non-fiction
  with a focus on women's lives.
  Includes the Virago Modern
  Classics series.

Little Tiger Press
(See Magi Publications)

Liverpool University Press
4 Cambridge Street,
Liverpool L69 7ZU
0151 794 2233
joanne.hart@liv.ac.uk
www.liverpool-unipress.co.uk

Lonely Planet Publications
2nd floor, 186 City Road,
London EC1V 2NT
020 7106 2100
go@lonelyplanet.co.uk
www.lonelyplanet.com
Travel guides

Longman
(see Pearson Education)

Lutterworth Press
(see James Clarke & Co Lutterworth
Press)

Macmillan Publishers
4 Crinan Street, London N1 9XW
020 7833 4000
www.macmillan.com
Nature Publishing Group
4 Crinan Street, London N1 9XW
020 7843 4000

www.nature.com
Scientific journals and reference
publishing
Macmillan Education
Macmillan Oxford,
Between Towns Road,
Oxford OX4 3PP
01865 405700
www.macmillaneducation.com
ELT learning materials for
international markets
Palgrave Macmillan
Brunel Road, Houndmills,
Basingstoke, Hampshire RG21 6XS
01256 329242
bookenquiries@palgrave.com
www.palgrave.com
Academic, scholarly and reference
publishing in the social sciences and
humanities. Publishing partners
for BFI
Pan Macmillan
20 New Wharf Road,
London N1 9RR
020 7014 6000
www.panmacmillan.com
Fiction and non-fiction for adults and
children. Imprints: Boxtree; Campbell
Books; Kingfisher; Macmillan;
Macmillan Children's Books;
Macmillan Digital Audio; Macmillan
New Writing; Pan; Picador; Sidgwick
and Jackson; Papermac; Rodale; Think
Books; Young Picador

Magna Large Print Books
(see Ulverscroft Group)

Maia Press
82 Forest Road, London E8 3BH
020 7683 8141
www.maiapress.com
Fiction from new and established
authors

Magi Publications
1 The Coda Centre,
189 Munster Road,
London SW6 6AW
020 7385 6333
www.littletigerpress.com
Children's Picture Books. Imprints:
Caterpillar Books; Little Tiger Press;
Stripes

**Mainstream Publishing Co
(Edinburgh)**
7 Albany Street, Edinburgh EH1 3UG
0131 557 2959
enquiries@mainstreampublishing.com
www.mainstreampublishing.com
Non-fiction: biography, autobiography,
art, sport and general

Management Books 2000
Forge House, Limes Road,
Kemble, Cirencester,
Gloucestershire GL7 6AD
01285 771441
info@mb2000.com
www.mb2000.com
Business and management

**Manchester University
Press**
Oxford Road, Manchester M13 9NR
0161 275 2310
mucp@manchester.ac.uk
www.manchesteruniversitypress.
co.uk

Manson Publishing
73 Corringham Road,
London NW11 7DL
020 8905 5150
www.mansonpublishing.com
Scientific, technical, medical and
veterinary

Marion Boyars Publishers
24 Lacy Road, London SW15 1NL
020 8788 9522
catheryn@marionboyars.com
www.marionboyars.co.uk
Formerly Calder and Boyars. Literary
fiction, fiction in translation, social
affairs, film, music, drama

Marshall Cavendish
5th Floor, 32-38 Saffron Hill,
London EC1N 8FH
020 7421 8120
infot@marshallcavendish.co.uk
www.marshallcavendish.co.uk
Adults' and children's and educational

McGraw-Hill Education
Shoppenhangers Road,
Maidenhead, Berkshire SL6 2QL
01628 502500
www.mcgraw-hill.co.uk
Business, economics, computing and
engineering

Higher Education
University textbooks on business, economics, accounting, finance, marketing, computing science, decision sciences. Imprints: McGraw-Hill Education, McGraw-Hill Irwin

Open University Press
Higher education, education, health and social welfare, cultural and media studies, psychology, criminology, sociology, counselling, study guides

Professional
Professional, business and general reference books covering computing, science, technical and medical, languages, architecture, careers, politics, management, finance, parenting, health, sports & fitness. Imprints: McGraw-Hill Professional, McGraw-Hill Trade, McGraw-Hill Osborne, McGraw-Hill Medical Publishing, McGraw-Hill Contemporary, Harvard Business School Press, Amacom, Berrett-Koehler, CMP

Schools
Early childhood, primary and secondary school books. Imprints: Kingscourt, Glencoe and SRA, Macmillan, The Learning Group

Meadowside
185 Fleet Street, London EC24 2HS
020 7400 1084
info@meadowsidebooks.com
www.meadowsidebooks.com
Fiction and non-fiction of Scottish interest

Mercat Press
Birlinn, 10 Newington Road,
Edinburgh EH9 1QS
0131 225 5324
enquiries@mercatpress.com
www.mercatpress.com
Fiction and non-fiction of Scottish interest

Merlin Press
99b Wallis Road, London E9 5LN
020 8533 5800
info@merlinpress.co.uk
www.merlinpress.co.uk
Economics, history, leftwing politics. Imprints: Green Print, Merlin Press, Crescent Books

Merrell Publishers
81 Southwark Street,
London SE1 0HX
020 7928 8880
mail@merrellpublishers.com
www.merrellpublishers.com
Art, architecture, design and photography

Methodist Publishing House
4 John Wesley Road,
Werrington, Peterborough,
Cambridgeshire PE4 6ZP
01733 325002
customer.services@mph.org.uk
www.mph.org.uk
Owned by the Methodist Church Christian books. Imprint: Epworth Press

Methuen Publishing
8 Artillery Row, London SW1P 1RW
020 7802 0018
info@methuen.co.uk
www.methuen.co.uk
General fiction and non-fiction. Imprint: Politicos (politics)

Michael Joseph
(see Penguin Books)

Michael O'Mara Books
9 Lion Yard, Tremadoc Road,
London SW4 7NQ
020 7720 8643
enquiries@mombooks.com
www.mombooks.com
Biography, popular history, humour, children's and pre-school

Michelin Travel Publications
Hannay House, 39 Clarendon Road,
Watford, Hertfordshire WD17 1JA
01923 205240
www.michelin.co.uk
Travel books and maps

Microsoft Press
Thames Valley Park, Reading,
Berkshire RG6 1WG
0870 601 0100
mspinfo@microsoft.com
www.microsoft.com/mspress/uk
Computing manuals to accompany Microsoft products; also system administration, business solutions and security

Miles Kelly Publishing
Unit 17 & 18, The Bardfield Centre,
Great Bardfield, Essex CM7 4SL
01371 811309
info@mileskelly.net
www.mileskelly.net
Children's titles

Milet Publishing
c/o Turnaround Publisher Services
Unit 3, Olympic Trading Estate,
Coburg Road, London N22 6TZ
020 8829 3000
Info@milet.com
www.milet.com
Children's books

Mills & Boon
(see Harlequin Mills & Boon)

Mira Books
(See Harlequin Mills & Boon)

MIT Press
(see Harvard University Press/
MIT Press)

Motor Racing Publications
PO Box 1318, Croydon,
Surrey CR9 5YP
020 8654 2711
mrp.books@virgin.net
www.mrpbooks.co.uk
Motor racing, road cars, performance and classic cars

Murdoch Books UK
Erico House, 6th Floor,
93–99 Upper Richmond Road,
Putney, London SW15 2TG
020 8785 5995
info@murdochbooks.co.uk
Food and drink, craft, gardening, fiction and non-fiction

National Trust
(See Anova Books)

Nautical Data
The Book Barn, Westbourne,
Emsworth, Hampshire PO10 8RS
01243 389352
info@nauticaldata.com
www.nauticaldata.com

NCVO Publications
Regent's Wharf, 8 All Saints Street,
London N1 9RL
020 7713 6161
ncvo@ncvo-vol.org.uk
www.ncvo-vol.org.uk

Publishing imprint of the National Council for Voluntary Organisations. Directories, public policy and governance; trusteeship and HR in the voluntary sector

Neil Wilson Publishing
G/2 19 Netherton Avenue,
Glasgow, G13 1BQ
info@nwp.co.uk
www.nwp.co.uk
Scottish and Irish interest: food and drink, outdoor pursuits, history, humour and biography. Imprints: The Angel's Share; 11:9; In Pinn; NWP; The Vital Spark

Nelson Thornes
Delta Place, 27 Bath Road,
Cheltenham,
Gloucestershire GL53 7TH
01242 267100
info@nelsonthornes.com
www.nelsonthornes.com
Part of the Wolters Kluwer Group. Educational

New Beacon Books
76 Stroud Green Road,
London N4 3EN
020 7272 4889
newbeaconbooks@btconnect.com
Black-oriented fiction, history, politics, poetry and language

New Cavendish Books
3 Denbigh Road, London W11 2SJ
020 7229 6765
sales@newcavendishbooks.co.uk
www.newcavendishbooks.co.uk

New Holland Publishers (UK)
Garfield House,
86–88 Edgware Road,
London W2 2EA
020 7724 7773
postmaster@nhpub.co.uk
www.newhollandpublishers.com
Non-fiction, lifestyle and self-improvement. Imprint: Cadogan Guides (travel guides and travel literature)
info@cadoganguides.co.uk
www.cadoganguides.com

New Rider
(see Pearson Education)

Nicholas Brealey Publishing
3–5 Spafield Street,
London EC1R 4QB
020 7239 0360
publicity@nicholasbrealey.com
www.nicholasbrealey.com
Includes Intercultural Press. Cultural business, self-help and travel. US imprint: Intercultural Press

Nick Hern Books
The Glasshouse,
49a Goldhawk Road,
London W12 8QP
020 8749 4953
info@nickhernbooks.demon.co.uk
www.nickhernbooks.co.uk
Theatre and film

Nielsen BookData
89-95 Queensway, Stevenage,
Hertfordshire, SG1 1EA
01483 712325
customerservices.book@nielsen.com
www.nielsenbookdata.com
The Directory of UK and Irish Book Publishers

NMS Enterprises
National Museums of Scotland,
Chambers Street,
Edinburgh EH1 1JF
0131 247 4026
publishing@nms.ac.uk
www.nms.ac.uk
History, art, archaeology, natural history, popular Scottish history, culture, biography and geology

Nottingham University Press
Manor Farm, Church Lane,
Thrumpton, Nottingham NG11 0AX
0115 983 1011
editor@nup.com
www.nup.com
Scientific textbooks

Oberon Books
521 Caledonian Road,
London N7 9RH
020 7607 3637
info@oberonbooks.com
www.oberonbooks.com
Play texts

Octagon Press
78 York Street, London W1H 1DP
020 7193 6456
admin@octagonpress.com
www.octagonpress.com
Philosophy, psychology, travel and Eastern religion

Octopus Publishing Group
2–4 Heron Quays, London E14 4JP
020 7531 8400
info@octopus-publishing.co.uk
www.octopus-publishing.co.uk
Owned by Hachette. Illustrated books. Imprints: Bounty; Cassell Illustrated; Conran Octopus (www.conran-octopus. co.uk); Gaia Books; Godsfield Press; Hamlyn (www.hamlyn.co.uk); Miller's; Mitchell Beazley (www.mitchell-beazley. co.uk); Philip's (www.philips-maps. co.uk)

Oldcastle Books
PO Box 394, Harpenden,
Hertfordshire AL5 1XJ
01582 761264
info@noexit.co.uk
info@pocketessentials.com
www.oldcastlebooks.com
Imprints: No Exit Press (www. noexit.co.uk) and Crime Time (crime/noir fiction); Pocketessentials (compact reference books on film, tv, literature, ideas and history www. pocketessentials.com); High Stakes (gambling www.highstakespublishing. com); Kamera (film-related titles www. kamerabooks.co.uk).

Omnibus Press
14–15 Berners Street,
London W1T 3LJ
01284 725 725
info@omnibuspress.com
www.omnibuspress.com
Imprints: Omnibus Press (music-related biography); Vision On (upmarket music-related photo books). US imprint: Schirmer Books (self-help books, music industry)

Oneworld
185 Banbury Road,
Oxford OX2 7AR
01865 310 597
info@oneworld-publications.com
www.oneworldpublications.com

Oneworld Classics

London House,
243-253 Lower Mortlake Road,
Richmond, Surrey TW9 2LL
020 8948 9550
info@calderpublications.com
www.calderpublications.com
*Biography, drama, music, poetry
and translations. Imprints: Oneworld
Classics; Calder Publications (both
co-owned by Alma Books)*

Onlywomen Press

40 St Lawrence Terrace,
London W10 5ST
020 8354 0796
onlywomenpress@btconnect.com
www.onlywomenpress.com
*Lesbian and feminist fiction, non-
fiction theory and poetry*

Open University Press

(see McGraw-Hill Education)

Orbit

(see Little, Brown Book Group)

Orchard Books

(See Hachette Children's Books)

Orion Publishing Group

Orion House,
5 Upper Saint Martin's Lane,
London WC2H 9EA
020 7240 3444
info@orionbooks.co.uk
www.orionbooks.co.uk
- Cassell Military – *Illustrated and
  paperback*
- Cassell Reference
- Everyman – *Classics in paperback*
- Gollancz – *Sci-fi and fantasy*
- Orion Audiobooks
- Orion Children's Books
- Orion Paperbacks – *fiction and
  non-fiction in paperback*
- Phoenix – *Contemporary fiction*
- Weidenfeld & Nicolson – *History,
  reference, non-fiction, illustrated and
  literary fiction, military*

Osprey Publishing

Midland House, West Way,
Oxford OX2 0PH
01865 727022
info@ospreypublishing.com
www.ospreypublishing.com
Military history, aviation

Oxford University Press

Great Clarendon Street,
Oxford OX2 6DP
01865 556767
enquiry@oup.com
www.oup.com
*A department of Oxford University.
Academic. Imprint: Oxford Children's
Books*

Palgrave Macmillan

(see Macmillan Publishers)

Pan/Pan Macmillan

(see Macmillan Publishers)

Papermac

(see Macmillan Publishers)

Paper Tiger

(see Anova Books)

Pavilion

(see Anova Books)

Peachpit Press

(see Pearson Education)

Pearson Education

Edinburgh Gate, Harlow,
Essex CM20 2JE
01279 623623
enquiries@pearson.com
www.pearsoned.co.uk
- Addison-Wesley – *Computer
  programming*
- Allyn & Bacon – *Education,
  humanities and social sciences*
- BBC Active – learning resources
- Benjamin Cummings – *Science*
- Cisco Press – *Cisco systems
  materials*
- FT Prentice Hall – *Global business*
- Harcourt – *Educational resources
  for teachers and learners. Imprints:
  Heinemann; Gallway; Ginn; Payne-
  Gallway; Raintree; Rigby;*
- Longman – *Educational
  materials for schools, English
  language teaching (ELT) materials,
  higher education textbooks (law,
  humanities, social sciences)*
- New Rider – *Graphics and design*
- Peachpit Press – *Web development*
- Penguin Books – *(see separate
  entry under Penguin Books)*
- Penguin Longman – *ELT books*
- Penguin English (for teachers) –

www.penguinenglish.com
- Penguin Readers (for students)
  – www.penguinreaders.com
- Prentice Hall – *Academic and
  reference textbooks: business,
  computer science, engineering
  and IT*
- Prentice Hall Business – *Practical
  and personal development*
- QUE Publishing – *Computing*
- SAMS Publishing – *Reference
  books for programmers and
  developers, web developers,
  designers, networking and system
  administrators*
- Wharton - *Business*
- York Notes – *Literature guides for
  students*

Pegasus Elliot & Mackenzie Publishers

Sheraton House, Castle Park,
Cambridge CB3 0AX
01223 370012
editors@pegasuspublishers.com
www.pegasuspublishers.com
*Fiction and non-fiction, crime and
erotica. Imprints: Chimera; Vanguard
Press; Nightingale Books, Pegasus*

Pen & Sword Books

47 Church Street, Barnsley,
South Yorkshire S70 2AS
01226 734222
editorialoffice@pen-and-sword.
co.uk
www.pen-and-sword.co.uk
*Military, naval and aviation history.
Imprints: Leo Cooper, Wharncliffe
Publishing*

Penguin Books

80 Strand, London WC2R 0RL
020 7010 3000
www.penguin.co.uk
Owned by Pearson
- Dorling Kindersley – *Information
  books and resources for children and
  adults. Imprint: Dorling Kindersley
  Books; DK Travel (travel guides and
  phrasebooks)*
- ePenguin – *ebooks*
- Penguin Audiobooks
- Penguin General Books –
  *Imprints: Fig Tree; Penguin
  Paperbacks; Hamish Hamilton;
  Michael Joseph; Viking*
- Penguin Press – *Imprints:*

Allen Lane *(reference inc. Roget's Thesaurus and Pears Cyclopaedia); Penguin Classics; Penguin Modern Classics*
• Puffin – *Children's*
• Rough Guides – roughguide@penguin.co.uk
  Travel guides, phrase books, music guides and reference
• Warne – *Children's, inc. Beatrix Potter, Spot, Ladybird*

Penguin Ireland
25 St Stephen's Green, Dublin 2
00 353 1 661 7695
info@penguin.ie
www.penguin.ie

Persephone Books
59 Lamb's Conduit Street,
London WC1N 3NB
020 7242 9292
info@persephonebooks.co.uk
www.persephonebooks.co.uk
Reprint fiction and non-fiction, focus on women

Perseus Books Group
69–70 Temple Chambers,
3–7 Temple Avenue,
London EC4Y 0HP
020 7353 7771
enquiries@perseusbooks.co.uk
www.perseusbooksgroup.com
UK office of US Perseus Books Group. Non-fiction. Imprints: PublicAffairs (current affairs); Da Capo Press (music, history, film and biography); Basic Books (current affairs, history, popular science); Counterpoint (literature and fiction); Basic Civitas Books (African American studies); Westview Press (social sciences, humanities, science)

Peter Haddock Publishing
Pinfold Lane, Bridlington,
East Yorkshire YO16 6BT
01262 678121
info@phpublishing.co.uk
www.phpublishing.co.uk
Children's books

Peter Owen Publishers
73 Kenway Road, London SW5 0RE
020 7373 5628
admin@peterowen.com
www.peterowen.com
Biography, non-fiction, literary fiction, literary criticism, history and the arts

Phaidon Press
18 Regent's Wharf, All Saints Street,
London N1 9PA
020 7843 1000
enquiries@phaidon.com
www.phaidon.com
Arts and culture

Philip Wilson Publishers
109 Drysdale Street,
The Timber Yard, London N1 6ND
020 7033 9900
pwilson@philip-wilson.co.uk
www.philip-wilson.co.uk
Art, museums and exhibition catalogues

Phoenix
(see Orion Publishing Group)

Piatkus Books
(See Little, Brown Book Group)

Picador
(see Macmillan Publishers)

Piccadilly Press
5 Castle Road, London NW1 8PR
020 7267 4492
books@piccadillypress.co.uk
www.piccadillypress.co.uk
Children's, teenage and parental books

Pimlico
(see Random House Group)

Pinwheel
(See Alligator Books)

Pluto Press
345 Archway Road,
London N6 5AA
020 8348 2724
pluto@plutobooks.com
www.plutobooks.com
Non-fiction:politics and social sciences

Pocket Books
(see Simon & Schuster UK)

The Policy Press
University of Bristol, Fourth Floor,
Beacon House, Queen's Road,
Bristol BS8 1QU
0117 331 4054
tpp-info@bristol.ac.uk
www.policypress.org.uk
Social sciences

Politico's Publishing
(see Methuen Publishing)

Polity Press
65 Bridge Street,
Cambridge CB2 1UR
01223 324315
info@polity.co.uk
www.polity.co.uk
General academic

Poolbeg Press
123 Grange Hill, Baldoyle,
Dublin 13, Republic of Ireland
00353 1832 1477
www.poolbeg.com
Popular fiction, non-fiction and current affairs

Portland Press
3rd Floor, Eagle House,
16 Proctor Street,
London WC1V 6NX
020 7280 4110
editorial@portlandpress.com
www.portlandpress.com
Biochemistry and medicine

Portobello Books
12 Addison Avenue,
London W11 4QR
0207 605 1380
mail@portobellobooks.com
www.portobellobooks.com
Fiction and non-fiction

Prentice Hall/Prentice Hall Business
(see Pearson Education)

Prestel Publishing
4 Bloomsbury Place,
London WC1A 2QA
020 7323 5004
editorial@prestel-uk.co.uk
www.prestel.com
Art, architecture, photography, design and fashion

Profile Books
3A Exmouth House, Pine Street,
Exmouth Market, London EC1R 0JH
020 7841 6300
info@profilebooks.com
www.profilebooks.com
Non-fiction. Publishers of The Economist books. Imprints: Green Profile (environmental issues); Serpent's Tail (fiction and non-fiction in paperback); Imprint: Five Star

Profile Sports Media
5th Floor, Mermaid House,
2 Puddle Dock, London EC4V 3DS
020 7332 2000
info@profilesportsmedia.com
www.profilesportsmedia.com
Sporting annuals and publications

Proquest Information and Learning
The Quorum, Barnwell Road,
Cambridge CB5 8SW
01223 215512
marketing@proquest.co.uk
www.proquest.co.uk
Educational

Psychology Press
(see T&F Informa)

Puffin
(see Penguin Books)

Pushkin Press
12 Chester Terrace,
London NW1 4ND
0207 730 0750
books@pushkinpress.com
www.pushkinpress.com
Translated classic and contemporary European literature

Quadrille Publishing
Alhambra House,
27–31 Charing Cross Road,
London WC2H 0LS
020 7839 7117
enquiries@quadrille.co.uk
www.quadrille.co.uk
Lifestyle

Quartet Books
27 Goodge Street,
London W1T 2LD
020 7636 3992
quartetbooks@easynet.co.uk
Part of the Namara Group.
Contemporary literary fiction

Quarto Publishing
226 City Road, London EC1V 2TT
0207 700 9000
info@quarto.com
www.quarto.com
Highly illustrated non-fiction.

QUE Publishing
(see Pearson Education)

Quercus Publishing
21 Bloomsbury Square,
London WC1A 2NS
020 7291 7200
www.quercusbooks.co.uk
Fiction and non-fiction. Imprint:
Maclehose Press

Radcliffe Publishing
18 Marcham Road, Abingdon,
Oxfordshire OX14 1AA
01235 528820
contact.us@radcliffemed.com
www.radcliffe-oxford.com

Random House Group
Random House,
20 Vauxhall Bridge Road,
London SW1V 2SA
020 7840 8400
enquiries@randomhouse.co.uk
www.rbooks.co.uk
Cornerstone
• Arrow – *Mass-market paperback fiction and non-fiction*
• Century – *General fiction and non-fiction including commercial fiction, autobiography, biography, history and self-help*
• Hutchinson – *General fiction and non-fiction including belles-lettres, current affairs, politics, travel and history*
• Random House Books and Random House Business Books – *Non-fiction and business books*
• William Heinemann – *non-fiction and literary fiction, crime, thrillers*
• Windmill – *quality fiction and narrative non-fiction paperbacks*
CCV
• The Bodley Head – *Non-fiction, history, current affairs, science*
• Chatto & Windus – *Memoirs, current affairs, essays, literary fiction, history, poetry, politics, philosophy and translations*
• Harvill Secker – *Literary fiction, literature in translation, English literature, quality thrillers, some non-fiction*
• Jonathan Cape – *Biography and memoirs, current affairs, fiction, history, photography, poetry, politics and travel*
• Pimlico – *Quality non-fiction paperbacks specialising in history, biography, popular culture and*

the arts
• Square Peg – *Commercial non-fiction*
• Vintage – *Quality paperback fiction and non-fiction*
• Yellow Jersey Press – *Narrative sports books*
Ebury Publishing
• BBC Books
• Ebury Press – *Autobiography, biography, popular history, cookery, popular science, humour, diet and health*
• Rider – *Mind, body and spirit*
• Time Out – *(publishing in partnership with Time Out Guides)*
• Vermilion – *Popular reference, lifestyle, crafts, interior design*
Preface Publishing
submissionspreface@randomhouse.co.uk
www.prefacepublishing.com
Commercial fiction and non-fiction

Random House Children's Books
Imprints: Bantam Press;BodleyHead Children's Books; Johnathan Cape Children's Books; Corgi Children's Books; Doubleday Children's Books; David Fickling;Hutchinson Children's Books; Red Fox Children's Books

Transworld Publishers
61–63 Uxbridge Road,
London W5 5SA
020 8579 2652
info@transworld-publishers.co.uk
www.booksattransworld.co.uk
Imprints:
• Bantam – *paperback general fiction and non-fiction*
• Bantam Press – *fiction and general non-fiction*
• Black Swan – *quality fiction in paperback*
• Channel 4 Books – *TV tie-in books in partnership with Channel 4*
• Corgi – *general fiction and non-fiction in paperback*
• Doubleday – *literary fiction and non-fiction*
• Eden – *books in partnership with the Eden Project*
• Expert Books – *gardening and DIY*
Virgin Books
www.virgin.com/books
• Virgin – *popular culture, autobiography, sport*

- **Black Lace** – *erotic fiction by women for women*
- **Nexus** – *erotic fiction*

Ransom Publishing
51 Southgate Street,
Winchester SO23 9EH
01962 862 307
ransom@ransom.co.uk
www.ransom.co.uk
Education and children's fiction

Reader's Digest Association
11 Westferry Circus, Canary Wharf,
London E14 1HE
020 7715 8000
gbeditorial@readersdigest.co.uk
www.readersdigest.co.uk
Cookery, history, reference, gardening and DIY

Reaktion Books
33 Great Sutton Street,
London EC1V 0DX
020 7253 1071
info@reaktionbooks.co.uk
www.reaktionbooks.co.uk
Architecture, asian and cultural studies, film, art and photography, history and geography, biography

Reardon Publishing
PO Box 919, Cheltenham,
Gloucestershire GL50 9AN
01242 231800
reardon@bigfoot.com
www.reardon.co.uk
Member of the Outdoor Writers Guild. Cotswold area local interest

Red Bird Publishing
Kiln Farm, East End Green,
Brightlingsea, Colchester,
Essex CO7 0SX
01206 303525
info@red-bird.co.uk
www.red-bird.co.uk
Special-effects books for children

Red Fox
(see Random House Group)

Redhat Press
(see Wiley Europe)

Reed Elsevier
1–3 Strand, London WC2N 5JR
0207 930 7077
www.reedelsevier.com
0207 930 7077
Butterworth-Heinemann
Linacre House, Jordan Hill, Oxford
OX2 8DP
01865 310 366
www.bh.com
Books and electronic products, business, technical
Elsevier
The Boulevard, Langford Lane,
Kidlington, Oxford OX5 1GB
01865 843 000
www.elsevier.com
Academic and professional reference books, scientific and medical books.
Elsevier Health Sciences
32 Jamestown Road, London
NW1 7BY
0207 424 4200
www.elsevierhealth.com
Health science books and journals
LexisNexis
Halsbury House, 35 Chancery Lane,
London WC2A 1EL
020 7400 2500
competitive.intelligence@lexis-nexis.com
www.lexisnexis.co.uk
Legal and business materials in print and online, including The Advertiser Red Books. Butterworths Services provide access to a library of UK law
RBI UK
Quadrant House, The Quadrant,
Sutton, Surrey SM2 5AS
020 8652 3500
www.reedbusiness.co.uk
Business directories, magazines, e-newsletters, websites and cd-roms

Regency House Publishing
The Red House, 84 High Street,
Buntingford, Hertfordshire SG9 9AJ
01763 274666
regency-house@btconnect.com
Art and transport.

Richmond House Publishing Company
70–76 Bell Street, Marylebone,
London NW1 6SP
020 7224 9666
sales@rhpco.co.uk
www.rhpco.co.uk
Theatre and entertainment directories

Rider
(see Random House Group)

Robert Hale
Clerkenwell House,
45–47 Clerkenwell Green,
London EC1R 0HT
020 7251 2661
enquiries@halebooks.com
www.halebooks.com

Robinson
(See Constable & Robinson)

Robson Books
(see Anova Books)

Rodale Books
The Boulevard, Orbital Park,
Ashford, TN24 0GA
08607 731 0622
rodalecs@omsg.co.uk
www.rodale.co.uk
Lifestyle

Roget's Thesaurus
(see Penguin Books)

Rough Guides
(see Penguin Books)

Roundhouse
Maritime House, Basin Road North,
Hove, East Sussex, BN41 1WR
01273 704 962
roundhouse.group@tiscali.co.uk
www.roundhousegroup.co.uk
Cinema and media

Routledge
(see T&F Informa)

Ryland Peters & Small
20–21 Jockey's Fields,
London WC1R 4BW
020 7025 2200
info@rps.co.uk
www.rylandpeters.com
Illustrated lifestyle

SAF Publishing
149 Wakeman Road,
London NW10 5BH
020 8969 6099
info@safpublishing.co.uk
www.safpublishing.co.uk
Experimental rock and jazz music.
Firefly Publishing (mainstream rock
and pop)

SAGE Publications
1 Oliver's Yard, 55 City Road,
London EC1Y 1SP
020 7324 8500
info@sagepub.co.uk
www.sagepub.co.uk
Social sciences and humanities.
Imprint: Paul Chapman (education
and training)

Samuel French
52 Fitzroy Street, London W1T 5JR
020 7387 9373
theatre@samuelfrench-london.co.uk
www.samuelfrench-london.co.uk
Plays

SAMS Publishing
(see Pearson Education)

Sangam Books
57 London Fruit Exchange,
Brushfield Street, London E1 6EP
020 7377 6399
sangambks@aol.com
Educational textbooks

Saqi Books
26 Westbourne Grove,
London W2 5RH
020 7221 9347
www.saqibooks.com
History, politics, art, cuisine etc. with
an international outlook. Imprint:
Telegram (International literary
fiction, www.telegrambooks.com)

SB Publications
14 Bishopstone Road, Seaford,
East Sussex BN25 2UB
01323 893498
sbpublications@tiscali.co.uk
www.sbpublications.co.uk
Local history, travel, guides

Scholastic
Euston House, 24 Eversholt Street,
London NW1 1DB
020 7756 7756
SCBenquiries@scholastic.co.uk
www.scholastic.co.uk
Education

Scholastic Children's Books
Euston House, 24 Eversholt Street,
London NW1 1DB
020 7756 7756
scbenquiries@scholastic.co.uk
www.scholastic.co.uk
Fiction. Imprints: Hippo, Point

SCM Canterbury Press
13-17 Long Lane, London EC1A 9PN
London N1 0NX
020 7776 7540
admin@scm-canterburypress.co.uk
www.scm-canterburypress.co.uk
Theology and hymn books

Scala Publishers
Northburgh House,
10 Northburgh Street,
London EC1V 0AT
020 7490 9900
info@scalapublishers.com
www.scalapublishers.com
Art

Scottish Cultural Press/
Scottish Children's Press
Unit 6, Newhattle Abbey Business
Park, Newbattle Road,
Dalkeith EH22 3LJ
0131 660 4666
info@scottishbooks.com
www.scottishbooks.com
Scottish-interest books for adult, tourist
and academic readers

Search Press
Wellwood, North Farm Road,
Tunbridge Wells, Kent TN2 3DR
01892 510850
searchpress@searchpress.com
www.searchpress.com
Art and crafts

SEMERC
Angel House, Sherston,
Malmesbury,
Wiltshire, SN16 0LH
01666 843 200
sales@semerc.om

www.semerc.com
ICT special needs

Seren
57 Nolton Street,
Bridgend CF31 3AE
01656 663018
general@seren-books.com
www.seren-books.com
Wales and Welsh authors

Serpent's Tail
(See Profile Books)

Severn House Publishers
9–15 High Street, Sutton,
Surrey SM1 1DF
020 8770 3930
info@severnhouse.com
www.severnhouse.com
Hardback fiction for the library
market: romance, science fiction,
horror, fantasy and crime

Shepheard-Walwyn
(Publishers)
15 Alder Road, London SW14 8ER
020 8241 5927
books@shepheard-walwyn.co.uk
www.shepheard-walwyn.co.uk
Ethical economics, perennial
philosophy, biography, gift books,
books of Scottish interest

Shire Publications
Midland House, West Way, Botley,
Oxford OX2 0PH
01865 811 332
shire@shirebooks.co.uk
www.shirebooks.co.uk
Original non-fiction paperbacks

Short Books
3a Exmouth House, Pine Street,
Exmouth Market, London EC1R 0JH
020 7833 9429
info@shortbooks.biz
www.shortbooks.co.uk
Non-fiction for adults and children

Sidgwick and Jackson
(see Macmillan Publishers)

Sigma Press
Pontyclerc, Penybanc Road,
Ammanford SA18 3HP
01269 593 100
info@sigmapress.co.uk

www.sigmapress.co.uk
Outdoor, heritage, myth, biography

Simon & Schuster UK
Africa House, 64–78 Kingsway,
London WC2B 6AH
020 7316 1900
enquiries@simonandschuster.co.uk
www.simonsays.co.uk
*General fiction and non-fiction.
Imprints: Simon & Schuster; Pocket
Books; Simon & Schuster Children's
Books; Free Press; Scribner, Simon &
Schuster Audio; A CBS Company*

Snow Books
120 Pentonville Road,
London N1 9JN
07904062414
info@snowbooks.com
www.snowbooks.com
*Independent publisher of fiction and
non-fiction*

Souvenir Press
43 Great Russell Street,
London WC1B 3PD
020 7580 9307
souvenirpress@ukonline.co.uk
*Academic. Imprints include: Condor,
Human Horizons, Independent Voices,
Pictorial Presentations, Pop Universal,
The Story-Tellers*

Sphere
(See Little, Brown Book Group)

Spon Press
(see T&F Informa)

Springer-Verlag London
Ashbourne House, The Guildway,
Old Portsmouth Road, Guildford,
Surrey GU3 1LP
01483 734433
www.springer.com
*Computer science, medical,
engineering, astronomy, maths*

Stainer & Bell
PO Box 110, 23 Gruneisen Road,
London N3 1DZ
020 8343 3303
post@stainer.co.uk
www.stainer.co.uk
Music and hymns

TSO (The Stationery Office)
St Crispins, Duke Street, Norwich,
Norfolk NR3 1PD
01603 622211
customer.services@tso.co.uk
www.tso.co.uk

Summersdale Publishers
46 West Street, Chichester,
West Sussex PO19 1RP
01243 771107
submissions@summersdale.com
www.summersdale.com
*Travel, martial arts, self-help, cookery,
humour and gift books*

Summertown Publishing
Aristotle House, Aristotle Lane,
Oxford OX2 6TR
01865 454130
louis@summertown.co.uk
www.summertown.co.uk
English-language teaching

Sweet & Maxwell Group
100 Avenue Road,
London NW3 3PF
020 7393 7000
www.sweetandmaxwell.co.uk
*Part of the Thomson Corporation.
Legal and professional. Imprints:
W Green (Scotland); Round Hall*

T&F Informa
Mortimer House, 37–41 Mortimer
Street, London W1T 3JH
020 7017 5000
professional.enquiries@informa.com
www.informa.com
- BIOS Scientific Publishers –
  Biology and medicine
- Brunner-Routledge – *psychology
  and counselling*
- Carfax – *Social science and
  humanities*
- CRC – *Science and medical*
- Curzon Press – *Asian and Middle
  Eastern studies*
- David Fulton Books – *teaching
  books and resources*
- Europa Publications –
  *International affairs, politics and
  economics*
- Frank Cass – *Military and
  strategic studies. Also Jewish interest
  imprints: Vallentine Mitchell, Jewish
  Chronicle Publications*
- Garland Science – *Biology*

- Lawrence Erlbaum Associates
  – *academic and professional books
  and journals*
- Martin Dunitz – *Medical*
- Psychology Press – *Psychology*
- Routledge – *Humanities & social
  sciences textbooks/ general non-
  fiction*
- Routledge-Cavendish – *Academic
  and practitioner law books*
- Routledge Curzon – *Politics and
  Middle Eastern studies*
- Routledge Falmer – *Education*
- Spon Press – *Architecture and
  planning*
- Taylor & Francis – *Science
  and reference esp. ergonomics,
  geographical information systems,
  biotechnology and engineering*

Taschen UK
1 Heathcock Court, 5th Floor,
415 Strand, London WC2R 0NS
020 7845 8585
contact-uk@taschen.com
www.taschen.com
*Architecture, art, atlases, collectors'
editions, film, lifestyle, photography
and pop culture*

Taylor & Francis
(see T&F Informa)

Templar
The Granary, North Street, Dorking,
Surrey RH4 1DN
01306 876361
rebecca.beves@templarco.co.uk
www.templarco.co.uk
*Illustrated and novelty books for
children*

Thalamus Publishing
4 Attorney's Walk, Bull Ring,
Ludlow, Shropshire SY8 1AA
01584 874977
www.thalamus-books.com
*Family reference. An imprint of
International Media Solutions*

Thames & Hudson
181A High Holborn,
London WC1V 7QX
020 7845 5000
mail@thameshudson.co.uk
www.thamesandhudson.com
Cultural non-fiction

Third Millennium Publishing
2–5 Benjamin Street,
London EC1M 5QL
020 7336 0144
info@tmiltd.com
www.tmiltd.com

Thomas Cook Publishing
PO Box 227,
Unit 15/16 Coningsby Road,
Peterborough PE3 8SB
01733 416477
publishing-sales@thomascook.com
www.thomascookpublishing.com
Guide books and timetables

Thorsons
(see HarperCollins Publishers)

Time Out
(See Random House Group)

Titan Books
144 Southwark Street,
London SE1 0UP
020 7620 0200
editorial@titanemail.com
www.titanbooks.com
Comic books, graphic novels, spin-offs

Top That! Publishing
Marine House, Tide Mill Way,
Woodbridge, Suffolk IP12 1AP
01394 386651
info@topthatpublishing.com
www.topthatpublishing.com
Children's imprints: Top that!, Kids and Tide Mill Press: Adult imprint: Kudos

Transworld Publishers
(see Random House Group)

Travel Publishing
Airport Business Centre,
10 Thornbury Road, Estover,
Plymouth, Devon PL6 7PP
01752 697 280
info@travelpublishing.co.uk
www.travelpublishing.co.uk
Imprints: Hidden Places; Country Living Rural Guides; Off the Motorway; Country Pubs and Inns; Garden Centre and Nursery Guides

Trentham Books
Westview House,
734 London Road, Stoke-on-Trent,
Staffordshire ST4 5NP
01782 745567
tb@trentham-books.co.uk
www.trentham-books.co.uk
Education, culture and law for professional readers

Trident Press
Empire House, 175 Piccadilly,
London W1J 9TB
020 7491 8770
admin@tridentpress.com
www.tridentpress.com
TV tie-ins, history, travel, geography, culture

Trotman & Co
Westminster House, Kew Road,
Richmond, Surrey TW9 2ND
020 8334 1600
info@trotman.co.uk
www.trotman.co.uk
Careers and education

Tucann Books
19 High Street, Heighington,
Lincoln LN4 1RG
01522 790009
sales@tucann.co.uk
www.tucann.co.uk
Self-publishing

Ulverscroft Group
The Green, Bradgate Road,
Anstey, Leicester LE7 7FU
0116 236 4325
sales@ulverscroft.co.uk
www.ulverscroft.com
Large print and audio, fiction and non-fiction

University of Hertfordshire Press
Hatfield Campus, Learning
Resource Centre, College Lane,
Hatfield, Hertfordshire AL10 9AB
01707 284000
www.herts.ac.uk
Literary criticism and theatre studies, Romani studies, regional and local history, parapsychology. Imprints: Hertfordshire Publications

University of Wales Press
10 Columbus Walk, Brigantine
Place, Cardiff CF10 4UP
02920 557 451
press@press.wales.ac.uk
www.uwp.co.uk
Imprints: GPC Books, Gwasg Prifysgol Cymru

University Presses of California, Columbia & Princeton
1 Oldlands Way, Bognor Regis,
West Sussex PO22 9SA
01243 843291
sales@upccp.demon.co.uk
www.ucpress.edu
www.columbia.edu/cu/cup www.pup.princeton.edu

Unofficial Guides
(see Wiley Europe)

Usborne Publishing
83–85 Saffron Hill,
London EC1N 8RT
020 7430 2800
mail@usborne.co.uk
www.usborne.com
Non-fiction books for children, including computer guides, puzzlebooks, pre-school and books on music

V&A Publishing
V&A Museum, South Kensington,
London SW7 2RL
020 7942 2966
vapubs@vam.ac.uk
www.vandabooks.com

Vallentine Mitchell
Suite 314, Premier House,
112-114 Station Road, Edgware,
Middlesex HA8 7BJ
020 8952 9526
info@vmbooks.com
www.vmbooks.com

Vermilion
(see Random House Group)

Viking
(see Penguin Books)

Vintage
(see Random House Group)

Virago
(see Little, Brown Book Group)

Virgin Books
(See Random House Group)

Visual
(see Wiley Europe)

Voyager Books
(see HarperCollins Publishers)

W Foulsham & Co
The Publishing House,
Bennetts Close, Slough,
Berkshire SL1 5AP
01753 526769
info@foulsham.com
www.foulsham.com
Lifestyle

Walker Books
87 Vauxhall Walk,
London SE11 5HJ
020 7793 0909
enquiry@walker.co.uk
www.walkerbooks.co.uk
*Children's big books, book charts,
game books. Series: Giggle Club*

Wallflower Press
6 Market Place, London W1W 8AF
020 7377 9797
info@wallflowerpress.co.uk
www.wallflowerpress.co.uk
Film, media and cultural studies

Warne
(see Penguin Books)

Weidenfeld & Nicolson
(see Orion Publishing Group)

Wharncliffe Publishing
(see Pen & Sword Books)

Which?
2 Marylebone Road,
London NW1 4DF
020 7770 7000
books@which.co.uk
www.which.co.uk
*Publishing arm of the Consumers'
Association. Imprint: Which? Books
(guides to restaurants, law, property
etc.)*

Whittet Books
BSP House, Station Road, Linton,
Cambs CB 21 4NW
01223 894 870
mail@whittetbooks.com
www.whittetbooks.com
*Natural history, pets and rural
interest, livestock and horticulture.*

Wild Goose Publications
Iona Community,
4th Floor, The Savoy House,
140 Sauchiehall Street,
Glasgow G2 3DH
0141 332 6292
admin@ionabooks.com
www.iona.books.com
*Publishing house of the Iona
Community. Religion, spiritualism and
human rights*

Wiley Europe
The Atrium, Southern Gate,
Chichester PO19 8SQ
01243 779777
cs-books@wiley.co.uk
www.wileyeurope.com
*Scientific, technical and medical;
professional and trade; textbooks and
educational materials.*
Imprints include:
- Capstone Publishing – *Business
  and personal development (*www.
  capstoneideas.com)
- Fernhurst Books – *Sailing and
  watersports*
- For Dummies – *Reference series*
- Frommer's – *Travel guides*
- Jossey-Bass – *Management,
  education and religion*
- The Unofficial Guide – *Travel,
  computing*
- Visual/Redhat Press/Wrox –
  Computing
- Wiley – *Scientific, technical and
  medical; professional and trade;
  textbooks and educational materials*
- Wiley Interscience – *Scientific,
  technical and medical; print and
  online reference materials*
- Wiley-Academy – *Architecture*
- Wiley-Liss – *Life and medical*
- Wiley-VCH – *Scientific, technical
  and medical*

William Heinemann
(see Random House Group)

**Wimbledon Publishing
Company**
75–76 Blackfriars Road,
London SE1 8HA
020 7401 4200
info@wpcpress.com
www.anthempress.com
*Textbooks for languages, maths,
biology and accountancy. Imprint:
Anthem Press*

Windhorse Publications
33 Newmarket Road,
Cambridge, CB5 8DT
01223 911 997
info@windhorsepublications.com
www.windhorsepublications.com
Meditation and Buddhism

WIT Press
Ashurst Lodge, Ashurst,
Southampton,
Hampshire SO40 7AA
02380 293223
marketing@witpress.com
www.witpress.com
Scientific and technical

Women's Press
27 Goodge Street,
London W1T 2LD
020 7636 3992
sales@the-womens-press.com
www.the-womens-press.com
*Part of the Namara Group. Imprint:
Livewire*

Woodhead Publishing
Abington Hall, Abington,
Cambridge CB1 6AH
01223 891358
wp@woodhead-publishing.com
www.woodheadpublishing.com
*Formerly Abington Publishing.
Engineering, textiles, finance and
investment, food technology and
environmental science*

Wordsworth Editions
8b East Street, Ware,
Hertfordshire SG12 9HJ
01920 465167
enquiries@wordsworth-editions.
com
www.wordsworth-editions.com
*Literary classics, reference, poetry,
children's classics, mystery and the
supernatural*

Working White
Chancery Court,
Lincolns Inn, Lincoln Road,
High Wycombe HP12 3RE
01494 429318
info@workingwhite.co.uk
www.workingwhite.co.uk
*Children's big books, book charts,
game books. Series: Giggle Club*

WW Norton & Company
Castle House, 75–76 Wells Street,
London W1T 3QT
020 7323 1579
office@wwnorton.co.uk
Academic and professional non-fiction

X Press
PO Box 25694, London N17 6FP
020 8801 2100
vibes@xpress.co.uk
www.xpress.co.uk
*Black interest. Imprints: Nia, 20/20,
Black Classics*

Y Lolfa Cyf
Talybont, Ceredigion SY24 5AP
01970 832304
ylolfa@ylolfa.com
www.ylolfa.com
*Welsh and Celtic interest. Imprints
and divisions include: Dinas*

**Yale University Press
(London)**
47 Bedford Square,
London WC1B 3DP
020 7079 4900
sales@yaleup.co.uk
www.yalebooks.co.uk

Yellow Jersey Press
(see Random House Group)

York Notes
(see Pearson Education)

Young Picador
(see Macmillan Publishers)

Zambezi Publishing
PO Box 221, Plymouth,
Devon PL2 2YJ
01752 367300
info@zampub.com
www.zampub.com
New-age and self-help

Zed Books
7 Cynthia Street, London N1 9JF
020 7837 4014
www.zedbooks.co.uk
*International and third-world affairs
and development studies*

Literary agents

Abner Stein
10 Roland Gardens, London SW7 3PH
020 7373 0456
abner@abnerstein.co.uk
US agents and authors, some full-length fiction and general non-fiction

The Agency (London)
24 Pottery Lane, Holland Park,
London W11 4LZ
020 7727 1346
info@theagency.co.uk
www.theagency.co.uk
Theatre, film, TV, radio and children's writers and illustrators; also film and TV rights in novels and non-fiction

Alan Brodie Representation
6th Floor, Fairgate House,
78 New Oxford Street,
London WC1A 1HB
020 7079 7990
info@alanbrodie.com
www.alanbrodie.com
Theatre, film, TV and radio scripts

Aitken Alexander Associates
18-21 Cavaye Place,
London SW10 9PT
020 7373 8672
reception@aitkenalexander.co.uk
www.aitkenalexander.co.uk
Fiction and non-fiction

Alexandra Nye
Craigower, 6 Kinnoull Avenue,
Dunblane, Perthshire FK15 9JG
01786 825114
Fiction and topical non-fiction, esp literary fiction and history

AM Heath & Co
6 Warwick Court,
London WC1R 5DJ
020 7242 2811
www.amheath.com
Fiction, general non-fiction and children's

Ampersand Agency
Ryman's Cottages, Little Tew,
Oxon OX7 4JJ
peter@theampersandagency.co.uk
www.theampersandagency.co.uk
Literary and commercial fiction and non-fiction

Andrew Mann
1 Old Compton Street,
London W1D 5JA
020 7734 4751
info@manscript.co.uk
Fiction; general non-fiction; film, TV, theatre and radio scripts

Andrew Nurnberg Associates
Clerkenwell House,
45–47 Clerkenwell Green,
London EC1R 0QX
0203 327 0400
contact@andrewnurnberg.com
www.andrewnurnberg.com
Foreign rights

Annette Green Authors' Agency
1 East Cliff Road, Tunbridge Wells,
Kent TN4 9AD
01892 514275
david@annettegreenagency.co.uk
www.annettegreenagency.co.uk
Literary and general fiction, non-fiction, fiction for teenagers, upmarket popular culture

Artellus
30 Dorset House, Gloucester Place,
London NW1 5AD
020 7935 6972
artellus@artellusltd.co.uk
www.artellus.co.uk
General fiction and non-fiction

Andrew Lownie Literary Agency
36 Great Smith Street,
London SW1P 3BU
020 7222 7574
lownie@globalnet.co.uk
www.andrewlownie.co.uk
Non-fiction

Anthony Harwood
103 Walton Street
Oxford OX2 6EB
01865 559 615
mail@antonyharwood.com
www.anthonyharwood.com
Fiction and non-fiction

AP Watt
20 John Street, London WC1N 2DR
020 7405 6774
apw@apwatt.co.uk
www.apwatt.co.uk
Full-length typescripts, including children's books, screenplays for film and TV

Barbara Levy Literary Agency
64 Greenhill,
Hampstead High Street,
London NW3 5TZ
020 7435 9046
General fiction, non-fiction, TV presenters, film and TV rights

Bell Lomax Moreton Agency
James House, 1 Babmaes Street,
London SW1Y 6HF
020 7930 4447
agency@bell-lomax.co.uk
Fiction and non-fiction, biography, children's, business and sport

Blake Friedmann
122 Arlington Road,
London NW1 7HP
020 7284 0408
info@blakefriedmann.co.uk

BookBlast
PO Box 20184, London W10 5AU
020 8968 3089
gen@bookblast.com
www.bookblast.com
Selective fiction and non-fiction

Brie Burkeman
14 Neville Court, Abbey Road,
London NW8 9DD
0870 199 5002
brie.burkeman@mail.com
*Commercial and literary fiction and
non-fiction, scripts. Independent film
and television consultant to literary
agents*

Campbell Thomson &
McLaughlin
50 Albemarle Street,
London W15 4BD
020 7493 4361
Fiction and general non-fiction

Capel & Land
29 Wardour Street,
London W1D 6PS
020 7734 2414
rosie@capelland.co.uk
www.capelland.com
*Fiction and non-fiction; film, TV, radio
presenters*

Caroline Davidson Literary
Agency
5 Queen Anne's Gardens,
London W4 1TU
020 8995 5768
cdla@ukgateway.net
www.cdla.co.uk
*High quality fiction of originality and
non-fiction*

Caroline Sheldon Literary
Agency
Thorley Manor Farm, Thorley,
Yarmouth PO41 0SJ
01983 760205
carolinesheldon@carolinesheldon.
co.uk
www.carolinesheldon.co.uk
*Fiction, commercial and literary
novels, especially women's and
children's fiction*

Casarotto Ramsay and
Associates
Waverley House, 7-12 Noel Street,
London W1F 8GQ
020 7287 4450
agents@casarotto.co.uk
www.casarotto.co.uk
Scripts for TV, theatre, film and radio

Cecily Ware Literary Agents
19C John Spencer Square,
London N1 2LZ
020 7359 3787
info@cecilyware.com
Scripts for TV and film in all areas

Celia Catchpole
56 Gilpin Avenue,
London SW14 8QY
020 8255 4835
celiacatchpole@yahoo.co.uk

Chapman & Vincent
7 Dilke Street, London SW3 5JE
020 7352 5582
info@chapmanvincent.co.uk
Non-fiction

Christine Green Authors'
Agent
6 Whitehorse Mews,
Westminster Bridge Road,
London SE1 7QD
020 7401 8844
info@christinegreen.co.uk
www.christinegreen.co.uk
*Literary and general fiction and
non-fiction*

Christopher Little Literary
Agency
10 Eel Brook Studios,
125 Moore Park Road,
London SW6 4PS
020 7736 4455
info@christopherlittle.net
www.christopherlittle.net
*Commercial and literary full-length
fiction and non-fiction; film scripts for
established clients*

Conville & Walsh
2 Ganton Street, Soho,
London W1F 7QL
020 7287 3030
sue@convilleandwalsh.com
*Literary and commercial fiction;
serious and narrative non-fiction;
children's books*

Curtis Brown Group
5th Floor, Haymarket House,
28/29 Haymarket, London SW1Y
4SP
020 7393 4400
cb@curtisbrown.co.uk
www.curtisbrown.co.uk

*Writers, directors, designers, presenters
and actors. Handles rights for ICM
Books.*

Darley Anderson Literary,
TV & Film Agency
Estelle House, 11 Eustace Road,
London SW6 1JB
020 7385 6652
enquiries@darleyanderson.com
www.darleyanderson.com
*Fiction: young male, American, Irish,
women's, crime/mystery and humour;
non-fiction; children's fiction; selected
scripts for film and TV*

DGA
55 Monmouth Street,
London WC2H 9DG
020 7240 9992
assistant@davidgodwinassociates.
co.uk
*Literary and general fiction, non-
fiction, biography*

David Grossman Literary
Agency
118b Holland Park Avenue,
London W11 4UA
020 7221 2770
*Full-length fiction and general non-
fiction, esp controversial*

David Higham Associates
5-8 Lower John Street,
Golden Square, London W1F 9HA
020 7434 5900
dha@davidhigham.co.uk
www.davidhigham.co.uk
*Fiction; general non-fiction: biography,
history, current affairs; children's;
scripts*

David O'Leary Literary
Agents
10 Lansdowne Court,
Lansdowne Rise, London W11 2NR
020 7229 1623
d.oleary@virgin.net
*Fiction (popular and literary) and
non-fiction, esp thrillers, history,
popular science, Russia and Ireland
(history and fiction)*

Deborah Owen
78 Narrow Street, Limehouse,
London E14 8BP
020 7987 51191

Dench Arnold Agency
10 Newburgh Street,
London W1F 7RN
020 7437 4551
www.dencharnold.com
Scripts for TV and film

Diane Banks Associates
submissions@dianebanks.co.uk

Dorian Literary Agency
Upper Thornehill, 27 Church Road,
St Marychurch, Torquay,
Devon TQ1 4QY
01803 312095
General fiction especially popular

Dorie Simmonds Agency
River Bank House, 1 Putney Bridge
Approach, London SW6 3JD
020 7736 0002
dhsimmonds@aol.com
*General fiction, including commercial
women's fiction, historical fiction,
thrillers; commercial non-fiction,
including historical and contemporary
biographies, self-help, cookery;
children's books and associated rights
throughout the world*

Duncan McAra
28 Beresford Gardens,
Edinburgh EH5 3ES
0131 552 1558
duncanmcara@hotmail.com
Literary fiction and non-fiction

Ed Victor
6 Bayley Street, Bedford Square,
London WC1B 3HE
020 7304 4100
*Mostly commercial fiction and
non-fiction; children's*

Edwards Fuglewicz
49 Great Ormond Street,
London WC1N 3HZ
020 7405 6725
ros@efla.co.uk
*Fiction: literary, some commercial;
non-fiction: biography, history, popular
culture*

Elaine Steel
110 Gloucester Avenue,
London NW1 8HX
020 8348 0918
ecmsteel@aol.com

*Writers and directors in film,
television and publishing*

**Elspeth Cochrane Personal
Management**
16 Trinity Close, The Pavement,
London SW4 0JD
020 7622 3566
elspeth@elspethcochrane.co.uk
*Fiction, non-fiction, biographies,
screenplays, scripts for all media*

Eric Glass
25 Ladbroke Crescent,
London W11 1PS
020 7229 9500
eglassltd@aol.com
Fiction, non-fiction and scripts

**Eunice McMullen Children's
Literary Agent**
Low Ibbotsholme Cottage,
Off Bridge Lane, Troutbeck Bridge,
Windermere, Cumbria LA23 1HU
01539 448551
eunicemcmullen@totalise.co.uk
www.eunicemcmullen.co.uk
Children's material

Faith Evans Associates
27 Park Avenue North,
London N8 7RU
020 8340 9920
Fiction and non-fiction

Felicity Bryan
2A North Parade, Banbury Road,
Oxford OX2 6LX
01865 513816
agency@felicitybryan.com
www.felicitybryan.com
Fiction and non-fiction

Felix de Wolfe
Kingsway House, 103 Kingsway,
London WC2B 6QX
020 7242 5066
info@felixdewolfe.com
Theatrical agency

**Fox & Howard Literary
Agency**
4 Bramerton Street,
London SW3 5JX
020 7352 8691
*Non-fiction: biography, history and
popular culture, reference, business
and lifestyle*

Frances Kelly Agency
111 Clifton Road,
Kingston-upon-Thames,
Surrey KT2 6PL
020 8549 7830
Illustrated and academic non-fiction

**Futerman, Rose &
Associates**
91 St Leonards Road,
London SW14 7BL
020 8255 7755
enquiries@futermanrose.co.uk
www.futermanrose.co.uk
*Commercial fiction, non-fiction,
biography, film and television scripts
specialising in book-to-film projects*

Greene & Heaton
37 Goldhawk Road,
London W12 8QQ
020 8749 0315
info@greeneheaton.co.uk
www.greeneheaton.co.uk
*Wide range of fiction and general
non-fiction (clients include Bill Bryson,
Hugh Fearnley-Whittingstall, Michael
Frayn, PD James and Sarah Waters)*

Gregory & Co
3 Barb Mews, London W6 7PA
020 7610 4676
info@gregoryandcompany.co.uk
www.gregoryandcompany.co.uk
*Fiction: literary, commercial, crime,
suspense and thrillers; general non-
fiction*

Hanbury Agency
27 Walcot Street, Oxford OX2 6EB
0207 630 6768
www.hanburyagency.com
maggie@hanburyagency.com
*Quality fiction and non-fiction);
children's books, plays/scripts and
poetry*

ICM Books
(See Curtis Brown Group)

IMG Literary UK
McCormack House,
Burlington Lane, Chiswick,
London W4 2TH
020 8233 5000
*Celebrity books, commercial fiction,
non-fiction, sports-related and how-to
business books*

Intercontinental Literary Agency
Centric House, 390–391 Strand,
London WCTR 0LT
020 7379 6611
ila@ila-agency.co.uk
www.ila-agency.co.uk
Translation rights only

Jane Conway-Gordon
1 Old Compton Street,
London W1D 5JA
020 7494 0148
jconway_gordon@dsl.pipex.com
Fiction and general non-fiction

Jane Judd Literary Agency
18 Belitha Villas, London N1 1PD
020 7607 0273
*General fiction and non-fiction:
biography, investigative journalism,
health, women's interests and travel*

Janklow & Nesbit (UK)
33 Drayson Mews, London W8 4LY
020 7376 2733
queries@janklow.co.uk
*Fiction and non-fiction, commercial
and literary; US and translation
rights handled by Janklow and Nesbit
Associates in New York*

Jeffrey Simmons
15 Penn House, Mallory Street,
London NW8 8SX
020 7224 8917
jasimmons@btconnect.com
*Biography, cinema and theatre, quality
and commercial fiction, history, law
and crime, politics and world affairs,
parapsychology and sport*

Jill Foster
9 Barb Mews, Brook Green,
London W6 7PA
020 7602 1263
Scripts for TV, film and radio

JM Thurley Management
Archery House, 33 Archery Square,
Walmer, Deal CT14 7JA
01304 371721
jmthurley@aol.com
*Full-length fiction, non-fiction, TV
and films*

Johnson & Alcock
Clerkenwell House,
45/47 Clerkenwell Green,
London EC1R 0HT
020 7251 0125
info@johnsonandalcock.co.uk
General fiction and non-fiction

John Welch, Literary Consultant & Agent
Mill Cottage, Calf Lane, Chipping
Camden, Gloucestershire GL55 6JQ
01386 840237
johnwelch@cyphus.co.uk
*Military, naval and aviation history,
general history, and a little biography*

Jonathan Clowes
10 Iron Bridge House,
Bridge Approach, London NW1 8BD
020 7722 7674
jonathanclowes@aol.com
*Fiction and non-fiction; scripts,
especially situation comedy, film and
television rights (clients include Doris
Lessing, David Nobbs, Len Deighton)*

Josef Weinberger Plays
12–14 Mortimer Street,
London W1T 3JJ
020 7580 2827
*Scripts for the theatre; play publisher
and licensor of stage rights; publishes
plays and acts as UK agent for US
agents including the Dramatists Play
Service*

Judith Chilcote Agency
8 Wentworth Mansions,
Keats Grove, London NW3 2RL
020 7794 3717
judybks@aol.com
*Commercial fiction, TV tie-ins,
biography and lifestyle*

Judith Murdoch Literary Agency
19 Chalcot Square,
London NW1 8YA
020 7722 4197
Full-length fiction only

Judy Daish Associates
2 St Charles Place,
London W10 6EG
020 8964 8811
judy@judydaish.com
Scripts for TV, theatre, film and radio

Jüri Gabriel
35 Camberwell Grove,
London SE5 8JA
020 7703 6186
Quality fiction and non-fiction

Juvenilia
Avington, near Winchester,
Hampshire SO21 1DB
01962 779656
juvenilia@clara.co.uk
*Baby to teen fiction and picture
books; non-fiction and scripts for TV
and radio*

Laurence Fitch
Mezzanine, Quadrant House,
80–82 Regent Street,
London W1B 5AU
020 7734 9911
information@laurencefitch.com
www.laurencefitch.com
*Children's and horror books, scripts for
theatre, film, TV and radio*

Lavinia Trevor Agency
29 Addison Place, London W11 4RJ
020 7603 5254
www.laviniatrevor.co.uk
*General literary and commercial
fiction; non-fiction including popular
science*

LAW (Lucas Alexander Whitley)
14 Vernon Street, London W14 0RJ
020 7471 7900
www.lawagency.co.uk
*Commercial and literary fiction, non-
fiction and children's books; film and
TV scripts for established clients*

LBLA
54 Hartford House,
35 Tavistock Crescent,
London W11 1AY
020 7727 8547
info@lorellabelliagency.com
www.lorellabelliagency.com
Fiction and general non-fiction

Limelight Management
33 Newman Street,
London W1T 1PY
020 7637 2529
limelight.management@virgin.net
www.limelightmanagement.com
General non-fiction

Lisa Eveleigh Literary Agency
c/o Pollinger Limited, 9 Staple Inn,
Holborn, London WC1V 7QH
020 7399 2803
lisaeveleigh@dial.pipex.com
*Literary and commercial fiction,
non-fiction and children's fiction*

Louise Greenberg Books
The End House, Church Crescent,
London N3 1BG
020 8349 1179
louisegreenberg@msn.com
Literary fiction and non-fiction

Lucy Luck Associates
(In association with Aitken
Alexander Associates)
18-21 Cavaye Place,
London SW10 9PT
020 7373 8672
lucy@lucyluck.com
www.lucyluck.com
Quality fiction and non-fiction

Luigi Bonomi
91 Great Russell Street,
London WC1B 3RS
020 7637 1234
info@bonomiassociates.co.uk
www.bonomiassociates.co.uk

Lutyens and Rubinstein
231 Westbourne Park Road,
London W11 1EB
020 7792 4855
susannah@lutyensrubinstein.co.uk
Adult fiction and non-fiction

Marjacq Scripts
34 Devonshire Place,
London W1G 6JW
020 7935 9499
enquiries@marjacq.com
www.marjacq.com
*Fiction and non-fiction, screenplays,
radio plays and film and TV rights*

Mary Clemmey Literary Agency
6 Dunollie Road, London NW5 2XP
020 7267 1290
mcwords@gmail.com
*Fiction and non-fiction, high quality
for an international market*

MBA Literary Agents
62 Grafton Way, London W1T 5DW
020 7387 2076
agent@mbalit.co.uk
www.mbalit.co.uk
*Fiction and non-fiction books, TV, film,
theatre and radio scripts*

Mic Cheetham Literary Agency
50 Albemarle Street,
London W1S 4BD
020 7495 2002
www.miccheetham.com
*General and literary fiction, fantasy
and science fiction, crime and some
specific non-fiction*

Micheline Steinberg Associates
Fourth Floor,
104 Great Portland Street,
London W1W 6PE
020 7631 1310
info@steinplays.com
Drama for stage, TV, radio and film

Michelle Kass Associates
85 Charing Cross Road,
London WC2H OAA
020 7439 1624
Literary fiction and film

Maggie Noach Literary Agency
Unit 4, 246 Acklam Road,
London W10
07506 717 726
info@mnla.co.uk
www.mnla.co.uk
Fiction and general non-fiction

Marsh Agency
50 Albemarle Street,
London W1S 4BD
020 7399 2800
submissions@marsh-agency.co.uk
www.marsh-agency.co.uk
*International rights specialists selling
English and foreign-language writing*

Paterson Marsh
50 Albemarle Street,
London W1S 4BD
020 7493 4361
www.patersonmarsh.co.uk
*World rights, especially psychoanalysis
and psychotherapy*

Peake Associates
14 Grafton Crescent,
London NW1 8SL
020 7482 0609
tony@tonypeake.com
www.tonypeake.com
Fiction and non-fiction

PFD (Peters Fraser & Dunlop Group)
Drury House, 34–43 Russell Street,
London WC2B 5HA
020 7344 1000
postmaster@pfd.co.uk
www.pfd.co.uk
*Fiction and children's, plus scripts for
film, theatre, radio and TV*

Peter Knight Agency
20 Crescent Grove,
London SW4 7AH
020 7622 1467
www.knightfeatures.com
*Motorsports, cartoon books, puzzles,
business, history, factual and
biographical material*

Pollinger
9 Staple Inn, Holborn,
London WC1V 7QH
020 7404 0342
info@pollingerltd.com
www.pollingerltd.com
*Formerly Laurence Pollinger and
Pearn, Pollinger & Higham. General
trade, non-fiction, children's fiction
and non-fiction*

Puttick Agency
46 Brookfield Mansions,
Highgate West Hill, London N6 6AT
020 8340 6383
enquiries@puttick.com
www.puttick.com
*General non-fiction, especially self-help,
mind, body and spirit, health and
fitness, lifestyle and business*

PVA Management
Hallow Park, Worcester WR2 6PG
01905 640663
md@pva.co.uk
Non-fiction only

Robert Smith Literary Agency
12 Bridge Wharf,
156 Caledonian Road,
London N1 9UU

020 7278 2444
robertsmith.literaryagency@
virgin.net
*Non-fiction; biography, health and
nutrition, lifestyle, showbusiness and
true crime*

Roger Hancock
4 Water Lane, London NW1 8NZ
020 7267 4418
info@rogerhancock.com
*Scripts for comedy, drama and light
entertainment*

Rogers, Coleridge & White
20 Powis Mews, London W11 1JN
020 7221 3717
www.rcwlitagency.com
*Fiction, non-fiction and children's
books*

Rosemary Sandberg
6 Bayley Street, London WC1B 3HE
020 7304 4110
rosemary@sandberg.demon.co.uk
Children's picture books and novels

Rosica Colin
1 Clareville Grove Mews,
London SW7 5AH
020 7370 1080
*Full-length manuscripts plus
theatre, film, television and sound
broadcasting*

Rupert Crew
1A King's Mews,
London WC1N 2JA
020 7242 8586
info@rupertcrew.co.uk
www.rupertcrew.co.uk
*Volume and subsidiary rights in fiction
and non-fiction properties*

Rupert Heath Literary Agency
177a Old Winton Road, Andover,
Hampshire SP10 2DR
020 7788 7807
rupert.heath@rupertheath.com
www.rupertheath.com
*Fiction, history, biography, science, arts
and popular culture*

Rod Hall Agency
6th Floor, Fairgate House,
78 New Oxford Street,
London WC1A 1HB
020 7079 7987

office@rodhallagency.com
www.rodhallagency.com
Drama for film, TV and theatre

Sayle Literary Agency
1 Petersfield, Cambridge CB1 1BB
01223 303035
www.sayleliteraryagency.com
*Fiction, crime and general; general
non-fiction*

Sayle Screen
11 Jubilee Place, London SW3 3TD
020 7823 3883
info@saylescreen.com
www.saylescreen.com
*Writers and directors for film, TV,
theatre and radio*

Sharland Organisation
The Manor House,
Manor Street, Raunds,
Northamptonshire NN9 6JW
01933 626600
tso@btconnect.com
www.sharlandorganisation.co.uk
*Scripts for film, TV, theatre and radio;
non-fiction; specialises in national
and international film, television and
theatre negotiations*

Sheil Land Associates
52 Doughty Street,
London WC1N 2LS
020 7405 9351
info@sheilland.co.uk
*Full-length general, commercial
and literary fiction and non-fiction,
including theatre, film, radio and
TV scripts*

Sheila Ableman Literary Agency
48-56 Bayham Place,
London NW1 OEU
020 7388 7222
sheila@sheilaableman.co.uk
*Non-fiction including history, science
and biography*

Shelley Power Literary Agency
13 rue du Pre Saint Gervais,
75019 Paris, France
00 33 1 42 383649
shelley.power@wanadoo.fr
*Fiction, business, true crime, film and
entertainment, architecture, self-help
and popular psychology*

Sinclair-Stevenson
3 South Terrace, London SW7 2TB
020 7581 2550
*Biography, current affairs, travel,
history, fiction, the arts*

Susijn Agency
3rd Floor, 64 Great Titchfield Street,
London W1W 7QH
020 7580 6341
info@thesusijnagency.com
www.thesusijnagency.com
*Sells rights worldwide in English and
non-English language literature:
literary fiction and non-fiction*

Tanja Howarth Literary Agency
19 New Row, London WC2N 4LA
020 7240 5553
tanja.howarth@btinternet.com
*Fiction and non-fiction from British
writers; represents German authors in
Britain on behalf of German publishers*

The Tennyson Agency
10 Cleveland Avenue,
Wimbledon Chase,
London SW20 9EW
020 8543 5939
submissions@tenagy.co.uk
www.tenagy.co.uk
Theatre, film, radio and TV scripts

Teresa Chris Literary Agency
43 Musard Road, London W6 8NR
020 7386 0633
teresachris@litagency.freeserve.co.uk
*Fiction: crime, general, women's,
commercial and literary and non-
fiction*

Toby Eady Associates
3rd Floor, 9 Orme Court,
London W2 4RL
020 7792 0092
toby@tobyeady.demon.co.uk
www.tobyeadyassociates.co.uk
*Fiction, non-fiction, especially China,
Middle East, Africa and India*

United Agents
130 Shaftesbury Avenue,
London W1D 5EU
020 7166 5266
info@unitedagents.co.uk
www.unitedagents.co.uk
Fiction and non-fiction

Valerie Hoskins Associates
20 Charlotte Street,
London W1T 2NA
020 7637 4490
vha@vhassociates.co.uk
Scripts for film, TV and radio,
especially feature films, animation
and TV

Vanessa Holt
59 Crescent Road, Leigh-on-Sea,
Essex SS9 2PF
01702 473787
General fiction especially crime,
commercial and literary; non-fiction;
non-illustrated children's

**Wade & Doherty Literary
Agency**
33 Cormorant Lodge,
Thomas More Street,
London E1W 1AU
020 7488 4171
rw@rwla.com
www.rwla.com
General fiction and non-fiction
including children's books

Watson, Little Limited
48-56 Bayham Place, London
NW1 0EU
020 7388 7529
office@watsonlittle.com
www.watsonlittle.co.uk
Commercial and literary fiction and
non-fiction for adults and children

The Wylie Agency (UK)
17 Bedford Square, London WC1B
3JA
020 7908 5900
www.wylieagency.co.uk
Fiction and non-fiction

**William Morris Agency
(UK)**
Centre Point, 103 New Oxford
Street, London WC1A 1DD
020 7534 6800
ldnmailroom@wma.com
www.wma.com
Fiction; general non-fiction; TV and
film scripts

William Neill-Hall
Old Oak Cottage, Ropewalk,
Mount Hawke, Truro,
Cornwall TR4 8DW
01209 891427
wneill-hall@msn.com
General non-fiction (clients include
George Carey, Philip Yancey and
Eugene Peterson)

Zebra Agency
Broadland House, 1 Broadland,
Shevington, Lancashire WN6 8DH
077193 75575
admin@zebraagency.co.uk
www.zebraagency.co.uk
Non-fiction and general fiction; scripts
for TV, radio, film and theatre

Trade press

**Annual Bibliography of
English Language and
Literature**
Modern Humanities Research
Association, Cambridge University
01223 333058
abell@bibl.org
www.mhra.org.uk/Publication/
Journals/abell.html
Annual. Editor: Gerard Lowe;
academic editor: Jennifer Fellows

The Bookseller
020 7420 6006
www.thebookseller.com
Editor-in-Chief: Neill Denny

**Booksellers Association
Directory of Members**
The Booksellers Association of the
UK and Ireland
020 7802 0802
mail@booksellers.org.uk
www.booksellers.org.uk
Annual. Editor: Meryl Halls

**Digital Demand – The
Journal of Printing and
Publishing Technology**
PIRA International
01372 802080
info@pira-international.com
www.piranet.com
12pa. Senior Editor: Sara Ver-Bruggen

London Review of Books
Nicholas Spice
020 7209 1101
edit@lrb.co.uk
www.lrb.co.uk
Fortnightly. Editor: Mary-Kay Wilmers

New Books Magazine
Guise Marketing
Editor-in-Chief: Elspeth Lindner

Writers Forum
Writers International
01202 586 848
chris@selectps.com
www.writers-forum.com
Monthly. Editor: John Jenkins

**Writers News/Writing
Magazine**
Warner Group Publications
0113 200 2929
hgray@writersnews.co.uk
www.writersnews.co.uk
Monthly. Editor: Hilary Gray

Societies and associations

Writers News/Writing Magazine
Warner Group Publications
0113 200 2929
hgray@writersnews.co.uk
www.writersnews.co.uk
Monthly. Editor: Hilary Gray

Academi (Yr Academi Gymreig)
Mount Stuart House, Mount Stuart Square, Cardiff CF10 5FQ
029 2047 2266
post@academi.org
www.academi.org
Welsh national literature promotion agency

Alliance of Literary Societies
22 Belmont Grove, Havant, Hampshire PO9 3PU
023 9247 5855
l.j.curry@bham.ac.uk
www.alllianceofliterarysocieties. org.uk

Arron Foundation
42a Buckingham Palace Road, London SW1W 0RE
020 793 7611
london@arronfoundation.org
www.arronfoundation.org
Charity running residential creative writing courses

Association for Scottish Literary Studies
c/o Department of Scottish Literature, 7 University Gardens, University of Glasgow, Glasgow G12 8QH
0141 330 5309
office@asls.org.uk
www.asls.org.uk
Charity promoting language and literature of Scotland

Association of Christian Writers
23 Moorend Lane, Thame, Oxon OX9 3BQ
01844 213 673
baynes@clearmail.net
www.christianwriters.org.uk
Support, training and encouragement

Association of Illustrators
150 Curtain Road, London EC2A 3AT
020 7613 4328
info@theaoi.com
www.theaoi.com
Trade association

Association of Learned and Professional Society Publishers
8 Rickford Road, Nailsea, North Somerset BS48 4PY
01275 856444
ian.russell@alpsp.org
www.alpsp.org
For not-for-profit academic and professional publishers

AuthorsOnline
19 The Cinques, Gamlingay, Sandy, Bedfordshire SG19 3NU
01767 652005
theeditor@authorsonline.co.uk
www.authorsonline.co.uk
Self-publishing and authors' services worldwide

Authors' Club
40 Dover Street, London W1S 4NP
020 7499 8581
authors@theartsclub.co.uk
www.authorsclub.co.uk
Anyone involved with written words; administers Best First Novel award and Sir Banister Fletcher award

Authors' Licensing & Collecting Society (ALCS)
The Writer's House, 13 Haydon Street, London EC3N 1DB
020 7264 5700
alcs@alcs.co.uk
www.alcs.co.uk
UK collecting society for writers and successors

Bibliographical Society
c/o The Institute of English Studies, University of London, Senate House, Malet Street, London WC1E 7HU
020 739 2150
secretary@bibsoc.org.uk
www.bibsoc.org.uk
Aims to encourage study of bibliography and history of publishing

Books 4 Publishing
Lasyard House, Underhill Street, Bridgnorth, Shropshire WV16 4BB
0870 777 3339
editor@books4publishing.com
www.books4publishing.com
Online showcase for unpublished writers

Booksellers Association of the UK & Ireland
Minster House,
272 Vauxhall Bridge Road, London SW1V 1BA
020 7802 0802
mail@booksellers.org.uk
www.booksellers.org.uk
Trade association. Coordinates World Book Day with Publishers' Association; administers Costa Book Awards

Booktrust
Book House, 45 East Hill, London SW18 2QZ
020 8516 2977
query@booktrust.org.uk
www.booktrust.org.uk
Educational charity

British Centre for Literary Translation
University of East Anglia, Norwich,
Norfolk NR4 7TJ
01603 592134/592785
bclt@uea.ac.uk
www.literarytranslation.com
Translation centre

British Copyright Council
Copyright House,
29–33 Berners Street,
London W1T 3AB
01986 788122
secretary@britishcopyright.org
www.britishcopyright.org
Liaison committee for copyright interest

British Science Fiction Association
39 Glyn Avenue,
New Barnet EN4 9PJ
London E17 9SE
bsfamembership@yahoo.co.uk
www.bsfa.co.uk
Also publishes Matrix, Vector and Focus magazines

British Society of Comedy Writers
61 Parry Road,
Ashmore Park, Wolverhampton,
West Midlands WW11 2PS
01902 722729
info@bscw.co.uk
www.bscw.co.uk
Society of comedy writers

Children's Books Ireland
First Floor,
17 North Great Georges Street,
Dublin 1, Ireland
00 353 1 872 7475
info@children'sbooksireland.com
www.children'sbooksireland.com
Promotes children's literature and publishes Inis magazine

Clé, The Irish Book Publishers' Association
25 Denzille Lane, Dublin 2,
Republic of Ireland
00 353 1 639 4868
info@publishingireland.com
www.publishingireland.com
Provides expertise and resources

Crime Writers' Association (CWA)
secretary@thecwa.co.uk
www.thecwa.co.uk
Professional group of crime authors

Critics' Circle
c/o William Russell
50 Finland Road, Brockley,
London SE4 2JH
020 7732 9636
www.criticscircle.org.uk
Critics of drama, music, cinema & dance, art and architecture

Directory & Database Publishers Association
Queens House, 28 Kingsway,
London WC2B 6JR
020 7405 0836
info@dpa.org.uk
www.dpa.org.uk
Trade association

Drama Association of Wales
The Old Library Building,
Singleton Road, Splott,
Cardiff CF24 2ET
029 2045 2200
aled.daw@virgin.net
www.amdram.co.uk/daw

English Association
University of Leicester,
University Road, Leicester LE1 7RH
0116 252 3982
engassoc@le.ac.uk
www.le.ac.uk/engassoc
Promotes knowledge, understanding and enjoyment of English language and literature

English PEN
6–8 Amwell Street,
London EC1R 1UQ
020 7713 0023
enquiries@englishpen.org
www.englishpen.org
Association of writers and literary professionals. Fights for right to freedom of expression

Federation of Worker Writers and Community Publishers (FWWCP)
Burslem School of Art, Queen
Street, Stoke on Trent ST6 3EJ
01782 822327

thefwwcp@tiscali.co.uk
For independent writing workshops and community publishers

Fellowship of Authors and Artists
PO Box 158, Hertford SG13 8FA
0870 747 2514
www.author-fellowship.co.uk
Promotes writing and art as therapy and self-healing

Garden Writers' Media Guild
Katepura House,
Ashfield Park Avenue, Ross-on-Wye,
Herefordshire HR9 5AX
admin@gardenmedia.guild.co.uk
www.gardenwriters.co.uk
Promotes high-quality garden writing, photography and broadcasting

Gaelic Books Council (Comhairle nan Leabhraichean)
22 Mansfield Street, Glasgow
G11 5QP
0141 337 6211
brath@gaelicbooks.net
www.gaelicbooks.org

Horror Writers Association
244 5th Avenue, Suite 2767,
New York, NY 10001 USA
hwa@horror.org
www.horror.org
Worldwide organisation of writers and publishing professionals

Independent Publishers Guild
P O Box 93, Royston,
Hertfordshire SG8 5GH
01763 247014
info@ipg.uk.com
www.ipg.uk.com

Independent Theatre Council
12 The Leathermarket,
Weston Street, London SE1 3ER
020 7403 1727
admin@itc-arts.org
www.itc-arts.org
Offers legal advice and training opportunities

Institute of Linguists
Saxon House, 48 Southwark Street,
London SE1 1UN
020 7940 3100
info@iol.org.uk
www.iol.org.uk
Professional association; accredited exam board; commercial contracts for government

Institute of Translation and Interpreting (ITI)
Fortuna House,
South Fifth Street, Milton Keynes,
Buckinghamshire MK9 2EU
01908 325250
info@iti.org.uk
www.iti.org.uk

International Booksearch Service
07939 711039
sarah.fordham@btinternet.com
www.scfordham.com
Finds out-of-print books

Irish Writers Centre
19 Parnell Square, Dublin 1,
Republic of Ireland
00353 1872 1302
info@writerscentre.ie
www.writerscentre.ie
Promotes Irish writers, living in Ireland, organises readings and workshops
Also houses:

Irish Translators' and Interpreters' Association
translation@eircom.net
www.translatorsassociation.ie

Irish Writers' Union
iwu@ireland-writers.com
www.ireland-writers.com

ISBN Agency
3rd Floor, Midas House,
62 Goldsworth Road,
Woking GU21 6LQ
0870 777 8712
isbn@nielsenbookdata.co.uk
www.nielsenbookdata.co.uk
Book numbering agency

Medical Writers' Group
The Society of Authors,
84 Drayton Gardens,
London SW10 9SB
020 7373 6642
info@societyofauthors.org
www.societyofauthors.org
Specialist group within Society of Authors

National Archives
Kew, Richmond, Surrey TW9 4DU
020 8876 3444
enquiry@nationalarchives.gov.uk
www.nationalarchives.gov.uk
National resource for documents relating to British history; brings together the Public Record Office and the Historical Manuscripts Commission

National Association for Literature Development
PO Box 49657, London N8 7YZ
020 7272 8386
admin@nald.org
www.nald.org

National Association of Writers' Groups
The Arts Centre,
Biddick Lane, Washington,
Tyne & Wear NE38 2AB
01262 609228
nawg@tesco.net
www.nawg.co.uk
Connecting writers' groups around the country; yearly festivals and competitions

National Association of Writers in Education
PO Box 1, Sheriff Hutton,
York YO60 7YU
01653 618429
www.nawe.co.uk

New Writing North
Culture Lab, Grand Assembly
Rooms, Newcastle University,
King's Walk, Newcastle upon Tyne
NE1 7RU
0191 222 1332
mail@newwritingnorth.com
www.newwritingnorth.com
Literature development agency for north-east arts region

Nielsen BookData
3rd Floor, Midas House,
62 Goldsworth Road, Woking,
Surrey GU21 6LQ
0870 7778710
info@nielsonbookdata.co.uk
www.nielsenbookdata.com
Bibliographic data

Nielsen BookScan
3rd Floor, Midas House,
62 Goldsworth Road, Woking,
Surrey GU21 6LQ
0870 7778710
info@nielsenbookscan.co.uk
www.nielsenbookscan.co.uk
International sales data monitoring

Player-Playwrights
37 Woodvale Way, London NW11 8SQ
020 8450 6112
www.playerplaywrights.co.uk
Gives opportunities to writers new to stage, radio and TV

Public Lending Right
Richard House, Sorbonne Close,
Stockton-on-Tees TS17 6DA
01642 604699
registrar@plr.uk.com
www.plr.uk.com
Distribute government funds to authors/libraries

Publishers Association
29B Montague Street,
London WC1B 5BH
020 7691 9191
mail@publishers.org.uk
www.publishers.org.uk
Trade association

Publishers Licensing Society
37–41 Gower Street,
London WC1E 6HH
020 7299 7730
pls@pls.org.uk
www.pls.org.uk
Licensing of photocopying materials in schools and universities

Publishers Publicity Circle
65 Airedale Avenue,
London W4 2NN
020 8994 1881
ppc-@lineone.net
www.publisherspublicitycircle.co.uk
Forum for book publicists and freelance PRs

Romantic Novelists' Association
Catherine Jones, 3 Griffin Road,
Thame, Oxon, OX9 3LB

01844 213 947
www.rna-uk.org

Royal Society of Literature
Somerset House, Strand,
London WC2R 1LA
020 7845 4676
info@rslit.org
*Holds monthly lectures promoting
literature and spoken word. Annual
prizes*

Science Fiction Foundation
28 St Johns Road,
Guildford GU2 7UH
sff.chair@gmail.com
www.sf-foundation.org
*Writers, academics and critics with an
active interest in science fiction*

Scottish Book Trust
Sandeman House, Trunk's Close,
55 High Street, Edinburgh EH1 1SR
0131 524 0160
info@scottishbooktrust.com
www.scottishbooktrust.com
*Arts organiser, promotes reading and
writing in Scotland; holds a resource
library*

**Scottish Print Employers
Federation**
48 Palmerston Place,
Edinburgh EH12 5DE
0131 220 4353
info@graphicenterprisescotland.
org.uk
www.spef.org.uk
*Advice, expertise, education and
training*

Publishing Scotland
Scottish Book Centre,
137 Dundee Street,
Edinburgh EH11 1BG
0131 228 6866
enquiries@publishingscotland.org
www.publishingscotland.org
*Networking and information services.
Lobbying organisation for book
publishing issues*

Scottish Youth Theatre
Old Sheriff Court,
105 Brunswick Street,
Glasgow G1 1TF
0141 552 3988
info@scottishyouththeatre.org
www.scottishyouththeatre.org

*Giving young people in Scotland
opportunity to explore and reach their
creative potential through art*

**Society of Children's Book
Writers & Illustrators**
36 Mackenzie Road, Beckenham,
Kent BR3 4RU
020 8249 9716
ra@britishscbwi.org
www.britishscbwi.org

Society of Editors
Bob Satchwell, University Centre,
Granta Place, Mill Lane, Cambridge
CB2 1RU
0123 304 080
info@societyofeditors.org
www.societyofeditors.org
*Non-profit body promoting high
editorial standards and recognition of
the professional status of its members*

Society of Authors
84 Drayton Gardens,
London SW10 9SB
020 7373 6642
info@societyofauthors.org
www.societyofauthors.org
Trade union for professional authors

**Society of Civil and Public
Service Writers**
Mrs JM Lewis, 17 The Green, Corby
Glen, Grantham, Lincs. NG33 4NP
www.scpsw.co.uk

Society of Indexers
Woodbourn Business Centre,
10 Jessell Street, Sheffield S9 3HY
0114 244 9561
admin@indexers.org.uk
www.indexers.org.uk

**Society of Young
Publishers**
Endeavour House,
189 Shaftesbury Avenue,
London WC2H 8TJ
info@thesyp.org.uk
www.thesyp.org.uk
*Provides a forum, organises readings
and meetings*

**Sports Journalists'
Association
of Great Britain**
Unit 92, Capital Business Centre
22 Carlton Road

Surrey CR2 0BS
020 8916 2234
www.sportsjournalists.co.uk

Translators Association
84 Drayton Gardens,
London SW10 9SB
020 7373 6642
info@societyofauthors.org
www.societyofauthors.org

**Welsh Books Council
(Cyngor Llyfrau Cymru)**
Castell Brychan, Aberystwyth,
Ceredigion SY23 2JB
01970 624151
castellbrychan@cllc.org.uk
www.gwales.com
For Welsh writers

**West Country Writers'
Association**
01566 773615
secretaryWCWA@fsmail.net
www.westcountrywriters.com
Annual congress in May

Women in Publishing
info@wipub.org.uk
www.wipub.org.uk

**Writers, Artists and their
Copyright Holders (Watch)**
David Sutton,
Director of Research Projects,
University of Reading Library,
PO Box 223, Whiteknights,
Reading RG6 6AE
0118 931 8783
D.C.Sutton@reading.ac.uk
www.watch-file.com
Database of copyright holders

**Writers' Guild of Great
Britain**
40 Rosebery Avenue
London EC1R 4RX
Tel: 020 7833 0777
Fax: 020 7833 4777
erik@writersguild.org.uk
www.writersguild.org.uk
Trade union for professional writers